# YOUR FORTUNE IN THE MICROCOMPUTER BUSINESS

## VOLUME I

## GETTING STARTED

by

VICTOR WILD

# YOUR FORTUNE IN THE MICROCOMPUTER BUSINESS

## VOLUME I

# GETTING STARTED

by

VICTOR WILD

This book is designed to provide information in regard to the subject matter covered. It is sold with the understanding that the publisher and author are not engaged in rendering legal, accounting, or other professional services. If legal advice or other expert assistance is required, the services of a competent professional should be sought.

Published by

WILDFIRE PUBLISHING COMPANY
P.O. Box 420
Carpinteria, California 93013



ISBN #0-938444-04-2

# Acknowledgements

Many thanks to the bright and delightful people who allowed me to enter details of their business in our interviews. Each interview was different but the common factor was the amount of intimate detail people in competitive and technically advanced businesses were willing to share.

Many thanks to Tom Pine of VITEK, Scott Daley of THE COMPUTER SHOP, Fred Bellomy of INFOMART, Dr. Bill Georgiou of VOICETEK, Marilyn Darling, Polly Sloane, Carmen Governale and Bill Smale of DIGITAL RESEARCH and Herb Schildt and Richard Balocca of SUPERSOFT for their time and patience.

Special thanks to Richard M. White, author of *The Entrepreneurs' Manual*, ISBN #0-8019-6454-7, published by Chilton Book Company, Radnor, PA 19089. Rich's book is a practical and complete guide to starting and finishing right in *any* kind of business. It is a hard act to follow but provided me with inspiration to keep writing during those times when I thought the subject of the microcomputer business was too vast to be comprehensible.

Richard White devoted much of his time explaining his new theories and outlining his thoughts on the complexities of marketing technical products.

Many of his ideas are included in this volume and in Volume II of this work. Many more of his innovative ideas are detailed in his new book soon to be released by Chilton.

*The Entrepreneurs' Manual* is recommended reading for anyone starting any kind of company. I have bought three, worn one out, given two to friends, and am on my way down to buy another.

Your Fortune in the Microcomputer Business

# VOLUME I: Getting Started

800
CADO
JADE
Computer Products
ComputerWorld
Computer Systems for Home and Office

# INTRODUCTION

"There is a tide in the affairs of men which, when taken at the flood, leads on to fortune." Shakespeare, *Julius Caesar.*

This book is about the most exciting change in civilization since the Renaissance. It is about the New Renaissance and the beginning of a world only described previously in Science Fiction.

This world has many progenitors. No single genius has brought it about. It has led step-by-step through Issac Newton, Neils Bohr, Michael Faraday, Ohm, Thevenin, Kirschoff, Zener and a host of other inspired contributors.

Large Scale Integration, Very Large Scale Integration, Winchester Drives and the stimulus of competition has brought the world of electronic miracle to the doorstep of every home and business in the country.

The decade of the 80's is witnessing electronic wonders which are creating huge and exponentially expanding market horizons. In terms of dollars, units or users the scale of this new industry is exciting.

What do all these orders of magnitude have to do with a person who would like to make a part-time or full-time career in the microcomputer business?

The industry will need increasing numbers of trained people but most needs are for warm bodies to fill pews in the corporate sanctuary. A corporate job can offer security and a comprehensible, sane and defined future. Most of the world needs that. How about you?

Business is a Grand Adventure. It is the ultimate computer game using software created by your own mind. Like any other game, business has rules, players and a field of action. You keep score by profits and a feeling of accomplishment.

Going into business for yourself is probably the most exciting adventure you will ever have. Add to that the excitement and power of starting your business in an industry which is bringing the world into the 21st Century and you have the stuff of religious conversion.

The excitement of quantum technology and industrial growth measured in orders of magnitude rather than percentage increase in attracting a growing legion of bright, adventuresome pioneers who want to be in business for themselves.

This book is written for these mavericks: The people who never fit comfortably into any mold — even one they made themselves. If the soles of your feet itch and you are ready for a ride in the fast lane, then come on along.

## Business Life Phases

In the first phase of your business life you try to understand the market you have settled your roving eye on. You spend lots of time going to trade shows, talking to shop owners, sending inquiry letters and filling out reader-response cards from trade magazines.

This phase of the action may make you frantic. You get overwhelmed with input and it is often difficult to find a thread of unification running through the mass of information. The panic stage will pass. Piece-by-piece you begin to find coherency in this world of information. A day eventually comes when you have a handle on it all. But don't relax yet; the feeling of control will pass when you learn more.

The second phase starts with the decision to enter the market with a goods or services product. A train of decisions then occurs: Facilities? Advertising? Equipment? Image? Full-Time? Part-Time? Money? Employees? Expansion? Oh God! How do I open a commercial bank account?

The third phase begins when your business is operating. You have a product, a place to work and some customers have been taking the bait. Cash starts to flow in (and out). You spend all your money on inventory and a new typewriter. Then two weeks go by and no money at all comes in. Panic time!

In phase four, things start happening. You wear all the hats, are totally busy and money comes in steadily. You face decisions like "Should I be a wholesaler or retailer? Right now I sell both trades, I hate to drop either, but I can't do both things competitively. I've got an extra thousand dollars but there are three places it needs to be spent." Life in phase four can be frustrating.

Phase five is when you start to fly. Money, expansion and growth all go together in this phase. Great! You are suddenly so busy taking care of details you begin to lose contact with the real world of marketplace. And your original contact with the market was largely responsible for your success.

Your new product line misses the mark and your money gets tied up in slow-moving inventory. At the same time your growth has outrun available cash so you need to find outside financing.

You step on to the outside financing treadmill. You learn how to work with bankers, lenders and investors. You learn the Golden Rule: *Those with the gold make the rules.* You feel like you are in a leaking rubber raft surrounded by Jaws and his friends. In phase five you learn a lot about the games the big kids play.

Phase six eventually happens in greater or lesser degree to every business. You solved your financing problems in phase five. Things go well and you become steadily profitable. Then things slow down or get downright bad. When hard times knock on your door it is time to polish up your survival kit. I call this high art of survival the RLC Factor. It is Rat-Like-Cunning. No business school teaches RLC. It is taught daily in the tough, no-margin-for-error businesses like sportswear and dry-cleaning equipment. My Uncle Henry used RLC for all phases of his business, mainly because he grew up in New York's Seventh Avenue Garment District where you need RLC just to get to work and home at night.

Things are quite different in the fresh and new micro-computer industry. But it doesn't hurt to know a little street fighting technique for use in emergencies. Volume II of this book, titled *Survival, Growth and Success* tells you how to be a black belt in RLC tactics.

Some of the methods described in Volume II aren't so nice and some are of questionable ethics. But the methods of RLC work and are used every day in the industry. You can use these techniques at your discretion. At the bottom line it is nice to know what may be done to you when things get tough for your customers or competitors. It also doesn't hurt to know a few deadly moves yourself, just for insurance.

Both volumes of this book make sweeping generalizations about character and personality types you will encounter in your business. All of these generalizations are both right and wrong. They are right when applied as an idea of attitudes and actions you will encounter. They are wrong in the degree you apply them to an isolated individual. Physics and business science predict the net result of mass action. They do not and cannot say how a single particle will behave.

Elementary particles and personality types are predictable.

While each sales rep, customer or employee will not necessarily display the traits described in these volumes, you will still be amazed by the fidelity of these descriptions to reality.

Much of what is said below could be taken as accounting or legal advice. I am not an accountant or lawyer and am unqualified to give specific advice on specific accounting or legal problems. I have discussed legal and accounting matters to give you a framework based on the real experiences of myself and people I have known or interviewed.

For legal and accounting advice you should go to the appropriate practitioner. But not just any of these professionals will do. Most attorneys and CPA's are quite ordinary mortals and produce mediocre results.

The ability to choose the *best* professional help grows only with business experience. You start your business assuming you are an excellent judge of horses and men. You will finish your business career being a truly good judge of professional help. It is an expensive education.

In summary, this book gives you a distillation of experience of seasoned and often battle-scarred veterans of chronic and infectious entrepreneurship. It talks about traps to avoid and clearly lays out the way to start and fly your business properly.

The world of microcomputers is exciting, brave and new. It will remain so for a long time to come. Why not take your place among those who will make it happen?

*How do you measure up to the role of microcomputer Entrepreneur?*

## Chapter One

# MOTIVATION

### Taking Your Measurements

How do *you* measure up to the role of Entrepreneur? What does it take to be self-directed and successful in your own business? How do you feel about taking risks? And finally, how do you feel about wealth? These questions all become important during the cycle of entrepreneurship.

To be prepared for what is to come you will need to know the demands you will make of yourself as your own boss. You need to know what will get you to work when you become the sole source of responsibility to the needs of your business.

Will you set your own timetable and meet your own goals? You will need the ability to push yourself when it's necessary. You alone will set and meet your own schedules when you are the boss.

You need to have an idea of the real feelings you and your spouse have about the risks ahead. Starting a business can be like jumping into a dark cave hoping to find a landing place on the way down.

Most of all you need to know your attitude toward wealth, success and money. Business is really all about making money. And money is the barometer of business success.

Many people have bad attitudes about money because they associate problems with it that do not necessarily belong there. A person who has neurotic ideas about money will do subtle unconscious things to keep himself from acquiring it. If you have these problems, now is the time to get them straightened out.

Your own motivation is a management task. This task requires you to discover what you are working with and secondly requires you to organize your discoveries to work for you.

When you manage people you are dealing with their motivations so they can do the tasks you want. When you manage yourself you deal with your own motivation so you can provide for yourself the things you want and need.

## Back to Basics

Below is a list of questions to help you clarify your feelings about starting your own business.

Answering these questions should make it clear that personal values and attitudes are primary in formulating your business approach.

What is your intended business? ____________________
In *exactly* what industry? ____________________
Local or national? ______________ Products or services?
(Explain) ____________________________________
____________________________________________
____________________________________________

Why do you want to be in business for yourself? ______
____________________________________________

Do you want to make a profit? How much per year? ____
________ Maximum % of sales: ________ Minimum % of sales: ____________ Only to make a living? ______ If so, how much per year? ____________ Maximum? ________
Minimum? ________ Other reasons? ______________
____________________________________________
____________________________________________

What are your objectives? ______________________
Sales anticipated the first year? __________ Second year?
____________ What does it take to be successful in your business? ______________________________________
____________________________________________
____________________________________________

Your own determination? ___ Your own product/service?
____________ Your experience and financial strength?
____________ Explain: __________________________
____________________________________________
____________________________________________
____________________________________________

What are your fears? ____________
Customer acceptance? ________ Competition? ________
Insufficient Financing? ________ People? ________
Other reasons? ____________
Explain: ____________

## Paying the Price

Are you willing to pay the price of being your own boss? How much of yourself do you want to give up to the business? This is an important decision and is best made with eyes wide open.

The growth of your business will have a direct effect on your freedom to do other things. It is a direct trade-off. If your company grows rapidly it will take all of you (and demand more) in order to insure its success. The greatest factor in the success or failure of a small business is the willingness of the founder to give of himself, his time, income, leisure and so on *ad infinitum.*

Studies by venture capital groups have shown entrepreneurs are successful in *direct proportion* to their willingness to give of themselves.

If you think you will prosper working at your business a few hours a week while watching TV you are in for a rude surprise! You may start out doing things casually but when the pot starts to boil, your business may demand many things of you.

Each business need you ignore limits your success. But where should you draw the line? In truth, most successful beginning business people don't draw the line—they give it all they have.

What are your real values? Values are so integrated into our lives we are largely unaware of them until they are questioned or challenged.

Your values are an important part of your personality—they form a sort of inertial guidance system your personality uses to make choices. If you know your values you know what decisions you will make in a given situation and thus you can predict your behavior.

In a later chapter of this book there is an analysis of six microcomputer-related businesses. The founder of each of these businesses has chosen a different path, a different level of commitment and has a different view of his business and the world.

The most successful of these entrepreneurs is the one who has most accurately aligned his business with his real needs.

When you read the practical parts of this book you will see the clear steps to start your business right. When you add confidence to this formula your efforts will become increasingly effective. You will be on the positive, ascending spiral of success.

## Setting Goals

The first step to starting a business and realizing financial success is to set some goals. What do you *really* want from your business? You better be careful on this one because your goal will come true. Set the things that will lead to real happiness for *you*, because if goals are set by a clear and purposeful mind they will surely come true!

The first step to setting goals is to write them down and be *specific*.

Do you want to make $10,000 a year from your hobby?

Do you want $50,000 or $100,000 a year from a full-time business effort?

Do you want a six-week vacation every year?

Do you want a totally equipped lab or facility?

The goals conjectured above are material in nature. The hardest goals to achieve are the non-material ones because of the more difficult problem of definition. The more clearly and realistically you see yourself, the easier it will be to define and achieve the satisfaction you want.

There are a number of paths to take realizing your dreams. The paths range from conservative, low-risk, low-profile and low-expectation of return ways, to risky high-powered schemes which hold great promise of rapid and high return. Your way will probably be somewhere between these extremes.

## Money

Being in business is, at the bottom line, about making money. If you don't make enough of it you won't be able to continue playing the game. Profits are the scorecounters of your success levels. Happiness, repose and rent are all satisfied by profitability.

How do you really feel about making money? If you think there is something dishonest about profits or that money is the root of all evil you are bound to land in the penalty box.

Incredible as it may seem, making money is the thing many new business owners have the most trouble with; I don't mean making money but the idea of whetherthey really *want* it. Many people go into business for reasons other than to make money and two-thirds of the people going into business go out of business in a short time.

If you have all sorts of neurotic problems about taking money for your efforts you better not invest your life savings in your business. If you aren't in business to make money you won't make it—simple as that. The *kind* of business is just the machine you use to get cash flowing to your account.

If you devote yourself to making money there is *no limit* to the amount you can make. Is this hard to believe? It's true and not only that but if you make lots of money your business will be more fun to run.

It all starts with the way you think about it. If you hear yourself saying "no" to being rich then your are putting a limitation on yourself from the outset.

## The Secret of Money

The Secret of Money has been known to only a few individuals in each society throughout the ages. These individuals had the "knack" of becoming wealthy. *The secret is that they believe they can make money and they use every talent they have to the max.* (The other part of the secret is the miracle of compound interest.)

Does this sound crazy? It's crazy only because the majority of people don't understand the power of belief in themselves. This book is all about how to make money with your talent, training, energy and willingness to take a chance. These are the ingredients which have undoubtedly taken other cultures to the stars and beyond.

This book is about how to have more success than you have dreamed of. And the secret lying underneath your ability to succeed is your own belief you can do it.

Are you the right person to be a computer entrepreneur? An unblinking desire for success is the price of admission.

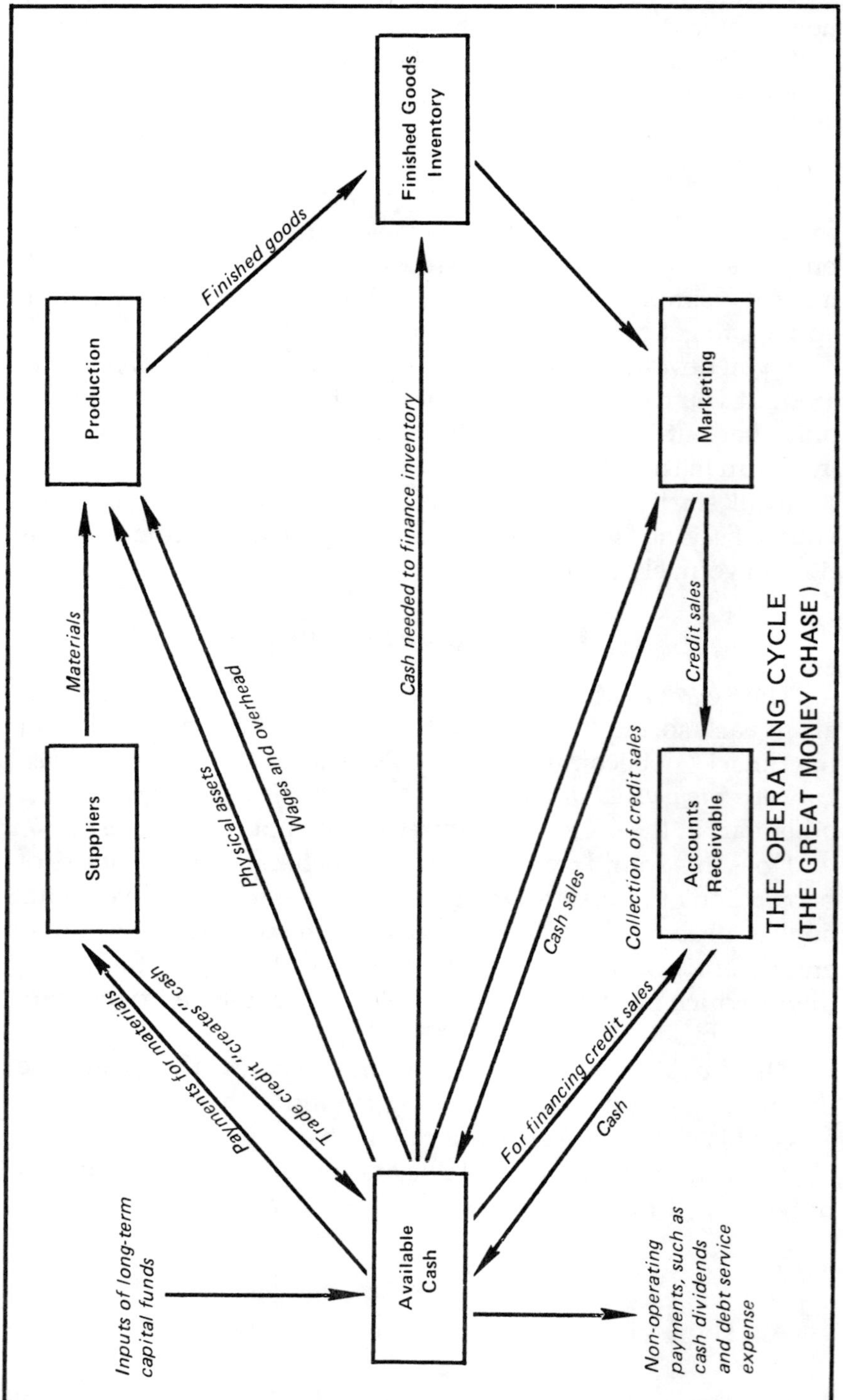


THE OPERATING CYCLE
(THE GREAT MONEY CHASE)

## Chapter Two

# START-UP CAPITAL

If you are starting your first business avoid start-up capital, loans and investors! It's as easy as that. It is safer and more educational. Starting broke saves your potential lenders until later when you will be a blooded veteran and can use the money more wisely.

By the time you are a legitimate credit or investment risk you will have developed a track record, have some of your own money and an even brighter future.

Engrave the words "Track Record" on the cover of your financial planning notebook. It is *the* most important factor when you are being scrutinized by potential investors or lenders.

One of the best features of the microcomputer business, besides an explosive market, unlimited future and high profits, is that you can get started in it with only a small investment of cash.

Each of the six businesses discussed in this book was started on a shoestring! DIGITAL RESEARCH, the largest and richest of the cases presented, was started by one person working from his home, generating capital from the high profits such a low-overhead operation can yield.

The microcomputer business is the epitome of the American Dream. Businesses in this industry are still founded on ingenuity, market savvy and entrepreneurial zeal!

How much capital is required to develop and market software? A little for the the time to get it done, a little for advertising and promotion, and a little for the package!

The consulting business has even smaller capital requirements. Fred Bellomy, who founded INFOMART, paid for his superb information gathering and disseminating facility by telling other people what to do with their computer systems!

Even if you choose to sell a hardware-based product like a voice synthesizer there are enough modular components, custom PCB houses and enclosures available so that you can assemble a few systems, sell them and make a few more with the profits.

In most of the microcomputer industry there is a low start-up capital requirement. It is possible to lay out big bucks getting started fast and furiously but it is possible and even preferable to get started in a limited way, bootstrapping your business with profitability.

It is by far the best approach to start small. Starting small will allow you to survive untutored judgment, market misappreciation, ignorance and mismanagement.

When you start small and take each step carefully you limit the scale of your problems. Small-scale problems are more easily dealt with by small scale finances and limited business experience. Real problems result from decisions taking you outside the scope of your present finances or track record.

## Starting on a Shoestring

The most asked question and the biggest worry in starting a new business is "Where is the money going to come from?"

We hear stories of fabulous start-ups financed by a friendly banker (?), eager investors, or a public offering. It must be so wonderful in the glamorous world of high finance!

Bullshit! The last thing you want when starting a new business is the burden of loan payments, investors jitters, or the requirements of the Securities and Exchange Commission.

When you start your business you will be quite busy getting a handle on your explosive and mobile market, developing your product and a base of customers to pay you for it.

The miracle of the microcomputer business is that you can start and succeed in your business on a shoestring! The best financing of all comes from your earnings and the most wisely spent money comes from your own savings!

As your products catch the consumers fancy they will see brisk and accelerating sales. Your overhead will be low (at first) and your profits high. You will experience some frustration because if you experience an extraordinarily successful product you won't be able to finance all possible sales. Other, better financed companies will jump on your product and you will eventually lose the market to them. You end up feeling all you have accomplished is to develop products and market share for your rich competitors.

When this inevitably happens you must be patient. The same ability that fostered the first product will engender a series of other even more powerful products or ideas.

You must remember the trade-off you have chosen. Your low investment and low working capital situation will save you from making disastrous mistakes. If your money is limited the scope of your activities will be limited and the quality of your decisions will be enhanced. If you start lean and mean you will be smarter about how you spend your money and your mistakes will cost you a lot less than if your first start-up is heavily financed.

## Cash Planning

### SOURCES AND APPLICATION OF FUNDS FOR A START-UP MANUFACTURER

Below is a cash flow chart for a hypothetical manufacturing operation. If you are planning a service business, the plan is the same but you don't have as many categories of expense.

This scenario assumes you work your regular job for three months full-time, and half-time for the next three months after starting Wonder Widget Company. You can see by the cumulative ten-month total you need just over ten kilobucks to start this enterprise.

Uncalculated overhead expenses can be a major expense factor. The numbers shown here for auto dues and insurance, for instance, are high—up to $500 per month. You will, however, be amazed when you see the gas and insurance bills you pay when things are in high gear!

On second thought, the figures shown here are probably representative of the proportional relationship of expenses in a typical mail-order hardware operation. Note particularly how overheads race with profits. This game is known affectionately as "Beat The Reaper."

Management is all about improving the relationship of expenses to income. Ruthless attention to overheads is one important key. The battle of overheads vs. expenses is a battle which rages every day in every business in every part of the world.

You can control and forecast all your expenses. By spreading your expected income and expenses on a Cash Flow Projection sheet you can get a remarkably good picture of the sort of cash requirements your proposed business will have.

Most of the figures in your cash flow sheet will be results from best-guesses. When the year is through and the dust has settled you'll be amazed at how accurate your projections were.

The microcomputer business is like a compelling lover; it sings a song of romance, power, success and easy entry. If you are willing to do the courting, it is yours for the taking.

| Exhibit I MONTH | 1 | 2 | 3 | 4 | 5 | 6 | 7 | 8 | 9 | 10 | 11 | 12 | TOTALS |
|---|---|---|---|---|---|---|---|---|---|---|---|---|---|
| **INCOME** | | | | | | | | | | | | | |
| Your Salary | 1500 | 1500 | 1500 | 750 | 750 | 750 | 0 | 0 | 0 | 0 | 0 | 0 | 6750 |
| Your Spouse's Salary | 1500 | 1500 | 1500 | 1500 | 1500 | 1500 | 1500 | 1600 | 1600 | 1600 | 1600 | 1600 | 18500 |
| Sales (Widgets Sell for $100) | 0 | 0 | 500 | 900 | 1500 | 2200 | 2600 | 3600 | 4600 | 5600 | 6600 | 7800 | 35900 |
| TOTAL INCOME | 3000 | 3000 | 3500 | 3150 | 3750 | 4450 | 4100 | 5200 | 6200 | 7200 | 8200 | 9400 | 61150 |
| **EXPENSES** | | | | | | | | | | | | | |
| Fixed Living Exp. (Rock Bottom) | 1500 | 1500 | 1500 | 1500 | 1500 | 1500 | 1500 | 1500 | 1500 | 1500 | 1500 | 1500 | 18000 |
| R&D | 1000 | 1000 | 1000 | 750 | 750 | 750 | 500 | 500 | 500 | 500 | 500 | 500 | 8250 |
| Advertising & Prom. | 1000 | 1000 | 1000 | 1400 | 1400 | 1400 | 1800 | 1800 | 1800 | 2200 | 2200 | 2200 | 19200 |
| Production Costs (Widgets Cost $25.00) to Make) | 0 | 0 | 125 | 225 | 375 | 550 | 650 | 900 | 1150 | 1400 | 1650 | 1950 | 8975 |
| Office Expenses (Typewriter, Office Equipment, Paper, Stamps) | 350 | 350 | 350 | 400 | 400 | 400 | 450 | 450 | 450 | 500 | 500 | 500 | 5100 |
| Production Expenses (Drill Press, Test Equip., Payments) | 300 | 300 | 300 | 400 | 400 | 400 | 500 | 500 | 500 | 500 | 500 | 500 | 5100 |
| Auto Expenses, Ins. Dues General Out of Pocket | 300 | 400 | 400 | 400 | 450 | 450 | 450 | 500 | 500 | 500 | 500 | 500 | 5350 |
| TOTAL EXPENSES | 4450 | 4550 | 4675 | 5075 | 5275 | 5450 | 5850 | 6150 | 6400 | 7100 | 7350 | 7650 | 69975 |
| TOTAL CASH POSITION (Income—Expenses) | -1450 | -1550 | -1175 | -1925 | -1525 | -1000 | -1750 | -950 | -200 | 100 | 850 | 1750 | -8825 |
| CUMULATIVE TOTAL | -1450 | -3000 | -4175 | -6000 | -7625 | -8625 | -10375 | -11325 | -11525 | -11425 | -10575 | -8825 | |

CASH FLOW ANALYSIS FIRST YEAR OPERATIONS HYPOTHETICAL MANUFACTURING COMPANY

*Every trade show has a pulse and a dominant theme. If you know where and how to look, you can discover the hot items and companies. By discovering these things you can get a picture of the future.*

## Chapter Three

# HOW TO SURVEY THE MICROCOMPUTER MARKET

*Venture* magazine published an article in 1980 in which they rated their estimate of the ten best business areas for the coming decade. Six out of ten were computer-related and the remaining four depend heavily on the computer market!

- Communications
- Consulting
- Computer Hardware
- Automation
- Computer Software
- Custom Interactive Services (controlling things with computers)
- Energy
- Investment Firms
- Leisure
- Medical Engineering

By 1985 the average U.S. household will spend $2000 annually on electronic products and services. The business market is already seeing increases of billions per year in spending for electronic communication, data and information services and equipment.

Electronics is seeing the most rapid advance in technology and applications of any industry. Any segment you look at has an open future. Some segments are important but so new that no one knows where the top will be. Optoelectronics, lasers and speech synthesis will have such an effect on the market that few forecasters are willing to say a number for fear it will be a gross understatement.

The home electronics market alone will probably be over $200 *billion* a year by 1985. And how much will business users add to that total?

So you are sniffing the right tree! Systems houses, time sharers, OEMers, dealers, distributors, graphics software houses and an endless list of microcomputer enterprises will thrive and multiply in the 80's.

Some of these businesses will go broke through bad management or bad breaks. Others will become billion dollar industries, and thousands of free-lance part-time businesses will grow and prosper in the market niches created.

Do any of these descriptions fit your personal picture for the decade of the 80's? No doubt! So let's take a closer look at the market and explore some ways you can put yourself into the picture.

## Understanding Market Change

Economies, the seasons and the tide all change. Change is unarguable and absolute; this is one constant for your predictive models. What must be calculated, however, is the pace, direction and effects of change.

To be a market predictor you need to be a part-time sociologist and see fundamental behavioral changes due to currents of history. An example is the way World War II caused the boom in jeans, coffee and donuts.

## Jeans, Coffee and Donuts

During the war years million of servicemen became accustomed to wearing fatigues. Also, every time they would get off a train or boat the Red Cross lady would be there handing out coffee and donuts. When the servicepeople came home they had acquired a taste for fatigue-type clothes (jeans and T-shirts) and donuts with coffee. Several new industries sprang up to meet this change. Donut shops, jean manufacturers and coffee plantations thrived.

## The Singles Industry

Another important historical event was the invention of the birth-control pill. This development caused enormous social and moral change in our culture. It created the singles industry. It also created the divorce industry supporting innumerable attorneys, real estate brokers, diet fads, mini-storage, day care centers, psychologists and so on, *ad infinitum*.

## Tracking Change

The way to track historic shifts and their concomitant effects on your industry is to be in close contact with change. There are some proven ways to do this:

1. *Read everything you possibly can:* spend four hours a week in a university library just exploring. Buy $10 worth of books (at least) per day and read a minimum of 50 magazines per month.

2. Go to *every* trade show even remotely connected with your industry. Collect, read and carefully file the literature you pick up at these shows. Talk to everyone there. At each show try to figure out the dominant theme—what is selling, who is selling it, who is dying on the vine. In effect you will be taking the pulse of the show. Every trade show has a pulse—and you should make it a point to find it every time you attend one.

3. Get on every government publication list you can afford. The Superintendent of Documents in Washington, D.C. has a monthly catalog of what has just been published—it currently costs $90 per year and can be a timely source of important information. The National Technical Information Service, phone # 703-487-4650, has a cataloging program to let you know what they receive each month in your subject area. This source lets you see research done by research companies like Rand, hardware people like Rockwell, all unclassified NASA documents and generally any paper which has been produced with government funding.

4. Subscribe to and read every trade publication you can find. In the advertising chapter of this book you will find an extensive listing of trade and consumer magazines serving the computer and electronics industries. Write for sample copies. Many offer free subscriptions or have "deals" which are designed to boost paid circulation (thus higher ad rates). Many of the industrial publications offer a free subscription if you "qualify" by filling the card out appropriately.

5. Travel and visit people related to your business. Many times a business owner is so proud of his R&D efforts he will show you every detail and answer every question fully. Exchanging information in this way can be a real boost for everyone. When you pay someone a personal visit it creates ties and an openness that otherwise might not exist.

When you travel you will run across new ideas from unexpected sources. When you are travelling, stop by the local university or college to say hello to a professor in the electronic engineering, computer science or physics department. He might be glad to see you; you will make valuable contacts and find out what is happening at the grass roots level of technology. Like business owners, many professors are proud of their work and might be willing to share it.

How many professors are there who are at this very moment wondering how to contact an entrepreneur to license his ideas? One of them might be waiting for you!

6. Study patent applications. These documents include a complete description of the idea, drawings included! There are thousands of patented ideas which have never been developed into a marketable product. At the very least, a study of patent records might stimulate you to think in new ways about old problems.

7. Talk with customers and end-users of your product. When you're at a trade show don't limit your attention to only the booth dwellers. Talk to the attendees to find out why they came, what they want and what they plan to buy. Remember, the end users' perception makes markets.

## Surveying Your Market

To survey any market you should first define the information you need. The next step is to prepare an information gathering campaign. Mailed questionnaires and customer interviews are the usual methods of the big-time market research companies. They spend enormous amounts of money gathering their information — probably more than you planned to spend starting your entire company. Besides, there are cheaper and better ways to gain clear understanding you your market.

A place to start is with the market summaries made by magazines, trade organizations, brokerage houses and market study firms. Many of these organizations publish results of their surveys of particular markets as a promotional tool.

How much good will these columns of figures and projections of industrial trends do you? You must already know your market has a strong future or you wouldn't be reading this book!

What kinds of data would be really helpful? The best kind of market data is from informed personal experience. One of the

### HOW TO SCOPE OUT THE COMPETITION

- Get competitors' price lists and promotional material at trade shows.
- Any way you can, get the competition's new-product announcements.
- If the competition is a public company, they must file a yearly Form 10-K with the Security and Exchange Commission. This document contains much valuable information and is available at many libraries.
- Credit reports from credit reporting companies such as Dun and Bradstreet and TRW.
- Interview past employees of the competitor.
- Much information can be gained from listings in industry trade association directories.
- Your customers who deal with your competitors can give you much valuable information.
- Salesmen who call on you and your competition are in a great position to tell you your competitors' plans.
- Many times a competitor's employees will publish articles about some phase of their activities in the trade journals.

best ways to get concentrated personal experience of your industry is at a trade show.

Trade shows are a great place to get information about a specific company's plans, products and promotion efforts. You can meet a company's top and middle managers at a show and they will be in a mood to talk. If you call these people on the phone while they are in their own office they aren't likely to tell you much (see exception below). The set and setting of a trade show opens the door to communication.

Of course, it may not be clever to tell the booth-dwellers you intend to compete with them or that you already are a competitor. I don't recommend outright lying or obvious deception because it is too embarrassing if you are caught.

If you are new in the industry, people won't recognize you and you needn't worry about disguises. It is most practical to pose as a potential buyer but there are two major drawbacks to this approach. If you appear too interested as a buyer, the salesperson will buttonhole you and it will be hard to get away without being rude. Remember you have many booths to check out and can't spend too much time in any one of them.

If your questions are too sharp and informed the salesperson might get suspicious. If he thinks you are making a fool of him by coming on deceptively he might try to turn the tables and embarrass you or make an unpleasant scene. This situation should be avoided at all costs.

If company management is in the booth you can try another approach: Honesty with moderation. You might not necessarily want to say you are already in the business but that you are interested and looking at it carefully with an eye to getting involved in some way.

This approach creates several hooks for the executive in the booth. He is probably tired of talking with "retail" customers and answering the same dumb questions over and over again. When you come along being humble but asking more interesting questions and not threatening him or his company, you are giving him an opportunity to show off his knowledge and his job. What bored executive can resist an intelligent, attentive and non-threatening listener?

The factor hugely in your favor is trade shows are a place where people are supposed to communicate.

## Telephone Technique

You can often get an incredible amount of information from a company executive by calling and presenting yourself and your questions in the right way.

Here is an example: I once needed information on digital control of stepping motors — a subject which at that time was quite novel and fairly proprietary.

There was little in the literature because the knowledge about the subject resided with the R&D departments of the motor control companies.

I looked up a group of these companies in the Los Angeles Yellow Pages, called the biggest and asked the receptionist for the name of the president—"Joe Doe." I then called the second company, asked to talk to the boss and told him, "I asked Joe Doe who was the most informed on Digital Motor Control in the whole industry and he said to call you." Ethical?

In Greek mythology, businessmen and thieves shared the same god: Lucre. Like other information in this book, the incident above tells you what *works*. How or if you use it is up to you.

When you begin to center on the sector of the industry that feels right you will want to find out all you can about the companies already working that field. Each of these companies will be a competitor should you decide this is where you belong.

## Growth Sectors in the Market

Which of these growth areas will see the strongest increases for you in the decade of the 80's?

Computers in the classroom? One of the biggest problems here is to get teachers to feel comfortable with their machines. The kids already do because of the success of the computer game arcades!

Classroom demos are a good idea—if you can get your foot in the door. Make the programs fun and easy for the teacher. Once a teacher is sold you can present a formal analysis of benefits, costs and maintenance to the School Board. Sell them first on a pilot program. The kids of today will surely be tomorrow's computer maniacs—you might as well start them out right.

Teaching? You might think of giving programming seminars and extention classes. Studies have shown a high school or college graduate gets $1000 per year more to start if they know *anything* about programming. This is a great selling feature for seminars and local classes.

Seminars on word processing? An important item. They will continue to be important through the 80's. These seminars can be set up in a high school or college meeting room and need only one CPU and a series of terminals (one per six students).

Innovations? Hand-held recall systems that can access information from a remote computer system. Think of the advantage for realtors, engineers, architects, builders, even the military. The potential is enormous!

Programming innovations? Computerize the computer manuals. It could make it easier to reference and thus easier to get more out of the computer. You would need permission of the computer manufacturers to do this. But why not re-write the manuals? Most need serious revision and clarification.

Research? Light Emitting Films are a billion dollar business for the organization that cracks the technical puzzle. Think of the market for a *thin* display. It would, for instance, make the hand-held recall system practical. Dick Tracy, here we come! Remember, the membrane keyboard was invented by a entrepreneur working in his garage. How about LEF?

Bubble memory? Rockwell has abandoned the project as too difficult. *All* of their research data is available from the National Technical Information Service on microfiche at a buck per two hundred pages. This knowledge is in the public domain because Rockwell's research was government funded. Were they going about the problem in the right way? Remember big companies sometimes have problems with simple ideas.

Organic computers? LSI and VLSI technology is essentially two dimensional. Brain tissue functions in three dimensions. The pea sized brain of a pigeon has *enormous* integrative, functional, storage and learning capacity when compared to our best technology on a size basis. It even has an inertial guidance system accurate to arc seconds over a thousand mile range!

Can a bacterial colony be "programmed" to store and integrate information? Can mammalian brain tissue be "genetically engineered" to perform anywhere near the vast functional capability of a natural organic system?

A book could be written about the technical, moral and ethical considerations of creating a synthesis of artificial intelligence and organic engineering. In fact I think *I'll* do it.

Information Brokerage? As more complete files become available to computer search the services of computer information retrieval specialists become more relevant and practical.

The decade of the 80's represents a technical revolution which consumes information by the bale. It is said if NASA stacked up the information generated by the Apollo projects they could have walked to the moon.

The information industry is only just awakening. The combination of necessary function and availability of networked retrieval systems will drive this industry to an important place in the microcomputer world.

## The Biggest Market Opportunity

The *biggest* problem in this industry is communications. Here is a typical letter from a business owner who just bought his first system:

John Semiwise
Semiwise Accounting Service
1233 Main Street
Skokie, IL 20234

*It is no wonder more businessmen don't buy computers. I just bought a word processor and things have turned out really badly with my purchase. I'm not only sorry I bought it but I have on several occasions considered cutting the machine in half with my chain saw and ritually burning the instruction mannual.*

*I have been a victim of false and misleading advertising by the computer manufacturers, the software vendors and the retail outlet where I purchased this disaster. The salesman at the store led me to believe the operation of my system would be easy. It certainly is not!*

*My system simply couldn't do what I had been led to believe it could do. I spent so many hours trying to get the machine to behave properly that my business began to suffer.*

*The instruction books that come with the machine were unclear, full of misleading cryptography and were obviously written with a nuclear physicist in mind as the reader. These "instruction manuals" seemed to assume I already knew an awful lot about computers–wrong!*

*I went back to the computer store salesman but he was busy playing lifesavers and toothbrushes on the store's new Atari. He was really put out that he had to interrupt the game–he had just won a toothbrush and was well out in front of the cavities.*

*I am forced to conclude the computer I bought is really just a hobbyists' toy. It's not suited to my needs because I can't operate the goddamn thing. This bad experience will probably prejudice my thinking about computers for a long time to come.*

*Very pessimistically yours,*

John Semiwise
Semiwise Accounting Service

I spoke with a representative of one of the big microsystem manufacturers about this problem. The manufacturer's attitude was that John expected more of his system than it could give. His processor, for instance, had only upper case capability and the software was written and marketed by a hobbyist who didn't work it out properly.

## Consumer Education

Part of the problem is the prospective buyer doesn't know what questions to ask. This brings us to the rate-limiting factor in today's computer industry: *Not* hardware reliability, *not* technology, but *consumer education*.

Computers are complicated and many of the ideas they operate on are new to our culture. The average person is intimidated by the complexity of the system and doesn't know enough about it to even begin to ask questions.

Word processors have been a boon to the industry because they provide a comprehensible, logical step between a typewriter and computer. As a business person becomes familiar with the workings of his word processor he begins to lose his fear of computers in general. He has now developed a basis to build his knowledge on. He is no longer bowled-over by cryptic phrases like boot, baud and byte.

A computer store manager told me: "Our biggest problem is getting a customer who is sufficiently informed to communicate with us. The manufacturers leave the burden of consumer education to us and it is too big a job for a single sector of the industry to handle. The key to real growth in this industry is consumer education. I agree, word processors have been useful to provide some of this education but it isn't enough. Give me a customer I can communicate with and I will be able to sell him a bigger system with greater expectation of satisfaction."

The real point of all this is: where there is a need there is a way to profit by filling the need. There is a great need for grassroots educational processing of potential computer purchasers. Said another way, more people would be able to avail themselves of the benefits a computer could lend their life if only they knew enough to take advantage of it.

This means there is a huge potential market for seminars, newsletters, books, pamphlets, tapes and talk shows on the subject of computer fundamentals. This idea has a golden lining. Are there any takers?

The following is an extensive list of trade shows, seminars and industry meetings scheduled throughout 1981. I used this year because it was the most recent year I could gather rather complete information for. I assume these same organizations will be sponsoring shows throughout the next few years and that many will be held on nearly the same dates and in the same locations as before. Please contact the sponsor or the people at the show location before you make plans to attend one of these events. They may have changed the meeting dates or location.

I will try to maintain an updated list of these meetings and their published date and location. If you find there is an error in what I have shown here please drop me a line. In return for one of these corrections I will send you my updated meeting list.

*Trade Shows Organizations:*

Consumer Electronics Show hosts trade shows around the country. Two Illinois Center, Suite 1601, 233 North Michigan Avenue, Chicago,IL 60601.

National Computer Shows, 824 Boylston Street, Chestnut Hill,MA 02167, (617) 739-2000.

Computer Swap America, John Craig, P.O. Box 52, Palo Alto, CA 94302.

JANUARY

*Sixth Semiannual ATE Seminar/Exhibit* — January 9-10 — Pasadena, California.
Features a comprehensive program of workshops, technical papers, and courses. Contact Sheila Goggin, ATE, 1050 Commonwealth Ave., Boston, MA 02215, (617) 232-5470.

*TV-MEX* — January 15-17 — Birmingham, England.
The TV-Microelectronics and Microprocessing Exhibit is Europe's only trade exhibition devoted to all aspects of microelectronics and microprocessing for home, business, and education. Contact Jane Buchanan, 11 Manchester Sq., London, W1M 5AB, 01-486-1951.

*Telecommunications/China* — January 17-25 — Peking.
The second of its kind, this exhibition is limited entirely to U.S. companies; it introduces American products in China and explains the products' uses. Contact Expoconsul, a Division of Clapp & Poliak, Inc., Princeton-Windsor Office Park, P.O. Box 277, Princeton Junction, NJ 08550, (609)448-3200.

*ATE Seminar/Exhibit* — January 18-21 — Pasadena Center, Pasadena, California.
Information: Elaine Bull, Promotion Coordinator, ATE Seminar/Exhibit, 1050 Commonwealth Ave., Boston, MA 02215, (617) 232-5470.

*SOUTHCON* — Orange County Convention Center — Orlando, Florida.
Information: Dale Litherland, Electronics Conventions, Inc., 999 N. Sepulveda Blvd., El Segundo, CA 90245, (213) 772-2965.

*P.A.T.H. Conference* — January 19-22 — Dallas, Texas.

The Bank Administration Institute sponsors this conference on Productivity through Automation, Technology, and Human Resources. Contact Alice M. Moore, P.O. Box 500, 303 S. Northwest Highway, Park Ridge, IL 60068, (312) 693-7300.

*Texas Computer Show* — January 20-22 — Dallas, Texas.
The Texas show is scheduled to become a yearly event, covering all aspects of computer and word processing equipment, peripherals, software, and services. Contact Intercontinental Trade Shows, Inc., P.O. Box 214035, Dallas, TX 75221, (214) 761-9108.

*Data & Telecommunications/Japan* — January 20-23 — Tokyo, Japan.
Suppliers of PABX equipment, modems, cables, etc., from all over the world will be exhibiting at the Tokyo exposition. A conference program is also scheduled. Contact Industrial & Scientific Conference Management, Inc., 222 West Adams St., Chicago, IL 60606, (312) 263-4866.

HISSG Winter Seminar — January 20-23 — Long Beach, California.
The Theme for the Hospital Information Systems Sharing Group seminar is "Cost Containment — The Legislative and Voluntary Aspects and Their Effect on Hospital Information Systems." Contact W. V. Rosqvist, Hospital Information Systems Sharing Group, 2415 South 2300 West, Salt Lake City, UT 84119, (801) 972-6099.

*ASEE* — January 26-28 — San Jose, California.
The Advanced Semiconductor Equipment Exposition is the fourth annual show and conference of semiconductor processing, production, and test equipment and materials supplies. Contact Cartlidge & Associates, Inc.,491 Macara Ave., Sunnyvale, CA 94086, (408) 245-6870.

*First Military Computers & Software Seminar* — January 27-28.
American Defense Preparedness Association (ADPA, 900 Rosslyn Center, 170 N. Moore St., Arlington, VA 22209, Sheraton National Hotel, Arlington, VA.

*Communications Networks* — January 28-30 — Washington, D.C.
The national business communication conference and exposition. Contact William Leitch, Conference Company, 60 Austin St., Newton, MA 02160, (617) 964-4550.

*WINCO* — January 29-30 — Los Angeles, California.
Scientists and engineers from government, military and industry will attend to prove new technology and developments in electronics and aerospace. Contact Richard L. Harmon, (714) 557-4700.

## FEBRUARY

*Microprocessor-Based Energy Management Systems* — February 2-4 — U. of Wisconsin-Madison, Madison, Wisconsin.
Information: Robert P. Madding, Dept. of Engineering, U. of Wisconsin Extension, 432 N. Lake St., Madison, WI 53706, (608) 263-7920.

*Aerospace and Electronic Systems Winter Convention* — February 3-5 — Sheraton Universal Hotel, North Hollywood, California.
Information: William H. Minshull, Bldg. A 107, Hughes Aircraft Corp., Culver City, CA 90230, (213) 391-0711.

*Invitational Computer Conference* — February 3 & 5 — Pier 66 Hotel, Ft. Lauderdale, Florida, and Radisson Inn Atlanta, Atlanta, Georgia.
Information: B. J. Johnson & Assoc., 2503 Eastbluff Dr., Suite 203, Newport Beach, CA 92660, (714) 644-6037.

*15th Annual Television Conference* — February 6-7.
Society of Motion Picture and Television Engineers (862 Scarsdale Ave., Scarsdale, NY 10583), St. Francis Hotel, San Francisco.

*Financial Information Systems Confernce* — February 9-11 — San Francisco, California.
Presented by the National Institute of Management Research, this three-day conference has various sessions and workshops concentrating on financial systems. Contact NIMR Systems, PR Dept., P.O. Box 3727, Santa Monica, CA 90403, (213) 450-0500.

*International Symposium on Information Theory* — February 9-12 — Santa Monica, California.
Information: Prof. Izhak Rubin or Kung Yao, System Science Dept., 4531 Boetler Hall, U. of Southern California, Los Angeles, CA 90024, (213) 825-2240.

*Los Angeles Technical Symposium* — February 9-13.
Society of Photo-Optical Instrumentation Engineers (P.O. Box 10, Bellingham, WA 98225), Sheraton-Universal Hotel, North Hollywood, CA.

*International Solid State Circuits Conference* — February 10-12 — Hilton Hotel, San Francisco, California.
Information: L. Winner, 301 Almeria Ave., Coral Gables, FL 33134, (305) 446-8193.

*DATA* — February 12-14 — Toronto, Canada.
The program will feature panel sessions, audiovisual presentations, workshops, and technical sessions related to the field of data communications. Contact Laurie Whitsed, 1 Bloor St. West, Suite 2504, Toronto, Ontario M4W 3E2, (416) 967-6200.

*IEEE Internatonal Solid-State Circuits Conference* — February 18-20 — IEEE, Grand Hyatt Hotel, New York, New York.
The ISSCC is sponsored by the IEEE and is currently running in its 28th year. Contact Lewis Winner, 201 Almeria Ave., Box 343788, Coral Gales, FL 33134, (305) 446-8193-4.

*The European Information and Management Exhibition and Conference* — February 18-21 — London, England.
The major European forum for all managers and equipment suppliers. Contact Linwood Williams, Expoconsul, 420 Lexington Ave., New York, NY 10017, (212) 953-1190.

*COMPCON Spring* — February 23-26 — IEEE Computer Society, Jack Tar Hotel, San Francisco, California.
The theme for the spring conference is VLSI and its future effects on design systems. Contact Harry Hayman, IEEE, P.O. Box 639, Silver Spring, MD 20901, (301) 589-3386.

*ACM Computer Science Conference and Technical Symposium on Computer Science Educaton* — February 23-26 — St. Louis, Missouri.
The Association for Computing Machinery sponsors this computer science conference. Contact John W. Hamblen, University of Missouri-Rolla, Computer Science Dept., Rolla, MO 65401, (314) 341-4491. Stouffer's Riverfront Towers, St. Louis, MO, Feb. 24-26 (conference) and 26-27 (symposium).

*NEPCON West* — February 24-26 — Anaheim, California.
The conference is directed toward all persons involved in manufacturing and testing printed circuits, multilayers, microelectronic circuitry, semiconductors, and other devices. Contact Industrial & Scientific Conference Management, Inc., 222 West Adams St., Chicago, IL 60606, (312) 263-4866.

MARCH

*Information Utilities '81* — March 2-4 — New York Hilton, New York, New York.
Online Inc. (11 Tannery Lane, Weston, CN 06883).

*Invitational Computer Conference* — March 3 & 5 — Dallas Marriott, Dallas, Texas, and Adams Mark Hotel, Houston, Texas.
Information: B.J. Johnson & Assoc., Inc., 2503 Eastbluff Dr., Suite 203, Newport Beach, CA 92660, (714) 644-6037.

*Manufacturing Management: The Japanese Formula* — March 6 — Hyatt Rickey's, Palo Alto, California.
American Electronics Association (2600 El Camino Real, Palo Alto, CA 94306).

*Conference on Application Development Systems* — March 9-11 — Santa Clara, California.
Contact Mitch Zolliker, IBM Research, San Jose, CA 95121, (408) 256-7582.

*Fifth International Conference on Software Engineering* — March 9-12 — Town & Country Hotel, San Diego, California.
The ACM sponsors this one. Contact Seymour Jeffrey, Director, Center for Programming Sciences & Technology, National Bureau of Standards, Washington, D.C. 20234, (301) 921-3531. Information: Harry Hayman, P.O. Box 629, Silver Spring, MD 20901, (301) 589-3386.

*Micro-Delcon '81—Fourth Annual Conference on Computer Technology* — March 10.
IEEE Computer Society, Delaware Bay Section (H.P. Morneau, E.I. du Pont de Nemours & Co., Engineering Department, Louviers 3113, Wilmington, DL 19898), John M. Clayton Hall, University of Delaware, Wilmington, Delaware.

*Fourth Electromagnetic Compatibility Symposium and Technical Exhibition* — March 10-12.
Institute for Communications Technology (T. Dvorak, The Federal Institute of Technology, Zurich, Switzerland), Federal Institute of Technology.

*SEMICON/EUROPA '81 and Second Semi European Symposium on Materials and Processing* — March 10-12 — Zuspa Convention Center, Zurich, Switzerland.
Semiconductor Equipment and Materials Institute Inc. (625 Ellis St., Suite 212, Mountain View, California 94043).

*The National Office Exhibition and Conference* — March 10-12 — Toronto, Canada.
The office of the future and methods of storage and transmission of information will be debated. Contact Paul Day, 2 Bloor St. West, Suite 2504, Toronto, Ontario M2W 3E2, (416) 967-6200.

*PRODUX 2000* — March 11-13 — New York, New York.
PRODUX consists of two separate shows — Business & Personal Computer Sales — Expo '81, and the 1981 New York Business Show. Contact George Pachter, PRODUX 2000, Inc., Roosevelt Blvd. & Mascher St., Philadelphia, PA 19102.

*California Computer Shows* — March 12 — Inn-at-the-Park, Anaheim, California.
Information: Norm De Nardi, 95 Main St., Los Altos, CA 94022, (415) 941-8440.

*Fifth West Coast Computer Faire* — March 14-16 — San Francisco, California.
Will focus on inexpensive computer power for home, business, and industry. Contact Computer Faire, 333 Swett Rd., Woodside,CA 94062, (415) 841-7075.

*Industrial and Control Applications of Microprocessors, IECI '81* — March 16-18 — Sheraton Hotel, Philadelphia, Pennsylvania.
Information: H. Troy Nagle, Dept. of Electrical Engineering, Auburn U., Auburn, AL 36830.

*Fourteenth Annual Simulation Symposium* — March 16-20 — Holiday Inn Resort, Tampa, Florida.
Part of Simulation Week, the symposium is sponsored by the IEEE, ACM, SCS, and IMAC. Contact Alexander Kran, IBM, B/300-4-E, East Fishkill Facility, Hopewell Junction, NY 12533, (914) 897-2121 x7142.

*Spring Conference, Sperry UNIVAC Series 1100 Users* — March 16-20 — Bahrain.
First international event of the kind held in the Persian Gulf. Will contain a comprehensive and modern range of products and services from the entire spectrum of the business equipment industry. Contact Stephen Powell, Arabian Exhibition Manager, 11 Manchester Square, London, Q1M 5AB, 01-486-1951.

*Third Annual Microelectronics Measurement Technology Seminar* — March 17-18 — San Jose Hyatt, San Jose, California.
Benwill Publishing Corp. (1050 Commonwealth Ave., Boston, MA 02215).

*Data Communications* — March 19-20 and May 7-8 — Worcester Polytechnic Institute, Worcester, Massachusetts.
Information: Ginny Bazarian, Office of Continuing Education, Worcester Polytechnic Inst., Worcester, MA 01609, (617) 753-1411.

*28th International Electronics, Nuclear, and Aerospace Exhibition* — March 20-29.
With conferences on computer and energy from space. REINA (9 Via Cresenzio, Rome, Italy), Palazzo dei Congressi, EUR, Rome, Italy.

*Status '81—A Report on the Integrated Circuit Industry.*
Integrated Circuit Engineering Corp. (15022 N. 75th St., Scottsdale, AZ 85260), Hyatt Rickey's, Palo Alto, CA, Jan. 28; Travelodge International Hotel, JFK International Airport, New York, NY, Feb. 11; Hotel International, Zurich, March 13; Hotel Nikko, Paris, March 20.

*Office Automation Conference* — March 23-25 — Albert Thomas Convention Center, Houston, Texas.
The major conference for users and designers of electronic office equipment, the OAC is produced yearly by AFIPS. Contact AFIPS, 1815 North Lynn St., Arlington, VA 22209, (703) 558-3620. Information: Kate Frye, Office Automation Conf., P.O. Box 9659, Arlington, VA 22209, (703) 558-3617.

*Error Correcting and Detecting Codes* — March 23-25 — Congress Building, International Fair of Genoa, Genoa, Italy.
Information: Manager, Rome Branch of Administrative Office, 5th ICDSC, Telespazio SPA, Corso D'Italia 43, 00198 Rome, Italy.

*Ditital Communications Techniques Seminar* — March 24 — Princeton University, Princeton, New Jersey.
IEEE and Princeton University Department of Electrical Engineering.

*FOC 81 East* — International Fiber Optics and Communications Exposition — March 24-26 — Hyatt Regency, Boston, Massachusetts.
Information: Gatekeepers Inc. (167 Corey Rd., Suite 111, Brookline, MA 02146).

*Printemps Informatique* — March 24-27 — Palais de Congre, Paris, France.
An international edp exhibit for computer oems. Contact Kallman Associates, 30 Journal Sq., Jersey City, NJ 07306, (201) 653-3304.

*High Temperature Electronics Conference* — March 25-27 — Ramada Inn, Tucson, Arizona.
IEEE, Department of Energy, and University of Arizona.

*VIEWDATA '80* — March 26-28 — London, England.
The first world conference and exhibition on computerized TV-based information, education, and entertainment. Contact TMAC, 680 Beach St., Suite 428, San Francisco, CA 94109, (800) 227-3477; in California (415) 474-3000.

*Semiconductor Microlithography VI Conference* — March 30-31 — San Jose Hyatt House, San Jose, California.
Society of Photo Optical Instrumentation Engineers (P.O. Box 10, Bellingham, WA 98225).

*1981 IEEE International Conference on Acoustics, Speech, and Signal Processing* — March 30-April 1 — Sheraton-Atlanta Hotel, Atlanta, Georgia.
Information: Ronald W. Schaefer, Dept. of Electrical Engineering, Georgia Inst. of Tech., Atlanta, GA 30332, (404) 894-2917.

*Data Communications* — March-April — (various dates and locations).
An Introduction to Concepts and Systems; Advanced Concepts and Systems; Effective Network Design; Systems Analysis and Design; Concepts and Effective Practice; and Advanced Techniques. Information: Datapor Research Corp., 1805 Underwood Blvd., Delran, NJ 08075, (609) 764-0100.

## MARCH SHORT COURSES

*Microprocessor Application Design* — March 2-4, 4-6, 5-6, 9-12, and 16-17.
Advanced Micro Devices, Inc., Customer Education Center, Sunnyvale, CA. Information: Advanced Micro Devices, Inc., Customer Education Center, 490-A Lakeside Dr., Sunnyvale, CA 94086, (408) 732-2400.

*Digital Electronics for Automation and Instrumentation* — March 23-24; *TRS-80 Radio Shack Microcomputer Interfacing and Programming for Scientific Instrumentation* — March 25-28; and *Motorola Single Chip Interfacing and Programming Using the 6801, 6809,and 6800* — March 25-28.
Virginia Polytechnic Inst. and State U., Blacksburg, VA. Information: Dr. Linda Leffel, CEC Virginia Tech., Blacksburg, VA 24061, (703) 961-5241.

*Custom Integrated Circuits and Integrated Circuits for Telecommunication* — March 24-25, San Francisco Hilton, San Francisco, California.
Information: Continuing Education in Engineering, U. of California Extension, 2223 Fulton St., Berkeley, CA 94720, (415) 642-3112.

## MARCH MEETINGS

*Sixth Annual Spring Financial Conference* — March 11-13, Del Monte Hyatt House, Monterey, California.
American Electronics Association (2600 El Camino Real, Palo Alto, CA 94306).

*Monaco Financial Conference* — March 15-18 — Loews Monte Carlo Hotel, Monte Carlo, Monaco.

American Electronics Association (2600 El Camino Real, Palo Alto, CA 94306).

*Leipzig International Spring Fair* — March 15-21 — Leipzig Fairgrounds, Leipzig, East Germany.
Leipziger Messeamt (P.O. Box 720, DDR-701, Leipzig, East Germany).

*SCTE Spring Engineering Conference* — March 16-17 — Opryland Hotel, Nashville, Tennessee.
Society of Cable Television Engineers Inc. (1900 L St. N.W., Suite 614, Washington, DC 20036).

*LSI Technology Conference: Circuit Design, Systems and Applications* — March 16-18 — Congress Hall, Baden-Baden, West Germany.
Verbland Deutscher Elektrotechniker (6000 Frankfurt 70, Stresemannallee, West Germany).

APRIL

*Interface '81—Ninth National Data Communications/Distributed Data Processing Conference* — March 30-April 2 — Las Vegas Convention Center, Las Vegas, Nevada.
The Interfacing Group (160 Speen St., Framingham, MA 01701).

*Optical Characterization Techniques for Semiconductor Technology Conference* — April 1-2 — San Jose Hyatt House, San Jose, California.
Society of Photo-Optical Instrumentation Engineers (P.O. Box 10, Bellingham, WA 98825).

*First International Conference on Robot Vision and Sensory Controls* — April 1-3 — Hilton Hotel, Stratford-Upon-Avon, England.
IFS Conferences Ltd. (35/39 High St., Kempston, Bedford MK42 7BT, England).

*International Conference on Distributed Computing Systems* — April 1-3 — Paris, France.
Information: E. Gelinbe, Univ.de Paris-Sud, LBI Batlment 490, 91405 Orsay Cedex, France.

*DPMA Quality Assurance Conference* — April 1-3 — Chicago, Illinois.
The objective of this conference, sponsored by the DPMA Education Foundation, is to explain methods, tools, and techniques for improving computerized applications. Contact DPMA, 12611 Davan Dr., Silver Spring, MD 20904, (301) 622-0066.

*Hanover Fair* — April 1-8 — Germany.
One of the world's largest technology exhibitions, it combines dp and office products as well as a variety of noncomputer-related pavilions. Conduct Deutsche Messe-und Ausstellungs-AG, Messegelande, D-3000, Hanover 82, Germany.

*Invitational Computer Conference* — April 2 — Sheraton Denver Tech Center — Denver, Colorado.
Information: B. J. Johnson & Assoc., Inc., 2503 Eastbluff Dr., Suite 203, Newport Beach, CA 92660, (714) 644-6037.

*6th West Coast Computer Faire* — April 3-5 — Civic Auditorium, San Francisco, California.
Since 1977, this small annual business and personal computing conference and exposition with a strong focus on micros has been held regularly. Contact Computer Faire, 333 Swett Rd., Woodside, CA 94062, (415) 851-7075.

Information: Ben Catanzaro, MCSD Customer Training SV3-1, 1350 Bordeaux Dr.,
*Computers in Manufacturing* — April 6-8 — New York, New York.
Computers and dp as tools in manufacturing. Contact NIMR Seminars, P.O. Box 3727, Santa Monica, CA 90403, (213) 450-0500.

*Industry Oriented Spring Conference and Exhibit* — April 6-9 — Cervantes Convention Center, St. Louis, Missouri.
Information: Instrument Society of America, 67 Alexander Dr., P.O. Box 12277, Research Triangle Park, NC 27709, (919) 549-8411.

*1981 AECT National Convention* — April 6-10 — Philadelphia, Pennsylvania.
The Association for Educational Communications and Technology produces this show, the largest gathering of structural media/AV professionals in the U.S. Contact AECT, 1126 16th St. N.W., Washington, DC 20036, (202) 833-4179.

*Tutorial Week—East* — April 6-10 — Orlando Marriott Inn, Orlando, Florida.
Information: Tutorial Week — East, P.O. Box 639, Silver Springs, MD 20901, (301) 439-7077.

*Survival and Growth of the Engineering Industries Through Integration of CAD/CAM Technology* — April 7-9 — Carlton Hotel, Cannes, France.
Information: Rhonda Gerganess, Computer-Aided Manufacturing International, Inc., 611 Ryan Plaza Dr., Suite 1107, Arlington, TX 76011, (817) 265-5328.

*Electro/81 Show and Convention* — April 7-9 — New York Coliseum and Sheraton Centre, New York, New York.
IEEE Information: Dale Litherland, Electronic Conventions Inc., 999 N. Sepulveda Blvd., El Segundo, CA 90245, (213) 772-2965.

*International Reliability Physics Symposium* — April 7-9 — Sheraton Twin Towers, Orlando, Florida.
Information: John Edwards, General Chairman, American Microsystems, Inc., 3800 Homestead Rd., Santa Clara, CA 95051, (408) 246-0330.

*Southwest Computer Show and Office Equipment Exposition* — April 9-12 — Market Hotel, Dallas Market Center, Dallas, Texas.
Information: Bill Mayhan, National Computer Shows, 824 Boylston St., Chestnut Hill, MA 02167, (617) 739-2000.

*Integrating Business Machines into Local and Intercity Networks* — April 14-15 — Harvard Club, New York, New York.
The Yankee Group (P.O. Box 43, Cambridge, MA 02138).

*Peripherals '80* — April 16-17 — London, England.
An Exhibition for purchasers of computer equipment. Contact Lliffe Promotions Ltd., Dorset House, Stamford St., London SE1 9Lu, 01-261-8437/8.

*The DOD FY '82 Research and Development Program* — April 21-23 — Stouffer's National Center Hotel, Arlington, Virginia.
EIA (2001 Eye St., N.W., Washington, DC 20006).

*California Computer Shows* — April 23 — Hyatt Palo Alto, Palo Alto, California.
Information: Norm De Nardi, 95 Main St., Los Altos, CA 94022, (415) 941-8440.

*Ninth Annual Telecommunications Policy Research Conference* — April 26-29, Annapolis, Maryland.

The object of this conference is to provide a forum for the analysis and discussion of telecommunications policy issues. Contact William E. Taylor, Bell Laboratories, 2C-258, 600 Mountain Ave., Murray Hill, NJ 07974, (201) 582-2108.

*Communicaciones Expo '81* — April 26-30 — Coconut Grove Exhibition Center, Miami, Florida.
Information: Gloria Gomez-Mena de Marina, Marketing and Promotion Div., City of Miami, Office of Trade and Commerce Dev., 100 N. Biscayne Blvd., Suite 901, Miami, FL 33132, (305) 579-3320. Communicaciones Expo '81, Gables One Tower, 1320 S. Dixie Highway, Coral Gables, FL 33146.

*IOCC '81—THIRD INTERNATIONAL CONFERENCE ON INTEGRATED OPTICS AND OPTICAL FIBER COMMUNICATIONS* — April 27-29 — Hyatt Regency, San Francisco, California.
Information: Barbara Hicks, Optical Society of America, 1816 Jefferson Pl., N.W., Washington, DC 20036, (202) 233-8130. IEEE.

## APRIL SHORT COURSES

*Data Communications Systems* — April 1-3 — Sheraton Tara Hotel, Farmington, Massachusetts.
Information: Amer. Inst. for Professional Education, Carnegie Bldg., Hillcrest Rd., Madison, NJ 07940, (210) 377-7400.

*Data Communications and Computer Graphics Series* — Spring-Summer '81 — (various locations)
Information: Karen Smolens, Center for Management Research, 850 Boylston St., Chestnut Hill, MA 02167.

## APRIL MEETINGS

*SOUTHEASTCON 81* — April 5-8 — IEEE, Von Braun Civic Center, Huntsville, Alabama.

*Electronic Warfare Conference* — April 5-9 — U.S.Naval Postgraduate School, Monterey, California.
American Electronics Association (2600 El Camino Real, Palo Alto, CA 94306).

*Second Oxford Conference on the Microscopy of Semiconducting Materials* — April 6-10 — St. Catherine's College, Oxford, England.
Royal Microscopial Society/UK Institute of Physics (A.G. Cullis, Royal Signals and Radar Establishment, St. Andrews Road, Malvern, Worc. WR14 3PS, England).

*Sixth International Symposium on Noise in Physical Systems* — April 6-10.
National Bureau of Standards (Building 221, Room B128, Washington, DC 20234) and Catholic University of America, NBS, Gaithersburg, MD.

*International Electronic Components Show* — April 6-11, Paris Fairgrounds, Porte de Versailles, Paris, France.
Societe pour la Diffusion de Sciences et des Artes (20 Rue Hamelin, F 75116 Paris, France).

*Second International Conference on Distributed Computing Systems* — April 8-10 — Paris, France.
IEEE et al. (Institute National de Recherche en Informatique et en Automatique,

Domaine de Voluceau-Rocquencourt, 78150 Le Chesany, France).

*59th Annual Convention of the National Association of Broadcasters* — April 12-15 — Las Vegas Convention Center, Las Vegas, Nevada.
NAB (1771 N St., N.W., Washington, DC 20036).

*1981 Engineers Public Affairs Forum* — April — Hyatt Regency Hotel, Washington, DC.
National Society of Professional Engineers (Public Relations Department, 2029 K St., N.W., Washington, DC 20006).

*Second International Conference on Antennas and Propagation* — April 13-16 — University of York, Heslington, England.
Institution of Electrical Engineers, (Savoy Place, London WC2R OB1, England).

*Federal DP Expo* — April 14-16 — Sheraton Washington Hotel, Washington, DC.
The Interface Group (160 Speen St., Framingham, MA 01701).

*Western Regional Technical Symposium* — April 19-22 — Marriott Hotel, San Antonio, Texas.
Association of Old Crows, (P.K. Weir, Hewlett-Packard Co., 205 Billy Mitchell Rd., San Antonio, Texas 78226).

*Technical Symposium East* — April 20-24 — Hyatt Regency Hotel, Washington, DC.
Society of Photo-Optical Instrumentation Engineers (P.O. Box 10, Bellingham, WA 98227).

*Department of Defense/Industry Fiber Optics Standards Conference* — April 21-23 — Sheraton Hotel, Washington, DC.
EIA (2001 Eye St., N.W., Washington, DC 20006).

*INFO/MFG (Information Management Expo and Conference for Manufacturing)* — April 27-29 — McCormick Place, Chicago, Illinois.
Information: Banner & Greif, Ltd., 110 E. 42nd St., New York, NY 10017, (212) 687-7730.

*ISCAS '81 — IEEE International Symposium on Circuits and Systems* — April 27-29 — Radisson Chicago Hotel, Chicago, Illinois.

*29th Annual National Relay Conference* — April 27-29
National Association of Relay Manufacturers and the School of Electrical Engineering, Oklahoma State University (Engineering Extension, 301 EN, Oklahoma State University, Stillwater, OK 74078), OSU.

*1981 International Tool and Manufacturing Engineering Conference and Exposition* — April 27-30 — Cobo Hall, Detroit, Michigan.
Society of Manufacturing Engineers (P.O. Box 930, Dearborn, MI 48128).

*1981 National Design Engineering Show and Converence* — April 27-30 — McCormick Place, Chicago, Illinois.
American Society of Mechanical Engineers (Clapp & Poliak Inc., 245 Park Ave., New York, NY 10167).

*POWERCON 8 — International Power Electronics Conference* — April 27-30 — Loews Anatole Dallas Hotel, Dallas, Texas.
Power Concepts, Inc. (P.O. Box 5226, Ventura, CA 93003).

*National Design Engineering Show & ASME Conference* — April 27-30 — McCormick

Place, Chicago, Illinois.
Information: Banner & Greif, Ltd., 110 E. 42nd St., New York, NY 10017, (212) 687-7730.

*POWERCON 8* — April 27-30 — Loew's Anatole Hotel, Dallas, Texas.
Information: POWERCON 8 Program Chairman, Power Concepts, Inc., P.O. Box 5226, Ventura, CA 93003, (805) 985-6978.

*27th Annual International Instrumentation Symposium* — April 27-30 — Hyatt Regency Hotel, Indianapolis, Indiana.
Information: Instrumentation Society of America (P.O. Box 12277, Research Triangle Park, NC 27709, Hyatt Regency Hotel.

*Society for Information Display International Symposium* — April 27-May 1 — Grand Hyatt Hotel, New York, New York.
Information: SID, 654 N. Sepulveda Blvd., Los Angeles, CA 90049.

*Society for Information Display International Symposium* — April 27-May 1 — Grand Hyatt Hotel, New York, New York.
Information: Lewis Winner, 301 Almeria Ave., P.O. Box 343788, Coral Gables, FL 33134, (305) 446-8193.

*Federal DP Expo* — April 28-30 — Washington, DC.
Information: Update trends, applications, and state-of-the-art of all facets of ADP. Contact Sheldon Adelson, Conference Director, 160 Speen St., Framingham, MA 01701, (617) 879-4502.

*Annual Executive Forum on International Telecommunications* — April 28-30.
Arthur D. Little Inc. (25 Acorn Park, Cambridge, MA 02140), Palais des Congres, Paris.

*26th National SAMPE Symposium and Exhibition* — April 28-30 — Hyatt Hotel, Los Angeles Airport, Los Angeles, California.
Society for the Advancement of Material and Process Engineering (P.O. Box 613), Azusa, CA 91702).

*Socety for Information Display International Symposium* — April 28-May 1 — Grand Hyatt Hotel, New York, New York.
Information: Lewis Winner, 301 Almeria Ave., P.O. Box 343788, Coral Gables, FL 33134, (305) 446-8193/4 (1 to 5 PM).

*Tenth Conference on Computer Audit, Control, and Security* — April 28-May 2 — San Francisco, California.
Jointly sponsored by 11a and ATC. Contact John Sheehan, Manager of Public Relations, the Institute of Internal Auditors, Inc., 249 Maitland Ave., Altomonte Springs, FL 32701, (305) 830-7600.

*An Assessment and Forecast of Computer Graphics Conference* — April 30-May1 — Saddle Brook Marriott, Saddle Brook, New Jersey.
Information: Bob Sanzo, Frost & Sullivan, Inc., 106 Fulton St., New York, NY 10038, (212) 233-1080.

MAY

*General Purpose Interface Bus Workshop* — May 4 — Intel Training Center, San Francisco, California.

Sunnyvale, CA 94086, (408) 734-8102.

*NCC*—National Computer Conference and Personal Computing Festival — May 4-7 — McCormick Place, Chicago, Illinois.
American Federation of Information Processing Societies (P.O. Box 9658, 1815 N. Lynn St., Arlington, VA 22209).

*NCC—National Computer Conference* — May 4-7 — McCormick Place, Chicago, Illinois
Information: Gerard Chiffriller, 1815 N. Lynn St., Suite 800, Arlington, VA 22209, (703) 558-3600.

*PICA — 12th Power Industry Computer Applications Conference* — May 5-8 — Marriott Hotel, Philadelphia, Pennsylvania.
IEEE.

*AEDS Annual Convention* — May 5-8 — Minneapolis, Minnesota.
This convention is sponsored by the Association of Educational Data Systems each year. Contact Dale Schneiderhan, MECC, 2520 Broadway Dr., St. Paul,MN 55113, (612) 376-1600.

*Intelcom* — May 5-8 — Paris, France.
One in a series of Intelcom International Telecommunications and Computer Expos addressing the developments occuring in Europe, the Mediterranean, the Mid-East and Asia. Contact Horizon House, 610 Washington St., Dedham, MA 02026, (617) 326-8220.

*The Seventh International Symposium on Computer Architecture* — May 6-8 — LaBaule, France.
Contact Jacques Andre, Campus de Beulieu, Avenue de General Leclerc, 35042-Rennes, Cedex, France, (99) 36 48 15.

*Association for Systems Management Annual Conference* — May 10-13 — Las Vegas, Nevada.
The conference emphasizes systems planning, concepts, and advanced office systems. Contact R. B. McCaffrey, ASM, 24587 Bagley Rd., Cleveland, OH 44138, (216) 243-6900.

*AAMI 16th Annual Meeting and Exhbit* — May 10-13 — Sheraton Washington Hotel, Washington, DC.
Association for the Advancement of Medical Instrumentation (1901 N. Fort Myer Dr., Suite 602, Arlington, VA 22209).

*The European Consumer Electronics Show* — May 10-13 — Nuremberg, West Germany.
Industrial and Trade Fairs Ltd. (Radcliffe House, Blenheim Court, Solihul, West Midlands B91 2Bg, England).

*34th Annual Conference* — May 10-14 — Grand Hyatt Hotel, New York, New York.
Society of Photographic Scientists and Engineers (7003 Kilworth Lane, Springfield, VA 22151).

*SNA: The Blueprint for IBM's Telecommunications Future* and *Managing the Data Base Environment* — May 11-13; *The IBM 4300 Series* — May 13-15 & 20-22; *Local Network Architecture* and *Strategies for Distributed Computing* — June 1-3 — (various U.S. cities)
Information: Technology Transfer Inst., 741 10th St., Santa Monica, CA 90403, (213) 394-8305.

*INTELEC (International Telecommunications Energy Conference)* — May 19-21 — Royal Lancaster Hotel, London, England.
Information: INTELEC Secretariat, The Inst. of Electrical Engineers, Savoy Pl., London WC2R OBL, England.

*31st ECC — Electronic Components Conference* — May 11-13 — Colony Square Hotel, Atlanta, Georgia.
EIA and IEE.

*Eighth Annual International Symposium on Computer Architecture,* — May 12-14 — Holiday Inn, Minneapolis, Missouri.
Association for Computing Machinery and IEEE.

*Intermag—International Magnetics Conference* — May 12-15.
IEEE et al., AlpesCongres, Grenoble, France.

*15th IEE Photovaltaic Specialists Conference* — May 12-15 — Hyatt Orlando, Orlando, Florida.
IEEE.

*Fifth International Conference on Computers and the Humanities* — May 17-20 — Ann Arbor, Michigan.
The ACM, the University of Michigan and the Association for Literary & Linguistic Computing put this one together. Contact R. W. Bailey, Department of English, University of Michigan, Ann Arbor, MI 48104, (313) 764-6354.

*Spring DECUS (Digital Equipment Computer Users Society) U.S. Symposium* — May 18-21 — Miami Beach, Florida.
Information: Paula Morin, DECUS, One Iron Way, MR2-3/E55, Marlboro, MA 01752.

*High Technology Export Seminars* — May 19 — Hyatt Rickeys, Palo, Alto, California; June 25 — Marriott O'Hare Inn, Chicago, Illinois; (dates to be announced) — Boston, Massachusetts; Dallas, Texas; and Los Angeles, California.
EIA (2001 Eye St., N.W., Washington, DC 20006).

*Automan* — May 19-21 — England.
This is the first European Automated Manufacturing Exhibition & Conference. It will be devoted to robotics and automated manufacturing. Contact Clapp & Poliak International, 7315 Wisconsin Ave., Washington, DC 21104.

*NCC* — May 19-22 — Anaheim, California.
Will cover the broad areas of management, applications, science and technology, and social implications. Contact AFIPS, 1815 North Lynn St., Arlington, VA 22209, (703) 243-4100.

*CECON* — May 20-22 — Cleveland, Ohio.
The exhibits will display new products related to instruments, comonents, and systems. Contact Cleveland Electronics Conference, Inc., 2728 Euclid Ave., 5th floor, Cleveland, OH 44115, (216) 241-5515.

*NAECON* — May 20-22 — Dayton, Ohio.
The National Aerospace and Electronics Conference is the oldest and best known specialized National forum for the exchange of information on aerospace electronics. Contact Gordon Rabarus, Air Force Avionics, 140 E. Monument Ave., Dayton, OH 45402, (513) 255-2802.

MINICOM (International Symposium on Mini and Microcomputers in Control and Measurement) — May 20-22 — Hilton Hotel, San Francisco, California.
Information: P. L. Hsu, McDonnell Douglas Astronautics Co., 5301 Bolsa Ave., Huntington Beach, CA 92647, (714) 896-3311.

*Canadian National Conference and Exhibition* — May 25-27 — Hamilton, Ontario.
The DPMA's Hamilton conference (also called "Hard Hat Solution") is geared toward enhancing the education of novices to professionals in dept. Contact W. B. Seifried, 1981 National Conference Committee, P.O. Box 814, Station A, Hamilton, Ontario L8N 3MS, Canada.

*Office Korea* — May 26-29 — Seoul, Korea.
The second in an annual series. Last year's participants included the U.S., the U.K., Japan, and Korea. Contact Clapp & Poliak, International, 7315 Wisconsin Ave., Washington, DC 20014, (301) 657-3090.

*International Symposium on Multiple Valued Logic* — May 27-29 — Oklahoma City, Oklahoma.
Information: Dr. S. C. Lee, School of Electrical Engineering & Computer Science, U. of Oklahoma, 202 W. Boyd, Rm. 219, Norman, OK 73109, (405) 325-4721.

*Telecommunications: Trends and Directions* — May 26-28 — Dunfey's Hyannis Hotel, Hyannis, Massachusetts.
EIA (2001 Eye St., N.W., Washington, DC 20006).

*Fiber Optic Communications and Sensor Applications for Military and Government Markets,* — May 28-29 — Sheraton Islander Inn, Newport, Rhode Island.
Kessler Marketing Intelligence (22 Farewell St., Newport, RI 02840).

*CCUC—Custom Integrated Circuits Conference* — May 11-13 — Americana Hotel, Rochester, New York.
IEEE.

*Introduction to Pascal* — May 16 — Squibb World Headquarters, Princeton, New Jersey.
Information: Bill Hafstad, EDUCOM, P.O. Box 364, Princeton, NJ 08540, (201) 457-4055.

*Thirteenth ACM Symposium on Theory of Computing* — May 11-13 — Milwaukee, Wisconsin.
STOC is sponsored by the ACM's Special Interest Group for Automata and Computability Theory. Contact George Davida, School of Information & Computer Science. Georgia Institute of Technology, Atlanta, GA 30332, (404) 894-3152.

*CompuFest* — May 11-13 — Louisville, Kentucky.
The exhibition will feature vendors of computer hardware, software, service bureau services and other related computer products. Contact Kathy Schoen, Kentucky Society of CPA's, 310 W. Liberty St., Louisville, KY 40202, (502) 589-9239.

*Association for Systems Management Annual Conference* — May 10-13 — Las Vegas, Nevada.
The conference emphasizes systems planning, concepts, and advanced office systems. Contact R. B. McCaffrey, ASM, 24587 Bagley Rd., Cleveland, OH 44138, (216) 243-6900.

*Basic Elements of Digital Systems* — May 4-5; *Principals and Applications of Digital Devices in*

*Monitor and Control Systems* — May 6-8; *Microprocessors in Control Systems* — May 13-14; *Computer Process Control Strategies* — May 28-29 & June 11-12 — Research Triangle Park, North Carolina; Minneapolis, Minnesota; or Wilmington, Delaware.
Information: Instrument Society of America, Administrator, Continuing Education, 67 Alexander Dr., P.O. Box 12277, Research Triangle Park, NC 27709, (919) 549-8411.

*ISA Power Industry Division's National Symposium* — May 18-20 — Hyatt Pittsburgh Hotel, Pittsburgh, Pennsylvania.
Instrument Society of America (67 Alexander Drive, P.O. Box 12277, Rsearch Triangle Park, NC 27709).

*Automan — First European Automated Manufacturing Exhibition and Conference* — May 19-21 — Exhibition Centre, Brighton, England.
British Robot Association and IFS Conferences Ltd. (35-39 High St., Kempston, Bedford MK42 7BT, England).

*First European Conference on Cineradiography with Protons or Particles* — May 19-22 — Tour Oliver de Serres, Paris, France.
L'Association Nationale de la Recherche Technique (ANRT, 109 Ave., Raymond Poincare', 75116 Paris, France).

*Naecon — National Aerospace and Electronics Conference* — May 19-21 — Dayton Convention Center, Dayton, Ohio.
IEEE et al.

*Semicon/West* — May 19-21 — Semiconductor Equipment and Materials Institute Inc. (625 Ellis St., Suite 212, Mountain View, CA 94043).

*Third European Conference on Hybrid Microelectronics* — May 20-22 — Palais de Papes, Avignon, France.
International Society for Hybrid Microelectronics (Conference and Technical Forum Secretariat, ISHM, 11 Rue Hameline, 75783 Paris Cedex 16, France).

*Videotex* — May 20-22 — Royal York Hotel, Toronto, Canada.
Informart (12 St. Patrick St., Toronto, Ontario M5T 2X8, Canada) and Online Conferences Ltd. (Argyle House, Northwood Hills, Middlesex HA6 ITS, England).

*Ninth World Congress of the International Measurement Confederation* — May 24-28 — International Congress Center, West Berlin, Germany.
VDI/VDE Gresellschaft Messund Regelungstechnik, Graf-Recke-Strasse 84, P.O. Box 1139, D-4000, Dusseldorf 1, West Germany.

*Melecon — Mediterranean Electrotechnical Conference* — May 25-28 — Tel Aviv Hilton, Tel Aviv, Israel.
IEEE and the Association of Engineers and Architects in Israel.

*Fourth Biennial University/Government/Industry Microelectronics Symposium* — May 26-28 — Mississippi State University, Starkville, Mississippi.
IEEE, National Science Foundation,and International Society for Hybrid Microelectronics.

*16th Symposium on Electron, Ion, and Photon Beam Technology* — May 26-29 — Loews Anatole Dallas Hotel, Dallas, Texas.
IEEE Electron Devices Group and American Vacuum Society.

*35th Annual Frequency Control Symposium* — May 27-29 — Marriott Hotel, Philadelphia, Pennsylvania.
U.S. Army Electronics Technology and Devices Laboratory Electronics Research and Development Command (Fort Monmouth, NJ 07703).

*Microcomputer Show* — May 27-30 — Tokyo Ryutsu Center, Ota-ku, Tokyo, Japan.
Japan Electric Industrial Development Association (3-5-8 Shiba Koen, Mino-to-ku, Tokyo 105, Tokyo, Japan).

*NCTA 30th Annual Convention* — May 29-31 — Los Angeles Convention Center, Los Angeles, California.
National Cable Television Association, 918 16th Street, N.W., Washington, DC 20006.

*12th International Television Symposium* — May 30-June 4 — Exhibition Center, Montreux, Switzerland.
Swiss Postal and Telecommunications Administration (Symposium Secretariat, P.O. Box 122, CH-18-20, Montreux, Switzerland).

*Instruments Fair* — May 13-15 — Science Museum, Chiyoda-Ku, Tokyo, Japan.
Japan Optical Measuring Instruments Manufacturers' Association '3-5-8 Shiba Koen, Minato-Ku, Tokyo 105, Japan).

*56th Business Show* — May 13-16 — Tokyo International Fair Grounds, Chuo-Ku, Tokyo, Japan.
Nippon Administrative Management Association (4-1-13 Sendagaya, Shibuya-Ku, Tokyo 151, Japan).

*Computer Security Initiative Seminar* — May 18-20 — Gaithersburg, Maryland.
National Bureau of Standards (NBS) and Department of Defense (D. K. Branstad, A-265 Technology Building, NBS, Washington, DC 20234).

*Introduction to Pascal* — May 16; *Distributed Processing* — June 6 — Princeton, New Jersey.
Information: Bill Hafstaud, EDUCOM, P.O. Box 364, Princeton, NJ 08540, (201) 457-4055.

*Advances in Software Technology* — May 28 — Gaithersburg, Maryland.
IEEE and National Bureau of Standards, NBS.

*Trends and Applications: Advances in Software Technology* — May 28 — Gaithersburg, Maryland.
The IEEE and the NBS Institute for Computer Sciences and Technology co-sponsors this symposium. Contact Stan Lichtenstein, National Bureau of Standards, U.S. Dept. of Commerce, Washington, DC 20234, (301) 921-3181.

JUNE

Components—*Electronic Components Industry Fair* — June 9-12 — Earls Court, London, England.
Kallman Associates (5 Maple Court, Ridgewood, NJ 07450).

*PSI — The Process Systems and Instrumentation Exhibition* — June 9-12 — Earls Court, London, England.
Industrial and Trade Fairs Ltd. (Radcliff House, Blenheim Court, Solihull, West Mid-

lands B91-2G, England).

*CLEO — Conference on Lasers and Electro-Optics* — June 10-12 — Washington Hilton, Washington, DC.
IEEE.

*Conpar—Conference on Analyzing Problem Classes and Programming for Parallel Computing* — June 10-12 — Faculty of Economics and Social Sciences Building, Langengasse 20, Nuremberg, West Germany.
University of Erlangen-Nuremberg (Dr. Wolfgang Handler, Martensstr. 3, 8520 Erlangen, West Germany).

*Motorcon International Conference and Exposition* — June 10-13 — Conrad Hilton Hotel, Chicago, Illinois.
Intertech Communications (2909 Ocean Dr., Oxnard, CA 93030).

*ICC—International Conference on Communications* — June 14-17 — Denver Hilton Hotel, Denver, Colorado.
IEEE.

*National Computer Graphics Association Conference and Exposition* — June 14-18 — Convention Center, Baltimore, Maryland.
Society of Manufacturing Engineers (1 SME Dr., P.O. Box 930, Dearborn, MI 48128).

*Nepcon East Conference/Exhibition* — June 16-18 — New York Coliseum, New York, New York.
Cahners Exposition Group (222 W. Adams St., Chicago, IL 60606).

*International Microwave Symposium* — June 16-19 — Bonaventure Hotel, Los Angeles, California.
IEEE.

*National Plant Engineering and Maintenance Show and Conference* — June 16-19 — McCormick Place, Chicago, Illinois.
Clapp & Poliak Inc. (245 Park Ave., New York, NY 10167).

*Comdex/Spring* — June 23-25 — New York Coliseum, New York, New York.
The Interface Group (160 Speen St., Framingham, MA 01701).

*Microprocessors: Hardware, Software and Applications* — June 1-2 — Worcester Polytechnic Institute, Worcester, Massachusetts.
Information: Ginny Bazarian, Office of Continuing Education, Worcester Polytechnic Inst., Worcester, MA 01609, (617) 753-1411, X517.

*Pascal Programming Workshop* — June 1-4; and *Ada: The Defense Department's New Standard Programming Language* — (various cities and dates).
Information: Prof. Donald D. Grench, Inst. for Advanced Professional Studies, 1 Gateway Ctr., Newton, MA 02158, (617) 964-1421.

*Symposium on Incremental Motion Control Systems and Devices* — June 1-4 — Hyatt Regency Hotel, O'Hare, Rosemont, Illinois.
Information: Dr. B. C. Kuo, P.O. Box 2772, Station A, Champaign, IL 61820, (217) 356-1523 or (217) 333-4341.

*SNA But Not All IBM* — June 1-5 — New York, New York.

Information: TCT International, 599 N. Mathilda Ave., Sunnyvale, CA 94086, (408) 735-9990.

*Europe Software* — June 2-4 — Utrecht, The Netherlands.
The show is limited strictly to software, and will have a US Exhibition section. Contact S. V. Smith, Consulate General of the US, Museuplein 19, 1070 DJ Amsterdam, The Netherlands.

*Automated Office Expo* — June 2-4 — Los Angeles, California.
Seminars and exhibits on technology plus employers interviewing for automated office jobs. Contact New Horizons, 6521 West Sixth St., Los Angeles, CA 90048, (213) 651-2096.

*CIPS (Canadian Information Processing Society) Conference* — June 8-10 — Waterloo, Ontario, Canada.
Information: CIPS, 243 College St., Toronto, Ontario M5T 2Y1, Canada.

*ATE Seminar/Exhibit* — June 8-12 — Hynes Auditorium, Boston, Massachusetts.
Information: Test Conferences Registrar, Benwill Publishing Corp., 1050 Commonwealth Ave., Boston, MA 02215, (617) 232-5470.

*Machine Vision, Automatic Assembly, and Productivity Technology* — June 8-12 — Massachusetts Institute of Technology, Cambridge, Massachusetts.
Information: Director of Summer Session, Rm. E19-356, MIT, Cambridge, A 02139.

*Understanding and Using Computer Graphics* — June 9-11 — Chicago, Illinois.
Information: Bob Sanzo, Frost & Sullivan, Inc., 106 Fulton S., New York, NY 10038, (212) 233-1080.

*Data Datacomm Conference and Exhibition* — June 9-11 — Winnipeg, Manitoba, Canada.
Information: Laurie Whitsed, 55 Bloor St. West, Toronto, Ontario M4W 3K2, Canada.

*CONPAR (Conference on Analyzing Problem-Classes and Programming for Parallel Computing)* — June 10-12 — Nurnberg, West Germany.
Information: Wolfgang Handler, Immd, Universitat Erlangen-Nuremberg, Martensstrasse 3, D-8520 Erlangen, West Germany.

*ICC* — June 14-17 — Denver, Colorado.
The International Conference on Communication is sponsored by the IEEE. Contact Robert Kian, SE, One SME Dr., P.O. Box 930, Dearborn, MI 48128, (313) 271-1500.

*Second Annual NCGA Conference* — June 14-18 — Baltimore Convention Center, Baltimore, Maryland.
Information: Society of Manufacturing Engineers, P.O. Box 930, Dearborn, I 48121, (313) 271-1500.

*Info System Technology: Database and Performance* — June 15-19 — University of Michigan, Ann Arbor, Michigan.
Information: Engineering Summer Confs., 200 Crysler Ctr., N. Campus, U. of Mich., Ann Arbor, MI 48109, (313) 263-4866.

*Computerfest* — June 20-22 — Columbus, OH. Fifth annual gathering of the Midwest Affiliation of Computer Clubs (MACC), focusing on small business and personal requirements and uses. Contact James Crowley, 4008 Rickenbacker Ave, Columbus, OH 43213.

*Digital Electronics for Automation and Instrumentation* — June 22-23; and *Microcomputer Design Interfacing, Programming, and Application using the Z80/8085/8080* — June 24-27 — Blacksburg, Virginia.
Information: Dr. Linda Leffel, CEC Virginia Polytechnic Inst. and U. Blacksburg, VA 24061, (703) 961-5241.

*Comdex/Spring, The Interface Group* — June 23-25 — New York Coliseum, New York, New York.
The Interface Group (160 Speen St., Framingham,MA 01701).

*39th Annual Device Research Conference* — June 22-24 — IEEE Electronic Devices Society, University of California at Santa Barbara, Santa Barbara, CA.

*COMDEX* — June 2-25 — New York, New York.
"Where vendors and ISOS (independent sales organizations) get together." Contact The Interface Group, 160 Speen St., Framingham, MA 01701, (617) 879-4502.

*World Computing Services Industry Congress* — June 23-25 — San Francisco, California. Geared toward the serious discussion of responsibilities as custodians of the international information resources. Contact ADAPSO, 1925 Lynn St., Arlington, VA 22209, (703) 522-5055.

*Syntopican VIII* — June 23-26 — Minneapolis, Minnesota.
The International Word Processing Association conference will feature four days of conference and three days of exhibits. Contact IWP, Maryland Rd., Willow Grove, PA 19090, (215) 657-3220.

*EMC—Electronic Materials Conference* — June 24-26 — University of California at Santa Barbara, Santa Barbara, California.
Metallurgical Society (P.O. Box 430, Warrendale, PA 15086).

*TCS-11—11th Annual International Symposium on Fault-Tolerant Computing* — June 24-26 — Holiday Inn Downtown, Portland, Maine.
IEEE Computer Society.

*Eighteenth Design Automation Conference* — June 29-July 1 — Nashville, Tennessee.
The major topic will be computer-aided design of digital systems. Contact Dave Hightower, Texas Instruments, Box 225621 MS 3907, Dallas, TX 75265.

*Syntopican IX* — June 29-July 2 — Atlanta, Georgia.
Presented by the International Word Processing Association. Conference will feature panels, sessions, and workshops on information processing topics. Contact Conference Services Dept., IWPA, 1015, North York Rd., Willow Grove, PA 19090, (215) 657-6300.

*Power Electronics Specialist Conference* — June 29-July 2 — University of Colorado, Boulder, Colorado.
IEEE Aerospace and Electronic Systems.

*Microcomputer System Design* — June 29-July 10 — University of Ireland, Dublin, Ireland.
Information: Dr. D. P. McCarthy, Dept. of Computer Science, Engineering School, Trinity College, Dublin 2, Ireland.

*Software Engineering* — June-July (various cities and dates).
Information: Renate Lammermann, Battelle Seminars and Studies Program, 4000 NE

41st St., Seattle WA 98105, (206) 525-3130.

*Laser—Fifth International Congress and Exhibition* — June 1-4 — Fairgrounds, Munich, West Germany.
Munchener Messeund Ausstellungs-GmbH (D-8000 Munich 12, P.O. Box 121009, West Germany) or Kallman Associates (5 Maple Court, Ridgewood, NJ 07450).

*Fourth International Printed Circuits Conference* — June 2-4 — New York Hilton, New York, New York.
Benwile Publishing Corp. (Promotion Coordinator, 1050 Commonwealth Ave., Boston, MA 02215).

Metalization of Advanced Semiconductor Devices — June 3 — Bell Laboratories, Murray Hill, New Jersey.
American Vacuum Society, Greater New York Chapter (J. L. Vossen, RCA Laboratories, Princeton, NJ 08540).

*CSC—22nd Annual Chicago Spring Conference on Consumer Electronics* — June 3-4 — Arlington Park Hilton, Arlington Heights, Illinois.
IEE.

*Electronic Test and Measuring Equipment Exhibition* — June 3-5 — Osaka Merchandise Mart, 1-7 Kyobashi, Higashi-Ku, Osaka, Japan.
Japan Electronic Measuring Instruments Manufacterers' Association (1-9-10 Toranomon, Minato-Ku, Tokyo 105).

*JPCA Show* — June 3-6 — Tokyo International Fair Grounds, Harumi, Chuo-Ku, Tokyo, Japan.
Japan Printed Circuit Association (5-11-10 Toranomon, Minato-Ku, Tokyo 105, Japan).

*Paris Air Show* — June 5-14 — Le Bourget Airport, Paris, France.
Groupement des Industries Francaise Aeronatuiques et Spatiales (GIFAS, 4 rue Galilee, 75116 Paris, France).

*ATE (Automatic Test Equipment) Seminar/Exhibit* — June 8-11 — Hynes Veterans Auditorium, Boston, Massachusetts.
Benwell Publishing Corp. (Promotion Coordinator, ATE Seminar/Exhibit, 1050 Commonwealth Ave., Boston, MA 02215).

*Printed Circuit World Convention II* — June 9-12 — Munich, Germany.
Institute for Interconnecting and Packaging Electronic Circuits (3451 Church St., Evanston, IL 60203) et al.

*20th Annual ACM Symposium—Crisis in Computing: Innovation in a Constrained Environment* — June 18 — University of Maryland, College Park, Maryland.
Association for Computing Machinery and National Bureau of Standards (W. Osborn, A-265 Technology Building, NBS, Washington, DC 20234).

*Teleconferencing and Satellites Systems Technology* — June 24-26 — Sheraton Centre, New York, New York.
Data Communications Magazine (McGraw-Hill Conference and Exposition Center, 1221 Ave. of the Americas, New York, NY 10020).

*18th Design Automation Conference* — June 29-July 1 — Opryland Hotel, Nashville, Tennessee.
IEEE and Association for Computing Machinery.

*Visual Psychophysics and Medical Imaging Symposium* — July 2-3 — Vrije University, Brussels, Belgium.
IEEE.

*Third International Conference on Hot Carriers in Semiconductors* — July 7-10 — Montpellier, France.
Center for the Electronic Study of Solids (Université des Sciences et Techniques du Languedoc, Centre d'Etudes Electroniques des Solides, 34060-Montpellier CEDEX, France).

*Concapan 1—First Convention-Exposition of Electrical and Electronic Engineering of Central America and Panama* — July 9-12 — Atalpa Convention Center, Panama City, Panama.
IEEE.

*Data Communications, Fiber Optics, and Spread Spectrum Techniques* — July 13-15; *Mini & Microcomputers: Their Structures, Characteristics, and Applications* — July 20-24; and *Microcomputer System Design and Applications* — July 27-31 — Ann Arbor, Michigan.
Information: Viola E. Miller, Engineering Summer Confs., 200 Chrysler Ctr., N. Campus, U. of Mich., Ann Arbor, MI 48109, (313) 764-8490.

*CALP* — July 13-17 — Haifa, Israel.
This is the 8th International Colloquium on Automata, Languages and Programming. Contact Dr. Oded Kariv, ICALP, Computer Science Dept., Technion-Israel nstitute of Technology, Technicon City, Haifa, Israel.

*Third Brazilian Workshop on Microelectronics* — July 13-24 — University of Campinas, Sao Palo, Brazil.
Laboratorio de Electronica c Dispositivos (Faculdade de Engenharia de Campinas, Unicamp, Caixa Postal 6061, 13100-Campinas-Sao Palo, Brazil).

*Fifth International Conference on Vapor Growth and Epitaxy and Fifth American Conference on Crystal Growth* — July 19-24 — Hotel del Coronado, Coronado, California.
American Association for Crystal Growth (Conference Secretariat, Anthony L. Gentile, Hughes Research Laboratories, 3011 Malibu Canyon Rd., Malibu, CA 90265).

*Microcomputers in Control Systems and Microcomputer Interfacing Methods* — July 20-22 & July 23-24 — George Washington University, Washington, DC.
Information: Dir., Continuing Engineering Education, George Washington U., Washington, DC 20052, (202) 676-6106.

*Fourth International Conference on Software Engineering for Telecommunications Switching Systems* — July 20-24 — University of Warwick, Warwick, England.
Institution of Electrical Engineers (Savoy Place, London WC2R OBL, England).

*Symposium on Reliability in Distributed Software and Database Systems* — July 21-22 — Pittsburgh, Pennsylvania.
Information: Marie S. Sreha, LRDC Bldg., U. of Pittsburgh, Pittsburgh, PA 15250, (412) 624-4908.

*Eighth Cranfield International Conference on Mechanized Information Transfer* — July 21-24 — England.
The conference is organized by the Information Div. of the Institution of Electrical Engineers. Contact The Marketing Dept., INSPEC, Station House, Nightingale Rd., Hitchin, Herts, SG5 IRJ, England.

*OCR Users Association's Summer Conference* — July 26-29 — Minneapolis, Minnesota. The conference theme is "Managing Data Entry Productivity in Turbulent Times," held in conjunction with EXPO. Contact OCR Users Assn., 10 Banta Bl., Hackensack, NJ 07601, (201) 343-4935.

*WCCE — Third World Conference on Computers in Education* — July 27-31 — Palais de Beaulieu, Lausanne, Switzerland.
International Federation for Information Processing (WCCE Organization Committee, Pierre Immer, 33 ave de Cour, CH-1007 Lausanne, Switzerland.

*Inst. in Computer Science* — Summer — (various locations).
Information: Mrs. Cynthia Johnson, Faculty Offices, Wang Inst. of Graduate Studies, Tyng Rd., Tyngsboro, MA 01879, (617) 649-9731.

*Introductory, 8080/8085 and 8086/8088 Systems Design. Single-Chip Microcomputer, Peripheral Chip Design, and Development Systems Workshops* — Summer/Fall — (various locations).
Information: Intel Training Center, San Francisco, CA, (408) 734-8102; Chicago, IL (312) 981-7250; or Boston, MA, (617) 256-1374.

*Harvard Computer Graphics Week* — July 28-August 1 — Cambridge, Massachusetts. Five day conference features business graphics and computer mapping in commercial, educational, and governmental areas. Contact Kathy Devaney, Center for Management Research, 850 Boylston St., Chestnut Hill, MA 02167, (617) 738-5020.

AUGUST

*Pattern Recognition and Image Processing* — August 3-5 — Sheraton Hotel, Dallas, Texas. Information: PRIP, P.O. Box 639, Silver Spring, MD 20901, (301) 589-3386.

*ACM SIGGRAPH Conference and Exposition* — August 3-7 — Callas.
ACM's Special Interest Group on Computer Graphics sponsors this annual event. This year's theme is "The Eighth Annual Conference on Computer Graphics and Interactive Techniques." Contact Henry T. Cronan, Robert T. Kenworthy, Inc., 866 United Nations Plaza, New York, NY 10017, (212) 752-0911.

*Thin Films and Solid Surfaces* — July 13-17 — Colby-Sawyer College, New London, New Hampshire; *Point and Line Defects in Semiconductors* — July 13-17 — Plymouth State College, Plymouth, New Hampshire; and *Nonlinear Optics and Lasers* — August 3-7 — Brewster Academy, Wolfeboro, New Hampshire.
Gordon Research Conferences (Pastore Chemical Laboratory, University of Rhode Island, Kingston, RI 02881).

*SYMSAC (Association for Computing Machinery)* — August 5-7 — Snowbird Ski Resort, Salt Lake City, Utah.
Information: Prof. B. F. Caviness, Dept. of Mathematical Sciences, Renssellaer Polytechnic Inst., Troy, NY 12181, (518) 270-6731.

*Impactless Printing* — August 9-11 — Highlands Inn, Carmel, California.
Institute for Graphic Communication Inc. (Richard D. Murray, IGC, 375 Commonwealth Ave., Boston, A 02115).

*16th Intersociety Energy Conversion Engineering Conference* — August 9-14 — Hyatt Regency Hotel, Atlanta, Georgia.
IEEE, American Society of Mechanical Engineers, American Institute of Aeronautics and Astronautics, et al.

*GPIB (General Purpose Interface Bus) Workshop* — August 10 — Sunnyvale, California.
Information: Ben Catanzaro, Instructor, Intel Corp., MCSD Customer Training SV3-1, 1350 Bordeaux Dr., Sunnyvale, CA 94086, (408) 734-8102, X375.

*20th General Assembly of the International Union of Radio Science* — August 10-19 — Hyatt Regency Hotel, Washington, DC.
c/o R. Dow, National Academy of Sciences, 2101 Constitution Ave. N.W., Washington, DC 20418.

*Contemporary Data Communication Networks: Planning Analysis and Design* — August 10-14 — University of Michigan, Ann Arbor, Michigan.
Information: Dixon R. Doll, Continuing Engineering Education, 300 Chrysler Ctr., N. Campus, Ann Arbor, MI 48109, (313) 764-8490.

*Electronics Mexico City* — August 11-14 — Mexico City, Mexico.
Information: Franc D. Manzolillo, Proj. Mgr., Rm. 6015, U.S. Department of Commerce, Washingtion, DC 20230, (202) 377-2991.

*NYCE (New York Computer Expo)* — August 12-15 — Sheraton Center, New York, New York.
Information: NYCE, 110 Charlotte Pl., Englewood Cliffs, NJ 07632, (201) 569-8542.

*Distributed Computer Control Systems* — August 15-17 — Beijing (Peking), China.
Information: Prof. Liu-Shi-hua, Chinese Assoc. of Automation, Research Inst. of Electronic Technic Application, P.O. Box 927, Beijing, China.

*Laser Optics Course* — August 17-21 — Los Alamos Inn, Los Alamos, New Mexico.
Laser Institute of America (P.O. Box 9000, Waco, TX 76710).

*Optical Information Processing for Aerospace Application* — August 18-19 — Hampton, Virginia.
H. Hendricks, Langley Research Center, Hampton, VA 23665.

*Office Automation and Integration of Word Processing and Data Processing* — August 19-21 — Holiday Inn, Fisherman's Wharf, San Francisco, California.
Frost & Sullivan Inc. (106 Fulton St., New York, NY 10038).

*International Conference on Cybernetics and Society* — August 24-27 — Atlanta Hilton Hotel, Atlanta, Georgia.
IEEE.

*Software Design, Reliability and Testing* — August 24-27 — Sheraton Motor Inn, Lexington, Massachusetts.
Information: Prof. Donald D. French, Inst. for Advanced Professional Studies, One Gateway Ctr., Newton, MA 02158, (617) 964-1412.

*Seventh International Joint Conference on Artificial Intelligence* — August 24-28 — Vancouver, British Columbia, Canada.
Computer applications for medical diagnosis, computer-aided design, robotics, programmable automation, speech understanding, and vision are some of the topics to be discussed in this five-day conference. Contact Richard Rosenberg, Computer Science Dept., U.B.C., Vancouver, B.C., Canada VT6T 1W5, (604) 228-3061.

*SPIE International Symposium an Instrument Display* — August 24-28 — Town and Country Hotel, San Diego, California.
Society of Photo-Optical Instrumentation Engineers (P.O. Box 10, Bellingham, WA 98227).

*IFAC (International Federation for Automatic Control) World Congress* — August 24-28 — Kyoto, Japan.
Information: IFAC Secretariat, Kinki Hatsumei Ctr., 14 Kawahara-cho, Yoshida, Sakyo-ku, Kyoto 606, Japan.

*International Conference on Parallel Processing* — August 25-28 — Shanty Creek Lodge, Bellaire, Michigan.
Information: Dr. M. T. Liu, Dept. of Computer and Information Science, Ohio State U., Columbus, OH 43210, (614) 422-1837.

*National Small Computer Show* — August 26-29 — New York, New York.
Free lectures are presented daily, and this year there will be a five-hour seminar on the understanding, acquisition, and use of small computers in business. Contact National Small Computer Show, 110 Charlotte Place, Englewood Cliffs, NJ 07632, (201) 569-8542.

*Real Time Programming* — August 31-September 1 — Kyoto, Japan.
Information: IFAC/IFIP Workshop on Real Time Programming Orig. Committee, c/o Prof. T. Hasegawa, Dept. of Applied Mathematics and Physics, Faculty of Engineering, Kyoto University, Kyoto 606, Japan.

*Software Management* — August 31-September 1 — The 57 Park Plaza, Boston, Massachusetts.
Information: EFDPMA Confs., Dept. SMC, P.O. Box 91295, Los Angeles, CA 90009, (213) 670-2973.

## SEPTEMBER

*Quartz Crystal Conference* — September 1-3 — Radisson Muehlenback Hotel, Kansas City, Missouri.
K-M Enterprises Inc. (630 South Rogers Rd., Olathe, Kansas 66061).

*FOC WEST (International Fiber Optics and Communications Expo)* — September 1-2 — Hyatt Regency Embarcaero, San Francisco, California.
Information: Information Gatekeepers, Inc., 167 Corey Rd., Suite 111, Brookline, MA 02146, (617) 739-2022

*European Conference on Electronic Design Automation* — September 1-4 — University of Sussex, Brighton, United Kingdom.
Institution of Electrical Engineers (Savoy Place, London WC2R OBL).

*Computer Communications Systems and Networks, The American and Russian Methods in Linear Programming and Applications, and Structured Programming and Software Engineering* — September 2-4, 9-11 & 21-25 — George Washington University, Washington, DC.
Information: Dir., Continuing Engineering Education, George Washington U., Washington, DC 20025, (202) 676-6106.

*Soft '81* — September 2-4 — London, England.
This isthe third in the international *Soft '81* series; each conference concentrates on the

software market of the country in which it is held. Previous conferences were held in Paris and Munich, and the fourth (and last) in the series is scheduled for Stockholm in November. Contact Soft '81, Acorn Studios, Barnes, London SW13 9HP, United Kingdom, (01) 748-0287.

*VHSIC Military and Commercial Applications* — September 3-4 — Howard Johnson's, Boston, Massachusetts.
American Institute of Aeronautics and Astronautics (AIAA Conferences, 5959 W. Century Blvd., Los Angeles, CA 90009).

*Electron 1—Home Video and Personal Computers Exposition* — September 4-6 — Convention Center, Los Angeles, California.
Epic Enterprises (6158 Mission Gorge Rd., San Diego, CA 92120).

*International Audio and Video Fair Berlin* — September 4-6 — West Berlin Fairgrounds, West Berlin, Germany.
AMK Berlin (Messedamm 22), West Berlin, Germany.

*Microprocessor Workshop on Microprocessor Applications* — September 7-8 — Liverpool University, Liverpool, England.
Information: Dr. M. J. Taylor, Microprocessor Workshop, Computer Laboratory, University of Liverpool, P.O. Box 147, Liverpool, L69 3BX, England.

*11th European Microwave Conference* — September 7-11 — RAI Congress Center, Amsterdam, The Netherlands.
Eurel, IEEE, et al. (M. T. Vlaardingerbroek, Philips, Elcoma EH5, 5600 MD Eindhoen, The Netherlands).

*Workshop for International Marketing Decision-Makers* — September 8-9 — Washington, DC.
Exportig products inthe '80's isthetheme co-sponsoredby DATAMATION and the U.S. Department of Commerce. Contact Graydon Associates, P.O. Box 566, Red Bank, NJ 07701, (201) 741-2690.

*Fifth International Conference on Computer Hardware Description Languages & Applications* — September 8-9 — Kaiserslautern, Germany.
Co-sponsored by the ACM, IEEE, and others, this conference features discussions on Hardware Description Language issues, design methodologies and applications, CHDL in Education, and CHDL-based tools. Contact Will Sherwood, Digital Equipment Corp., 75 Reed Rd., MS HL1-1/Q05,Hudson, MA 01749, (617) 568-4316.

*International Conference on Computer Hardware Description Languages and Their Applications* — September 8-9 — Kaiserslautern University, Federal Republic of Germany.
Information: Prof. Melvin Breuer, Dept. of Electrical Engineering, USC, Los Angeles, CA 90007, (213) 743-2308.

*Third Symposium on Automation Technology in Engineering Data Handling* — September 8-10 — NPS, Monterey, California.
Naval Postgraduate School (Peter Wang, Code 53Wg, Department of Mathematics, NPS, Monterey, CA 93940).

*Seventh European Conference on Optical Communication* — September 8-11 — Bella Center, Copenhagen, Denmark.
Electromagnetics Institute, Technical University of Denmark (M. Danielsen, Electromagnetics Institute, Technical University of Denmark, DK-2800 Lyngby, Denmark).

*Ineltec and Swiss Data (Exhibitions for industrial electronics and for data processing in technical applications)* — September 8-12 — Basel Fairgrounds, Basel, Switzerland.
Schweizer Mustermesse (CH-4021, Basel, Switzerland).

*NECOM* — September 9 — Marriott Hotel, Newton, Massachusetts.
Information: Margo Landrum, Norm DeNardi Enterprises, Suite 204, 289 S. San Antonio Rd., Los Altos, CA 94022, (415) 941-8440.

*MIMI* — September 9-10 — Montreal, Quebec, Canada.
13th International symposium and exhibition on mini and microcomputer applications. Contact Prof. M.H. Hamza, Department of Electrical Engineering, the University of Calgary, Calgary, Alberta, Canada T2N 1N4.

*Eurographics—International Congress for Computer Graphics and Exhibition* — September 9-11 — Technical University of Darmstadt, West Germany.
International Federation for Information Processing et al., (J. Vlietstra, c/o NV Philips Gloeilampenfabrieken, Bldg. VO-124, NL-5600 MD Eindhoven, The Netherlands).

*Integrated Systems Expo* — September 9-11 — Washington, DC.
The National Micrographics Association will feature the development and promotion of the effective uses of micrographics, including interfaces with other information processing technologies. Contact John Bidwell, NMA, 8719 Colesville Rd., Silver Spring, MD 20910, (301) 587-8202.

*Internepcon/Semiconductor International Taiwan* — September 9-12 — CETDC Exhibition Center, Taipei, Taiwan.
Kiver Organization (Industrial & Scientific Conference Management Inc., 222 West Adams St., Chicago, IL 60606).

*Midwest Computer Show* — September 10-13 — McCormick Place, Chicago, Illinois.
Information: The National Computer Shows, 824 Boylston St., Chestnut Hill, MA 02167, (617) 739-2000.

*Internepcon/Semiconductor International Expo* — September 11-13 — Singapore.
Keyed to the specific needs of engineering, manufacturing and support personel of Southeast Asia. Contact Industrial and Scientific Conference Management, Inc., 222 W. Adams St., Chicago, IL 60606, (312) 263-4866.

*Invitational Computer Conference* — September 14; October 1, 27 & 29 — Newton, Massachusetts; Minneapolis, Minnesota; Valley Forge, Pennsylvania; and Washington, DC area.
Information: B. J. Johnson & Assoc., Inc., 2503 Eastbluff Dr., Suite 203, Newport Beach, CA 92660, (714) 644-6037.

*Standard Architecture, Interface, and Protocols* — September 14-16 — New York Hilton Hotel, New York, New York.
Information: McGraw-Hill Conf. Ctr., 1221 Ave. of the Americas, Suite 3677, New York, NY 10020, (212) 997-3928.

*Software Info (The National Software Package Conference and Exposition)* — September 14-17 — Merchandise Mart Expocenter, Chicago, Illinois.
Information: Software Info, 1730 N. Lynn St., Suite 400, Arlington, VA 22209, (703) 521-6209.

*11th European Solid State Device Research Conference and 6th Symposium on Solid State Device Technololgy* — September 14-17 — University Paul Sabatier, Toulouse, France.

National Societies of Electrical and Electronics Engineers of Western Europe (Eurel) (ESSDERCSSSDT Secretariat, Laboratories d'Automatisme et d'Analyses de Systemes, 7 Ave. du Colonel-Roche, 31400 Toulouse, France).

*Intelexpo — International Telephone Exposition and Symposium* — September 14-17 — Convention Center, Los Angeles, California.
U.S. Telecommunications Suppliers Association (333 N. Michigan Ave., Suite 1618, Chicago, IL 60601).

*IPA National Symposium* — September 17-19 — Denver, Colorado.
NASA and an Industry Technical Advisory Board (ITAB) to report on progress of the joint industry/government computer aided design project called IPAD (Integrated Programs for Aerospace-Vehicle Design). Contact IPAD Project Office, Mail Stop 246, NASA Langley Research Center, Hampton, VA 23665, (804) 827-2888.

*New York Computer Showcase Expo* — September 17-19 — Pier 92 Passenger Terminal, New York, New York.
The Interface Group (160 Speen St., Framingham, MA 01701).

*Federal Computer Conference* — September 21-23 — Washington, DC.
The fourth annual conference providing a forum for information by Federal ADP users. Contact Federal Education Programs, P.O. Box 368, Wayland, MA 01778, (617) 358-5181.

*International Micrographic Congress* — September 21-24 — Mexico City, Mexico.
"Technologies Today an Tomorrow" is the theme of the congress. Contact IMC Public Relations Committee, P.O. Box 33600, St. Paul, MN 55144, (612) 733-9534.

*ISS — International Switching Symposium* — September 21-25 — Hotel Bonaventure, Montreal, Canada.
IEEE (General Secretariat-ISS, Box 56, Station Ile des Soeurs, Verdun, P.Q.H3E IJ8, Canada).

*Federal Compute Conference* — September 22-24 — Washigton, DC.
Co-sponsored by Datamation. Will address the management of change in the 1980's for federal dp users. Contact Ms. Lynn Green, P.O. Box 368, Wayland, MA 01778, (617) 358-5181.

*Semicon/East* — September 22-24 — Hynes Auditorium, Boston, Massachusetts.
Semiconductor Equipment and Materials Institute (625 Ellis St., Suite 212, Mountain View, CA 94043).

*Electrical Overstress/Electrostatic Discharge Symposium* — September 22-24 — Aladdin Hotel, Las Vegas, Nevada.
IIT Research Institute (Nan Pfrimmer, Rome Air Development Center/RBRAC, Griffiss Air Force Base, NY 13441).

*12th Annual Conference of the Society for Management Information Systems* — September 22-25 — Philadelphia, Pennsylvania.
The conference theme will be "MIS Management in the Emerging Information Age" and will examine the challenges facing the MIS Executive. Emphasis will be on the impact of converging technologies on the role of the MIS executive in the 1980's. Contact M. Rippey, the Society for Management Systems Information, 11 East Wicker Dr., Chicago, IL 60601, (312) 644-6610.

*Digital Control* — September 23-25 — Holiday Inn, Newton, Massachusetts; and *Error*

*Correcting and Detecting Codes* — September 28-30 & October 26-28 — Holiday Inn, Palo Alto, California and Arlington, Virginia.
Information: Hellman Assoc., 299 S. California Ave., Palo Alto, CA 94306, (415) 328-4091.

*COMPSON FALL* — September 14-18 — Capital Hilton Hotel, Washington, DC.
Information: Harry Hayman, IEEE Computer Society, P.O. Box 639, Silver Spring, M 20901, (301) 589-3386.

*WESCON* — September 15-17 — Brooks Hall and Civic Auditorium, San Francisco, California.
Information: Dale Litherland, Electronic Conventions Inc., 999 N. Sepulveda Blvd., El Segundo, CA 90245, (213) 772-2965.

Compcon Fall—*22nd IEEE Computer Society International Conference* — September 15-17 — Capitol Hilton Hotel, Washington, DC.
IEEE (Victor Basili, Department of Computer Science, University of Maryland, College Park, MD 20742).

*First International Conference on Measurement Problems in Medicine and Biology* — September 15-17 — Tourist Center, Suzdai, USSR.
International Measurement Confederation (Imeko Secretariat, 1371 Budapest 5, Hungary).

*DPMA Symposium on Office Automation* — September 15-17 — Chicago, Illinois.
The Education Foundation of the DPMA announces a one-day series of workshops, followed by two days of general conference. Contact DPMA, 12611 Davan Dr., Silver Spring, MD 20904.

*Wescon* — September 16-18 — Anaheim, California.
This convention is the largest high technology assembly in the U.S. Contact Robert Myers, Communications Counsel, Wescon, 999 N. Sepulveda Blvd., El Segundo, CA 90245, (213) 772-2965.

*Eurodisplay — First European Display Research Conference* — September 16-18 — Hilton Hotel, Munich, West Germany.
Society for Information Display and Nachrichtentechnische Gesellschaft im VDE (Gerhard Meier, Eckerstr. 4, D-7800 Freiburg, West Germany).

*Third AFCET Congress on Pattern Recognition and Artificial Intelligence* — September 16-18 — Palais des Congres, Nancy, Fance.
Association Francaise pour la Cybernetique Economique et Technique (Jean-Paul Haton, 156 Blvd. Pereire, 75017 Paris, France).

*31st Annual Broadcast Symposium* — September 16-18 — The Washington Hotel, Washington, DC.
IEEE (R. A. O'Connor, CBS-TV Network, 51 W. 52nd St., New York, NY 10019).

*Design/Testing of Computer Devices per FCC Docket 20780, Product Safety Standards for Electronic Equipment* — September 17-18 & 21-22 (dates tenative); and *How to Meet VDE and Requirements for Computer and Other Electronic Devices* — September 22-25 — Chicago, Illinois; Boston, Massachusetts; and Philadelphia, Pennsylvania.
Information: Leonard Levin, R and B Enterprises, 050 Colwell Ln., Conshohocken, PA 19428, (215) 828-6236.

*SICOB* — September 17-26; and *Convention Informatique* — September 15-19 — Paris,

France
These back-to-back exhibitions and conferences cover personal computing to office equipment, and constitute the largest French international show. Contact Pierre Wagner, International Trade Shows in France, 1350 Sixth Ave., New York, Y 10019, (212) 582-4960.

*Mid-Atlantic Computer Show* — September 24-27 — DC Armory, Washington, DC.
Information: The Nat'l. Computer Shows, 824 Boylston St., Chestut Hill, MA 02167, (617) 739-2000.

*Comparative Database Management Systems; Computer Performance Evaluation; Configuration Management; Microprocessors and Microcomputers: Theory and Applications;* and *Computer Graphics Systems: Design and Applications* — September 28-October 2, September 30-October 2, October 5-7, October 12-16, & October 20-23 — George Washington University, Washington, DC.
Information: Director Continuing Engineering Education, George Washington U., Washington, DC 20052, (202) 676-6106.

*COMSEC* — September 29-October 1 — Chicago, Illinois.
This is the International Communications and Security Conference and Exposition featuring exhibits, meetings, and courses examining communications security implementation and cost in industrial and government areas, etc. Contact Michael A. O'Bryant, Information Gatekeepers, Inc., 167 Corey Rd., Brookline, MA 02146, (617) 739-2022.

*Microprocessor Software, Hardware, and Interfacing; Computer Graphics, Hands-on Pascal Workshop;* and *Distributed Processing* — September-December — (various cities and dates).
Information: Cassie Mason, Integrated Computer Systems, Inc., 3304 Pico Blvd., P.O. Box 5339, Santa Monica, CA 90405, (213) 450-2060.

Intel Corp. offers a wide selection of workshops during the fall and witer dealing with its microcomputer components, boards, software, operating systems, and design tools. The workshops are held frequently in cities that include Boston, New York, Chicago, Dallas, and San Francisco. Sessions are offered as well as customers' facilities. For more information write to Intel Corp., Customer Training, 27 Industrial Way, Chelmsford, MA 01824.

## OCTOBER

*National Conference on Software* — October 5-6 — Shoreham Hotel, Washington, DC.
Commission on Software Issues in the '80's (U.S. Professional Development Institute, 12611 Davan Dr., Silver Spring, MD 20904).

*International Electrical and Electronics Conference and Exposition* — October 5-7 — Canadian National Exhibition, Toronto, Canada.
IEEE (IEEE Canada Ofice, 7061 Yonge St., Thornhill, Ontario L3T 2A6, Canada).

*Electronics Test and Measurement Conference* — October 5-8 — Hyatt Regency, Chicago, Illinois.
Information: Dona Atwood, Registrar, Electronics Test and Measurement Conf., 1050 Commonwealth Ave., Boston, MA 02215, (617) 232-5470.

*Industry Applications Society Annual Meeting* — October 5-9 — Marriott Hotel, Philadelphia, Pennsylvania.

IEEE (S. P. Axe, Arco Chemical Co., Room 3010-G, 1500 Market St., Philadelphia, PA 19101).

*Computing Applications in Engineering* — October 6-7, November 2-3 & 5-6 — Boston, Massachusetts; Dallas, Texas; and Houston, Texas.
Information: Educational Programs Mgr., Engineering Systems Group, MR1-1/75, Digital Equipment Corp., 200 Forest St., Marlboro, MA 01752.

*Electronics Test and Measurement Conference* — October 6-8 — Hyatt Regency Hotel, Chicago, Illinois.
Benwill Publishing Corp. (Tillie Najjar, Benwill, 1050 Commonwealth Ave., Boston, MA 02215).

*ECOMA-9* — October 6-9 — Copenhagen, Denmark.
"Evaluation, Implementation, and Improvement of Contemporary Information Processing Systems" is the theme for this year's Ninth Europea Conference on Computer Measurement. Contact Scott Yasler, CDP, ECOMA-9 Conference, Scheuchzerstrasse 5, CH-8006 Zurich, Switzerland, 01-362-1268).

*BIAS* — October 6-10 — Milan, Italy.
The International Meeting Exhibition of Automation, Instrumentation, and Microelectronics is the only one of its kind to take place in Europe this year. Contact FAST (Union ofthe Scientific & Technical Associations), p. 13, Morandi 2, 20121, Milan, Italy.

*ISHM* — October 12-14 — Palmer House, Chicago, Illinois.
International Society for Hybrid Microelectronics (P.O. Box 3255, Montgomery, AL 36109).

*6th Conference on Local Computer Networks* — October 12-14 — Hilton Inn, Minneapolis, Minnesota.
IEEE (Abe Franck, University of Minnesota, 227 Experimental Engineering, 208 Union St. S.E., Minneapolis, MN 55455).

*INFO* — October 12-15 — New York, New York.
"Increasing the Responsiveness of Information Systems" will be the theme of the Information Management Exposition and Conference. A special section will be devoted to prepackaged and customized software. Contact Clapp and Poliak, Inc., 245 Park Ave., New York, NY 10167, (212) 661-8410.

*India Industrual Exhibition* — October 12-16 — Atlanta, Georgia.
Information: Alan Isacson, A. B.Isacson Assoc., Inc., 331 Park Ave. S., New York, NY 10010, (212) 475-1771.

*Fall Conference of Use Inc.* — October 12-16 — Sheraton Centre, Toronto, Canada.
Sperry Univac users Association (Box 461, Bladenburg, MD 20710).

*Semicon/Southwest* — October 13-14 — Market Hall, Dallas, Texas.
Semiconductor Equipment and Materials Institute (625 Ellis St, Suite 212, Mountain View, CA).

*WPOE* — October 13-15 — San Jose, California.
This is the fourth annual Word Processing and Office/Business Equipment Trade Show and Conference featuring equipment, products, and sessions geared to the automated office. Contact Cartlidge and Associates, Inc., 491 Macara Ave, Suite 1014, Sunnyvale, CA 94086, (408) 245-6870.

*Understanding and Using Computer Graphics* — October 13-15 & November 17-19 — New York, New York and Atlanta, Georgia.
Information: Bob Sanzo, Dir. of Marketing, Frost & Sullivan, Inc., 106 Fulton St., New York, NY 10038, (212) 233-1080.

*2nd Annual North Atlantic Organization Symposium* — October 14-16 — Brussels Sheraton Hotel, Brussels, Belgium.
Armed Forces Communications and Electronics Association (N. Allen, AFCEA, 5205 Leesburg Pike, S. 300, Fall Church, VA 22041).

*Northeast Computer Show* — October 15-18 — Hynes Auditorium, Boston, Massachusetts.
Information: The National Computer Shows, 84 Boylston St., Chestnut Hill, MA 02167, (617) 739-2000.

*27th Annual Vhf Conference* — October 17 — Kohrman Hall, Western Michigan University, Kalamazoo, Michigan.
Western Michigan University (Glade Wilcox, Department of Electrical Engineering, WMU, Kalamazoo, MI 49008).

*ACM Symposium on the Impact of Small Computer Systems (Sigsmall)* — October 19-20 — Orlando, Florida.
Information: S. Ron Oliver, The Mitre Corp., 433 N. Circle Dr., Colorado Springs, CO 80908, (303) 471-0102.

*Digital Speech Codig* — October 19-21; and *Speech Vocoders* — October 21-23 — Atlanta, Georgia
Department of Continuing Education—R, Georgia Institute of Technology, Atlanta, GA 30332.

*Autotestcon—International Automatic Testing Conference* — October 19-21 — Myatt House, Orlando, Florida.
IEEE (Autotestcon, P.O. Box 5837, MP 362, Orlando, FL 32855).

*7th Annual Symposium* — October 19-21 — Marriott Hotel, Los Angeles, California.
International Society for Testing and Failure Analysis (P.O. Box 742, Lawndale, CA 90260).

*Systems* — October 19-23 — Munich, West Germany.
Both the conference and exhibition Systems will strongly emphasize telecommunications. "Thinking in Systems" is the theme. Contact Kallman Associates, 30 Journal Sq., Jersey City, NJ 07306, (201) 653-3304.

*JEMIMA (Japan Electric Measuring Instruments Manufacturers' Association) International Exhibition* — October 19-23 — Tokyo International Trade Center, Tokyo, Japan.
Information: 19th JEMIMA International Exhibition, Secretariat of the Administration Committee, 1-9-10, Toraomon, Minato-Ku, Tokyo 105, Japan, 03/502-01, X4.

*San Fransciso Bay Area Computer Showcase Expo* — October 21-23 — Brooks Hall, San Francisco, California.
Information: Peter B. Young, The Interface Group, 160 Speen St., Framingham, MA 01701, (617) 87-4502 (outside Massachusetts).

*Careers Conference* — October 22-24 — Stouffer's Inn, Denver, Colorado.
IEEE (Jill Gerstenzang, Suite 609, 1111 19th St., N.W., Washington, DC 20036).

*123rd Technical Conference and Equipment Exhibit* — October 25-30 — Century Plaza Hotel, Los Angeles, California.
Society of Motion Picture and Television Engineers (Conference Department, 862 Scarsdale Ave., Scarsdale, NY 10583).

*37th Annual National Electronics Conference and National Communications Forum* — October 26-28 — Hyatt Regency O'Hare Hotel, Chicago, Illinois.
National Engineering Consortium Inc. (Oak Brook Executive Plaza No. 2, 1211 W. 22nd St., Oak Brook, IL 0421).

*5th International Printed Circuits Conference/Exhibition* — October 26-28 — Los Angeles Convention Center, Los Angeles, California.
Benwell Publishing Co. (1050 Commonwealth Ave., Boston, MA 02215).

*Data Communications Symposium* — October 27-29 — Mexico City, Mexico.
Information: Dr. Wushow Chou, General Chariman, Seventh Data Commnications Symposium, P.O. Box 5490, North Carolina State U., Raleigh, NC 27650.

*Gallium Arenide Integrated Circuit Symposium* — October 27-29 — Town and Country Hotel, San Diego, California.
IEEE (Varley L. Wrick, Westinghouse Research and Development Center, 1310 Beulah Rd., Pittsburgh, PA 15235).

*Symposium on Adaptive hf/vhf Systems* — October 27-29 — site in Washington not yet selected.
Defense Nuclear Agency (Patrick Crowley, Defense Nuclear Agency (RAAE), Atmospheric Effects division, Washington, DC. 20305).

*Defense Department Electronics Market: Impact of the Administration* — October 27-29 — Hyatt Union Square Hotel, San Francisco, California.
Electronic Industries Association (Frank A. Mitchell, EIA, 2001 Eye St. N.W., Washington, DC 20006).

*International Test Conference* — October 27-29 — Franklin Plaza Hotel, Philadelphia, Pennsylvania.
Cherry Hill, IEEE (Doris Thomas, P.O. Box 371, Cedar Knools, NJ 07927).

*CAD/CAM Graphics Users Expo* — October 27-30 — Fort Worth, Texas.
The expo is held in conjunction with Computer Aided Manufacturing-International, Inc.'s 10th annual meeting. The conference will focus on various graphics systems' capabilities relative to manufacturing users' needs. Contact CAM-1, Suite 1107, 611 Ryan Plaza Dr., Arlington, TX 76011, (817) 265-5329.

*Western Computer Show* — October 28-29 — Calgary, Alberta, Canada.
Information: Laurie Whitsed, Computing Equipment Assoc., 55 Boor St. W., Suite 1201, Toronto, Ontario M4W 3K2, Canada.

*FOCS (IEEE Symposium on Foundations of Computer Science)* — October 28-30 — Nashville, Tennessee.
Information: Prof. R. Book, Dept. of Mathematics, U. of California, Santa Barbara, CA 93106.

*Southeast Computer Show* — October 29-November 1 — Atlanta Civic Center, Atlanta, Georgia.
The National Computer Shows, 824 Boylston St., Chestnut Hill, MA 02167, (617) 739-2000.

*South Florida Computer Showcase Expo* — October 30-November 1 — Miami Expo/Center, Miami, Florida.
Information: Peter B. Young, The Interface Group, 160 Speen St., Framingham, MA 01701, (617) 879-4502; (800) 225-4620 (outside Massachusetts).

Fall training seminars and workshops, including courses on semicustom and custom large-scale integrated-circuit implementation, gate array design, bipolar linear circuit design, MOS digital circuit design, and new IC product testing, begining in September in Boston, Massachusetts; Scottsdale, Arizona; and Sunnyvale,California.
Integrated Circuit Engineering Corp., 15-22 N.75th St., Scottsdale, AZ, or call (602) 988-9780.

## NOVEMBER

*Data Base Technology* — November 2-5, December 1-4 & January 19-22 — Chicago, Illinois; Washington, DC; and San Francisco, California.
Information: Digital Equipment Corp., Educational Services, Seminar Programs, 12 Crosby Dr., BU/E58, Bedford, MA 01730, (617) 276-4949.

*Federal Office Automation Conference* — November 3-5 — Washington, DC.
The conference program provides coverage of issues including management, applications, technology, equipment, and systems and services. Contact Federal Office Institute, P.O. Box E, Wayland, MA 01778, (617) 358-5119.

*Management of CAD/CAM* — November 4-6 — Los Angeles, California.
Information: Marc Rosenberg, UCLA Extension Short Course Program Office, 6266 Boelter Hall, UCLA, Los Angeles, CA 90024, (313) 825-1047.

*Invitational Computer Conferences* — November 5, 12 & 17 — Amsterdam, The Netherlands; Paris, France; and Milan, Italy.
Information: B. J.Johnson & Assoc., Inc., 2503 Eastbluff Dr., Suite 203, Newport Beach, CA 92660, (714) 644-6037.

*ACM* — November 8-11 — Los Angeles, California.
Exhibits, tutorials, workshops, panels, plus a number of social events will be part of this year's ACM. Contact ACM, P.O. Box 24059, Village Station, Los Angeles, CA 90024, (213) 536-9735.

*15th Asilomar Conference on Circuits, Systems, and Computers* — November 9-11 — Asilomar Conference Center, Pacific Grove, Califoria.
IEEE (Harry Hayman, P.O. Box 639, Silver Spring, D 20901).

*Autofact III* — November 9-12 — Detroit, Michigan.
New technological refinements and management approaches to the automatic factory are the major subjects of this year's conference and exposition, sponsored by the Computer and Automated Systems Association of the Society of Manufacturing Engineers. Contact SME Public Relations, One SME Dr., P.O. Box 930, Dearborn, MI 48128, (313) 271-1500.

*Isratech* — November 9-12 — Binyanei Ha'ooma Convention Center, Jerusalem, Israel.
Information: Joan Leavitt, Ruder & Finn, 1225 19th St., N.W., Suite 270, Washington, DC 20036, (202) 466-7800.

*IECI (International Conference and Exhibit on Industrial Control and Instrumentation Applications of Mini and Microcomputers)* — November 9-13 — Hyatt Regency Hotel, San

Francisco, California.
Information: LeRoy Bushart, FMC, 328 Brokaw Rd., Santa Clara, CA 95051, (408) 289-3871.

*Making Silicon Talk—and Listen* — November 9-13 — Santa Barbara, California.
Information: A. H. (Steen) Gray, Jr., Signal Technology, Inc., 15 W. De la Guerra, Santa Barbara, CA 93101, (805) 963-1552; (800) 235-5787 (outside California).

*MIDCON* — November 10-12 — O'Hare Expo Center and Hyatt Regency O'Hare Hotel, Chicago, Illinois.
Information: Robert Myers, Electronic Conventions Inc., 999 N. Sepulveda Blvd., El Segundo, CA 90245, (213) 772-2965.

*27th Annual Conference on Magnetism and Magneticc Materials* — November 10-13 — Sheraton-Atlanta Hotel, Atlanta, Georgia.
IEEE et al. (H. C. Wolfe, American Institute of Physics, 335 E. 45th St., New York, NY 10017).

*Interface West* — November 10-12 — Los Angeles Convention Center, Los Angeles, California.
Information: The Interface Group, 160 Speen St., Framingham, MA 01701, (617) 879-4502; (800) 225-4620 (outside Massachusetts).

*Productronica — 4th International Trade Fair for Manufacture in Electronics* — November 10-14 — Trade Fair Center, Munich, West Germany.
Munchener Messe and Ausstellungsgesellschaft GmbH (Postfach 12 10 09, D-800 Munich 12, West Germany).

*14th Annual Connectors and Interconnectors Symposium* — November 11-12 — Franklin Plaza Hotel, Philadelphia, Pennsylvania.
Electronic Connector Study Group, Inc. (P.O. Box 167, Fort Washington, PA 19034).

*Eascon—Electronics and Aerospace Systems Conference* — November 16-19 — Washington Hilton Hotel, Washington, DC.
IEEE (Robert D. Briskman, Comsat General Corp., 950 L'Enfant Plaza S.W., Washington, DC 20024).

*Integrated Optics and Millimeter and Microwave Integrated-Circuits Conference* — November 16-19 — Von Braun Civic Center, Huntsville, Alabama.
International Society for Optical Engineering et al., (SPIE, P.O. Box 10, Belligham, WA 98227).

*CPEUG (Computer Performance Evaluation Users Group)* — November 16-19 — St. Anthony Hotel, San Antonio, Texas.
Information: Theodore F. Gonter, U.S. General Accounting Office, Rm. 6011, 441 G St. N.W., Washington, DC 20548, (202) 275-5040.

*Introduction to FORTH Programming Language* — November 16-20 — Belmont, California.
Information: Inner Access Corp.,517 Marine View, Suite K, Belmont, CA 94002, (415) 591-8295.

*Invitational Computer Conference* — November 17 — Hyatt Palo Alto, Palo Alto, California.
Information: B. J. Johnson & Assoc., Inc., 2503 Eastbluff Dr., Suite 203, Newport Beach, CA 92660.

*4th Digital Avionics Systems Conference* — November 17-19 — Stouffer's Inn, St. Louis, Missouri.
IEEE (Cary R. Spitzer, Mail Stop 472, National Aeronautics, and Space Administration Langley Research Center, Hampton, VA 23665).

*Electronic Display Device Exhibition* — November 17-20 — Science Museum, Tokyo, Japan.
Electronic Industries Association of Japan (3-2-2 Marunouchi, Chiyoda-Ku, Tokyo 100, Japan).

*Western Educational Computer Conference* — November 19-20 — San Francisco, California.
Sponsored by the California Educational Computing Consortium, this is the CECC's fifth year. Contact Ron Langley, Director, Data Processing Services, California State University, Long Beach, 1250 Bellflower Blvd., Long Beach, CA 90840, (213) 498-4111.

*COMDEX* — November 19-22 — Las Vegas, Nevada.
This is the third annual conference and exposition geared to the needs of independent sales organizations. Contact The Interface Group, 160 Speen St, Framingham, MA 01701, (617) 879-4502.

*National Telecommunications Conference* — November 29-December 3 — New Orleans, Louisiana.
"Innovative Telecommunications—Key to the Future" is the conference title. Topics include using communications technology to develop energy resources, and other innovative uses of telecommunications products and services. Contact Kenneth Black, New Orleans Public Office, 365 Canal St., Rm. 950, New Orleans, LA 70140, (504) 586-2173.

Fall Courses—including digital filters and spectral analysis; voice input/output for computers; digital image processing and analysis, microprocessor software, hardware, and interfacing; and computerized robots. Given in various cities.
Integrated Computer Systems (P.O. Box 5339, Santa Monica, CA 90405). For information call (800) 352-8251.

*Information processing seminars and management briefings.*
*Datapro Research Corp. (1805 Underwood Blvd., NJ 08075). For fall catalog call (800) 257-9406; in New Jersey, (609) 764-0100.*

*Electronics magazine has scheduled a series of seminars for engineers and managers running through January 1982. Topics include microprocessor design, single-chip microcomputers, power amplifier design, speech recognition and synthesis,anddigital filters. They are given at cities that include New York, Chicago, Boston, Atlanta, and Toronto. For information write to McGraw-Hill Seminar Center, 305 Madison Ave., Room 3112, New York,NY 10017, or phone (212) 687-9211.*

DECEMBER

*National Telecommunications Conference and Exhibition* — November 29-December 3 — Marriott Hotel, New Orleans, Louisiana.
IEEE (J. W. Joyner, South Central Bell Telephone Co., 518 Baronne St., Room 1035, New Orleans, LA 70140).

*Twelfth International Conference on Computer Performance Evaluation* — December 1-4 — New Orleans, Louisiana.
The conference is sponsored by the Computer Measureent Group, and will feature

CPE sessions from three viewpoints — technical, managerial, and tutorial. Contact Donald Deese,FEDSIM, 6118 Franconia Rd., Alexandria, VA 22310, (202) 274-8461.

*Writing for Results: A Course for Computer Professionals* — December 7-9; January 18-20; February 1-3 & 17-29; and March 15-17 — San Francisco, California; Atlanta, Georgia; Phoenix, Arizona; New York, New York; and Boston, Massachusetts.
Information: American Management Assoc., 135 W.50th St., New York,NY 10020, (212) 586-8100.

*International Electron Devices Meeting* — December 7-9 — Washington Hilton Hotel, Washington, DC.
IEEE (Melissa Widerkehr, Courtesy Associates,1629 K St., N.W., Washington, DC 20006).

*Infrared and Millimeter Waves Conference and Exhibitio* — December 7-11 — Carillon Hotel, Miami Beach, Florida.
IEEE (K. J. Button, Massachusetts Institute of Technology, National Magnet Laboratory, Cambride, MA 01239).

*Computer Networking Symposium* — December 8 — NBS, Gaithersburg, Maryland.
National Bureau of Standards and IEE's Computer Society. Contact Claude Delfosse, CACI, Inc., 1815 North Fort Myer Dr., Arlington, VA 22209.

*Introduction to Micro/Personal Computers: Application, Selection and Usage Guidelines* — December 14-16 — Chicago, Illinois.
Information: Datapro Research Corp., 1805 Underwood Blvd., Delran, NJ, (609) 764-0100; (800) 257-9406 (outside New Jersey).

*Software Design for Data Communications Systems* — December 14-16 — George Washington University, Washington, DC.
Information: Director, Continuing Engineering Education, George Washington University, Washington, DC 20052, (202) 676-6106.

*Gulf Computer Exhibition* — December 15-19 — Dubai International Trade Center, Dubai, U.A.E.
Information: Seymour House, 17 Waterloo Pl., London SEIY 4AR, England, Tel: 01/930-3881; or Trade Center Management Co., P.O. Box 9292, Dubai, U.A.E., Tel: 472200.

*Data Communications for Minicomputer Users* — November-December — (various U.S. cities).
Information: For dates and locations, contact Seminar Administrator, Micom Systems, Inc., 20151 Nordhoff Ave., Chatsworth, CA 91311, (213) 882-6890.

The following list was retrieved from the National Newsletter Index:

Experts Say IBM's Entry Will Buoy Already Booming Software Industry
Anders, George
Wall Street Journal v105 Section 2 p25(W) p31(E) Aug. 19, 1981
Descriptions: International Business Machines Corp. — management; microcomputers—marketing; computer programs—marketing; Peachtree Software Inc. —contracts and specifications; computers—home use; lifeboat associations—management; personal software—management; minicomputer—computer programs

IBM Set to Announce Entry Into Home-Computer Field
Anders, George
Wall Street Journal v105 Section 2 p25(W) p35(E) Aug. 11, 1981
Descriptions: International Business Machines Corp.—planning; computer industry —planning; computers—home use

New Mighty Mite: I.B.C. (Personal Computers)
New YorkTimes v130 Section 3 pF20(N) pF20(LC) Aug. 16, 1981
Descriptions: International Business Machines Corp.—manufactures; computers—home use

IBM Unveils New Home Computer Line
Scherer, Ron
Christian Science Monitor v73 p5 Aug. 13, 1981
Descriptions: International Business Machines Corp. — technological innovations; computers—home use; computer industry—technological innovations

Personal-Computer Field Dominated by 3 Firms, But Battle Royal Looms as Others Enter Market (Column)
Elia, Charles J.
Wall Street Journal v104 Section 2 p47 April 24, 1981
Descriptions: International Business Machines Corp.—planning; Digital Equipment Corp.—planning; computer industry—forecasts; computers—home use

In Buying That First Computer, Some Homework Can Be Crucial (Small Business)
Bulkeley, William M.
Wall Street Jurnal v103 Section 2 p29(W) p37(E) Oct. 6, 1980
Descriptions: computers—purchasing; small business—automation

The Computer Revolution—Work, School, Play, All In Your Home
Terry, Sara
Christian Science Monitor v72 pl Sept.24, 1980
Descriptions: telecommunications systems — forecasts; computers — forecasts; data transmissions systems—forecasts

She Takes Her Computers Home
Shabecoff, Philip
New York Times v128 Section 3 pF7 July 22, 1979
Descriptions: United States Bureau of Labor Statistics—officials and employees

Texas Instruments Pounces on Market in Home Computers: Its Debut in Surging Business Costs $1,150, is Aimed at People Lacking Expertise
Shaffer, Richard A.
Wall Street Journal v100 p26(W) p29(E) June 1, 1979
Descriptions: Texas Instruments Inc.—marketing; computers—home use; minicomputers—technological innovations

Electronics Speed Cross-Country Home Buying: Mobile Americans Generate Sales for Computer-Linked Brokers
Dole, Charles E.
Christian Science Monitor v71 Section B pB2 Jan. 30, 1979
Descriptions: real estate business — technological innovations; house buying — technological

Next, A Computer on Every Desk: A New Industry Has Burst Out, with Big-Time Players Like I.B.M.an Xerox and No Ceiling in Sight. In the wings are the Japanese.
Pollack, Andrew
New York Times v130 Section 3 pF1(N) pF1(LC) Aug. 23,1981
Descriptions: computers—marketing

Interface Age, Magazine for Home and Small Business Computers
New York Times v128 Section D pD7 Sept. 4, 1979
Descriptions: Interface Age (periodical)—aims and objectives; computers—periodicals

Portable Workplaces: Computer Terminals Allow More People to Work at Home Instead of Commuting
Vicker, Ray
Wall Street Journal v105 Section 2 p46(W) p56(E) Aug. 4,1981
Descriptions: home labor—innovations; computers—home use; work environment—innovations; Digital Equipment Corp.—innovations

Rising Trend of Computer Age: Employees Who Work at Home
Pollack, Andrew
New York Times v130 p1(N) pA1(LC) March 12, 1981
Descriptions: home labor—innovations; computer—home use; telecommunications—home use; office practice—automation

## Chapter Four

# SOME TRADITIONAL COMPUTER BUSINESSES

### Time Sharing/Service Bureaus

The best way to find out more about selling time on your computer or doing batch processing is to write BTI COMPUTER SYSTEMS, 870 West Maude Avenue, Sunnyvale, CA 94086, or call them at 408-733-1122. Ask for Downey Overton, the National Sales Manager and ask him to send you the BTI booklet *How To Start A Time Sharing Service.*

This booklet is written like an SBA Management Manual but it is well intentioned and has a lot of basic information on TS service markets, operations and some help on forecasting your financing requirements.

The real intention of this booklet is to get you to buy a 50 kilobuck mini system from BTI. If you decide to be a computer time vendor it might not be a bad idea. BTI obviously has a big stake in your success and they offer a good sounding set of support services like remote diagnostics for your machine and even management help.

It is estimated by mid-decade that 18% of the total data processing goods and services will be time shared. Batch services are phasing out, probably due to the great ease of having a terminal and printer in your office that can instantly input and access information to the big mother downtown.

It is thought the microcomputer explosion will not reach the time sharing market because time sharing frees business managers from the hassle of maintenance and programming updates; he doesn't have to become a computer expert.

A time sharing service can offer a standard business package modified around the edges to fit the exact business addressed. The more recent services have tended toward specialization. There are services specializing in agriculture, insurance and chiropractors.

According to BTI the most successful time sharers recently have been those who started from a perception of the market rather than the concept of time sharing. An entrepreneur who starts with the idea of providing a medical billing service is more liable to success than someone who has only vague and generalized ideas about "providing shared computer time to industry."

The basic hardware package costs 50 KB. If you have ten KB to put down you can get by with payments of about $1400/month. Add the other costs and the negative cash flow reasonably expected in the first nine months of operation and you get a minimum cash requirement of 52 KB to start up a first class time sharing operation.

BTI shows the following 5-year projection for a hypothetical time sharing start-up:

## HYPOTHETICAL TIMESHARING START-UP

| | YEAR 1 | YEAR 2 | YEAR 3 | YEAR 4 | YEAR 5 |
|---|---|---|---|---|---|
| REVENUE | | | | | |
| ●Timesharing & Storage | 59000 | 119000 | 153000 | 213000 | 250000 |
| ●Other Operations | 20000 | 59000 | 70000 | 100000 | 120000 |
| GROSS INCOME | 79000 | 178000 | 223000 | 331000 | 370000 |
| EXPENSES | | | | | |
| ●Operating Exp. | -82000 | -110000 | -125000 | -140000 | -155000 |
| ●Depreciation | -12000 | -16000 | -21000 | -30000 | -30000 |
| ●Interest | -11000 | -9000 | -13000 | -16000 | -16000 |
| TOTAL EXPENSES | -105000 | -135000 | -159000 | -186000 | -201000 |
| INCOME: | | | | | |
| ●Before Taxes | -26000 | 43000 | 64000 | 127000 | 169000 |
| —Income Taxes | — | -2000 | -10000 | -51000 | -75000 |
| NET INCOME | -26000 | 41000 | 54000 | 76000 | 94000 |

This illustration is meant to show relationships between numbers and doesn't mean that if you start a time sharing service it will work out this way for you. So much depends on you, luck, time and the tide.

There are several franchising operations specializing in setting up time sharing operations. They are listed in the Franchising Chapter a little further on.

If you actually start a time sharing service you should absolutely join ADAPSO. (The Association of Data Processing Service Organizations, 1925 North Lynn Street, Arlington, VA 22209, 703-522-5055.)

Joining this organization gets you into contact with others in your same business and allows you to help ADAPSO lobby in DC for the rights and protection of Time Sharing Service Organizations. It's important in this system to have a loud voice in the decision-making process and ADAPSO does just that.

ADAPSO has newsletters, reports and sales brochures that can be of help to you and your new data processing venture. If you're going to be a pro in your new venture the best first step is to meet the other pros in the business and get access to the same information they have.

## Service Bureaus

Service Bureaus are mostly for business customers who don't want the perceived hassle of owning or operating their own computer. Some large multi-location businesses like retail chains want terminals in the store feeding data into a remote CPU. There is usually a lot of hand-holding, consulting and customized programming necessary in this type of business.

To run a service bureau you need to be willing to deal with sometimes unpleasant business people who may disdain your expertise and string out your payments with stories instead of cash.

There are many old timers fiercely battling each other for traditional-style service bureau business. For a newcomer the Service Bureau concept is OK but needs to be approached with a fresh concept and marketing ideas. Never forget: novelty and inventiveness are your strongest assets. When you are uncommitted and have *low overheads* you are maximally flexible and can design your business around your innovations.

## Information Database Services

The whole world is growing for the people in this business. As access to computer networked databases and consumer awareness of informational possibilities grow, the information business will boom.

Right now the information business is a multi-billion dollar business; the future possibilities made possible by microcomputers are endless.

There are two organizations devoted to the computer information business. If you're interested contact them—they have a whole world of information for you.

Information World
1022 Wilson Blvd., Arlington, VA 22209

The Information Industry Association
4720 Montgomery Lane, Bethesda, MD 20014

## How About Being a Sales Rep?

Do you like plenty of money, adventure and travel? Being a sales rep looks great from the outside. When Arthur Miller wrote the character Willy Loman into his book *The Death of a Salesman,* he had it right.

In the garment business a sales rep is called a "Schlepper"—Yiddish for "to carry." Schleppers can be spotted rolling black, wheeled suitcases down the street on hot, muggy summer days.

Some Schleppers make big bucks. It is this carrot which keeps them wheeling those heavy suitcases. The dream of that big account just ahead keeps 'em moving right along.

Please don't get me wrong. Being a rep is not all bad. Many of them spend six months a year "on the road" (three months each, two seasons) and spend the rest of the time vacationing or making money in some other activity. In a way they are like firemen—total time on the job and then lots of time off.

Reps typically like to carry many manufacturers in their catalog books, but are somewhat shy about schlepping the actual items around with them. If an item is a big mover they will keep it in the back of the station wagon and if it is hot they will carry it into a call as a door kicker.

Reps like to "tie up" the lines in their geographic range. If they can, most reps would be a traveling medicine show and offer a little something for everybody.

They have a practical reason for wanting all the lines. If there are *any* sales of the carried item for mail-in, phone-in or house salesmen they want credit for the commission. Also carrying competing lines gives them creditability with the customers. If one line is slow paying commissions or if the home-office sales manager pinches the territory the salesman can move another line into place. If things get nasty he can tell the customer the manufacturer is having "trouble," the product is becoming unreliable and he should shift to this new line which is better, cheaper and is in stock. The variations of this game are endless and should someday be the subject of a full book (or Gothic novel).

It is sometimes said the rep and manufacturer are natural adversaries though each needs the other (neither will admit it when sober). The manufacturer's view is typically: "Anyone can take orders—my product is so underpriced and so hot, people line up to buy it—so why can't you sell more?" The salesman comes back with: "Your stuff is obsolete and overpriced—the only reason *anyone* buys it is to do me a personal favor." The truth swings eternally somewhere between these extremes.

Reps have to be careful about being ripped-off. Manufacturers often pinch territories and skim orders if they can get away with it. If there is a new customer who phoned or mailed in his order the salesman might not hear about it for a long time. You can imagine the sort of scenes acted out upon discovery of these dishonesties.

Most reps want geographic territorial rights. They want commissions from every sale transacted in their territory, no matter the source of the order. The reasoning is the salesman will have to spend money and time developing this customer and the order most likely came in, in any case, due to prior missionary work of the salesman in the territory.

You can see the problems already. The manufacturer is required to pay a commission (up to 25% with some lines); he is worried his product is selling itself and the salesman is milking the cow by taking commissions he has done *nothing* to earn.

The salesman feels he has done extensive missionary work in the territory and when it starts to pay off the manufacturer starts screwing him.

Contracts between reps and manufacturers are notoriously difficult to enforce. There are so many extenuating circumstances and special situations created in the sales arena it is almost impossible for a judge or jury to follow the story. In fact, in too many cases jurors take the "let dogs eat dogs" attitude when arbitrating disputes between litigious commercial entities.

The *Big Fear* an independent sales rep has is that he will spend time and money developing a territory, and the manufacturer will kick him out and turn the now fat territories into house accounts.

In fact this happens often, especially when the rep starts making more money than the president. Small companies, large corporations, nations and history itself often pivot on petty jealousies, envy and greed. What? That will never happen in your company? I genuinely hope not, but it does happen elsewhere.

All companies do not behave as I have described above. But every one of the sharp practices I have mentioned and more happen every day in every industry.

The key to successful repping is to be good at your profession and carry solid lines, backed-up by companies you know you can work with. It costs a lot of time and aggravation to get to this point.

## Selling to Small Businesses

Today's business person is characteristically intimidated by the prospect of bringing a computer into the business. He has heard too many horror stories and the complexity and jargon of computer technology is new and awesome. At the same time the business person knows computerization is the future and he will eventually have to deal with the dragon.

Sometime in the future small business owners will order data processing equipment as they now order typewriters and office furniture. But *today* the reserve is strong.

What makes a business owner cave in? The personal touch of a salesperson who can convince him of the necessity and relieve his anxieties is a critical factor.

A potential computer system buyer wants to know the equipment he buys will be backed up by a stable manufacturer. He wants to know service help will arrive within hours of his call or that he can carry the unit to the shop for immediate attention.

The computer buyer wants access to software support appropriate to his needs and the periodic presence of a technical consultant to hold his hand and interpret the instruction manuals.

The average business system purchaser wants flashing lights and a *Star Wars* look to his equipment. He wants to show it off. A computer installation is a sign of sophistication, technological currency and business success. The stuff needs to look professional and modern to fill this desire.

If you are willing to realistically address the above cited needs you can build a thriving business from the referrals of your first, happy customer.

Being a rep has promise of great rewards. You have seen a sampling of the price that may be exacted for success in this field.

All that's left is to total the score and see if the bottom line has your name on it.

## Supplies Distributor

Being a full-line supplies dealer takes a fair amount of front-end money. There is a growing number of large, well-organized, well-financed and aggressive supply houses competing ruthlessly with one another on price and delivery. To compete in this arena you need a substantial amount of inventory and rapid turnover of your stock. This business requires megabucks to be competitive.

But if you are already dealing with a group of customers by way of seminars, a newsletter or such, you might consider selling a line of paper goods and supplies under your own label.

Paper goods, diskettes, cassettes, printer ribbons and software packages are needed in some volume by all computer users. You might not be able to compete by pricing but you can offer quick personal service and quality advice.

You will want to answer some important questions before you strike a deal with a supplies manufacturer. Will they allow you to distribute under your own label? What is the discount structure? Return policy? Magnetic disk and cassette certifications available? Price change policy? Do they let you know in advance? Exclusive territory? (Good Luck.)

The nice thing about this business approach is it is an add-on to your regular activities you can start small and carefully. The disadvantage of this approach is it adds one more distractor to take you away from your main line of business. Many people in the computer business are jacks-of-all-trades because they can't live on any one activity. This approach might doom you to a too-diversified business forever.

## Being a Systems House

These companies sell, program, maintain and upgrade entire computer installations for the user.

Many small manufacturers are currently encouraging freelancers to perform this service for them because it's expensive to maintain a manufacturer-supported hand-holding function all over the country.

This approach keeps the end user off the manufacturer's back. Remember manufacturers have essentially the same goal

Reprinted by permission of **INMAC Corporation.**

as the retailers: selling equipment and giving a friendly pat on the back as the unit disappears forever.

There are three definite levels of involvement a small operator can have with a manufacturer:

1. The freelancer can supply sales leads and get a commission (usually a 5% standard finders fee).

2. You provide complete sales service. You deliver signed qualified orders to the manufacturer. The commission for this runs from 10-20%.

3. Being a distributor. In this relationship you sell and install the manufacturer's equipment. You make money from buying equipment with OEM discounts and selling the equipment at retail prices. You also collect money from the end user for implementing programs and providing a maintenance service if you wish.

The systems house approach can work well if you orient your efforts to a specialized market. Can you make a business of selling and installing dedicated equipment in a particular industry to control their processes or equipment? Can you specialize in dentists' offices or church donations programming and implementation? You bet! As this industry grows an increasing number of specialized applications will become whole businesses.

Dealing with the manufacturer is probably the hardest place in this scheme. No two manufacturers have the same policies regarding pricing, discounts or technical back-up. The OEM is in a jungle inside and outside of the tent.

## Retail Store Owner Interview

THE COMPUTER SHOP, 2007 State St., Santa Barbara, CA 93101, (805) 963-1325—Scott Daley, proprietor.

"I was a music major with an emphasis toward electronics. I started working with computers in the last couple of years of my degree and had an electronics background before that. I got out of college with a degree in music, but that is hard to make a living with. I saw the writing on the wall.

About that time I decided to open a computer store and happened to meet Paul Terrell, the founder of the Byte Shop chain, at a convention. He showed me, among other things, the first Byte Shop in San Jose and a wooden cased computer he called an "Apple." I wasn't impressed even though Paul said it was a hot little computer.

I took out a franchise with Paul and within a few months hired a

*Scott Daley of* **The Computer Shop**

few people and things got rolling. I knew very little about maintenance then and a lot of mornings found me still at the shop trying to figure out the problems with a customer's machine. Every problem seemed to take twice as long as I expected. It was an adventure though. The biggest display in our Grand Opening was an old Teletype hooked up to a KIM I board. It spewed randomly generated gibberish and no one, including myself, could understand a word of it. But everyone thought it was great. Within a week or two we had a Polymorphic computer—still one of the best machines around.

We did very well when we started. I opened the store for about $20 thousand. We did over $100 thousand the first year, mainly Polymorphics, IMSAI, a smattering of printers and a few terminals. At the end of '77 we were introduced to a new computer called the Alpha Micro. A large photography school here needed a multi-terminal computer so I set them up with an Alpha Micro. The machine had a few bugs and the customer earned five gold stars for patience.

This business is really geared toward business applications. We sold a few IMSAI machines to hobbyists, but things have gone more and more over to business applications. 50% of our total volume now is to businesses. Typically these customers are doing from half a million to four million dollars a year. Along the way I have become rather an expert in horse breeding and architectural estimating applications and have in fact developed special programs for these businesses.

As a computer dealer you are a half-breed—half professional and half business hawker. You have to act like a professional accountant or lawyer when you are dealing with someone's business. There are some strong constraints, much like the situation of a consultant, where you have entree to a business' vital numbers and then next week you do the same thing with their fiercest competitor just down the street. It requires a stiff upper lip. This situation indicates the dilemma many shops are faced with. What are you? A consultant? Programmer? Equipment salesperson? Software house? It is some combination of all these things. It remains to be seen what the computer store of the future will be like.

Are there big problems in the retail business? One of the biggest is trying to define the cut-off point of a sale. You aren't just selling equipment. You are selling equipment plus a service. That service very often includes modification and customization of the software. You install the system and then it's really difficult to say where is the point you draw the line and start charging them extra for services like training and adding to their program. Many customers require "hand-holding." The only problem here is whether or not you charge for the time taken to do it. Fewer than 10% of the contracts I have signed specify a formal cut-off point. It has mostly been on faith and I have never been sued by anyone.

Poor manuals are a problem. I usually plan to go out and explain the manual. I have even revised a few manuals. For example, I installed a system a few months ago and wrote a 35 page manual to go with it. The quality of many manufacturer-supplied manuals drives both the store and the user crazy. The problem is that manufacturers don't know exactly how the equipment is going to be used. They are having enough problems just keeping the machines running and out the door at a low price.

Many manufacturers sell too low and don't have the money to spend on good technical writers. The machine gets to someone like myself and I sell it to someone as, for instance, an accounts receivable system. Depending on the software used, that manual might not be appropriate to the specific use we are making of the machine. Even if the manual that came with the software is explicit, chances are they forgot to explain something. The customer needs the information so the store winds up bridging the gap. You hopefully know enough about the software to answer the questions over the phone or make a quick visit to the location. There are some really bad manuals out there!

The basic problem is that the type of person who excels at writing software or manufacturing hardware is typically very poor at being able to explain those things. It's like an artist coming up with a picture. That's not the hard part. For them the hard part would be how to write a manual of how they arrived at the picture.

Why not an "Idiot's Guide to Fixing Your Volkswagen"-type series of simplified manuals? The trick would be to take someone who is not in the business and have them write the manual. I think it was somewhat of an advantage I only knew a little about computers before I got into selling them.

I have a formula for how much time to spend with a customer. Generally if I sell a strictly hardware package the person already knows enough to fly solo. If it's a system sale it is typically to someone who is not buying a computer but an accounting function. We typically schedule four hours' training per software module.

Is it difficult to get qualified sales and repair people? Sales personnel are the most difficult because it is such a specialized thing. To sell computer hardware off the floor you can't afford to pay much more than hi-fi clerk wages. Wages vary—I use a system based on draw against commission. Max $200 per week draw. In some circumstances I pay a salary, but of course I would rather pay based on performance. Some salesmen have five thousand dollar months. That suits me just fine. Percentage is based on 25% of margin. If we sell a $10,000 system it typically costs us $6,000. We have about a 40% spread on a big custom system. We don't make that much money on a smaller system like an Apple. A $30,000 system can yield a 40% margin, 12K. Of that 12K 25%, or 3K, goes to the salesman. Keep in mind these numbers vary usually on the down side.

If the salesman takes an active follow-up role, helping with the installation and training the customer on the system, then I pay them more. On the other hand, some of the people are able to only point to the equipment and answer a few questions. That person is doing a function but is not worth the same dollars as a total service type. I have had a wide spectrum of sales people. Some just had effective sales personalities, knew little about computers but were effective in sales. Some learn on their feet in the store.

Service has been a lot easier than sales. There are quite a few technical types around. Typically it is someone who knows a bit about radios and TV's, TTL Logic, has fooled around with kit building, etc., subscribes to *Popular Electronics* and hopefully even owns a computer. They come to work for us and it isn't much different from what they are used to doing.

My philosophy is that service is a necessary evil. We can't make sales unless the customer feels there is service back-up. We therefore support a complete service function. The customer can come in and talk to the service manager at any time and get his problem solved.

Competition: Smaller stores sometimes have a harder time. To sell effectively you need to have inventory and even loaners so the customer has something to use if there is a serious service difficulty. The most successful stores are the ones who have oriented to business buyer rather than the hobbyist.

Interest rates have been a factor in limiting sales. People who want a system can't afford it, and those who can afford it don't want to. The effect of the prime rate has had more effect than competition.

I have lost a few sales to competition, but we emphasize after-sales service. That emphasis reduces the effect of price competition and most other kinds of competition, too.

There are two factors governing the kinds of stores that will be around in the future. The vertical marketness of the store—are they reaching a certain clientele and doing a complete job with them? The other factor is their capital structure. The stores that will really make it are diverse and almost exclusively big corporations or franchises.

It is difficult for an independent retailer like myself to handle a lot of lines. We handle three major lines plus a smattering of printers, modems, software and books. It is difficult to keep up with that. New models and the back-up required is a problem. A large store might have twenty of one model available. If one breaks down they send it to the main repair center and give the customer another one over the counter. In our case we have to try to repair the customer's equipment right in the shop. If we can't repair it, it has to be sent to L.A. and we often have to loan the customer our floor demo unit. The best thing is to have enough back-up stock to take care of this problem. It gets down to capital. With enough capital you can stock the units you need to deliver fast and give excellent service back-up. These things are the key to staying ahead of the competition. Delivery has characteristically been slow in this industry. If we come up with a unit in a shorter time than that, it put us ahead of the competiton.

What about the discounters who advertise in the computer magazines? Who needs business like that? There is no margin in it. We want the business user who is buying a systems function. We are really in that business rather than the hardware business. As soon as someone starts mentioning brand names, I know I have my work cut out for me. I then have to explain why my unit is the one for the job. I sell a service rather than a piece of equipment.

The biggest problem is when a customer is having a problem with his software and he doesn't write down what the screen said the moment the problem happened. They try to fix it and usually make it worse. By the time it has gone through several passes you get a call. The first thing they say is "it just stopped."

I charge $30 per hour to do work like that. I try to give people the benefit of the doubt. I charge for how much time the problem should have taken. That way, if it takes longer because I don't know how to approach the problem, the customer doesn't have to pay for my learning curve. Some businessmen might think this is a terrible thing to do, but when a repair comes in you try to fix it and get the customer operational as fast as possible. If you can do it in fifteen minutes and send them on their merry way they are happy. Even if the machine is out of warranty, we repair it on a complimentary basis. In some cases we do this even if they didn't even buy the machine from us. We buy goodwill by doing this. Typically I find I like to work on this stuff. You sit around, maybe business is slow, and this customer comes in with what amounts to a puzzle. Everybody crowds around and offers an opinion, we find the problem, and the customer gets his unit repaired on the spot. It's that kind of rapport that creates good business relations with the customer.

Customers are becoming more educated. More TV shows and print media articles are coming out about computer operation. The more education there is, the more units we will sell because the intimidation barrier will be breached. I personally see buying a computer as buying a car which has a few features on it. The person already knows how to drive and knows what the words tire, engine and gear mean. They know the fundamentals of maintenance, such as putting in oil, gas and coolant when necessary. You might have to learn a couple of the new features (cruise control?), but you already have an essential feeling for it and already have your license to drive the bloody thing. We are in the position now of teaching the very basics of machine operation. We start from scratch. This button is called the reset—if you push it, the computer will start up. What does that mean, "start up"? It's not fair for anyone, including the dealer. I have spent thousands of hours teaching all these fundamental things about computers.

The future of the retail business is in a vertical market or with back-up of lots of inventory. I feel you will have to be one of those two things. The corporate stores will have a strong capital base to allow them to have appropriate inventory levels. The vertical idea is the only place small companies are going to be able to exist.

They will also do very well at it if they "have their heads screwed on right," as Richard White said in the opening chapter of the *Entrepreneur's Manual.* It means in this case to go after a vertical market, architectural firms for example. Don't get lured into some other area. Get a good software selection and learn the needs and language of your selected market and sell especially to them. If a roller skate manufacturer drops in and says, "Here is some money—I want to buy a computer," what are you going to do?

It's ultimately a mistake when you don't follow your vertical format because you will eventually to do better by becoming an expert in a specific area. A store should specialize in a maximum of three or four areas and then have five other areas that are subsidiary. As an example, we have become expert in architectural job costing, manufacturing, distributorships and horse ranches. We have four areas where I feel strong enough to call on one of these kinds of companies and tell them we are experienced and competent in their area. It is a great entree.

If you have several other areas to fall back on, such as accounting firms, law offices or medical offices, it is helpful. Those are easier because there has been a lot of software already written for them. You can pull something off the shelf and offer them a specialized system. An expert in a specific area will always outsell the bigger companies like IBM and XEROX unless the salesman for them is an expert in that particular field. In most cases, a businessman will be more likely to trust you if you can talk his language.

The machines are getting more and more similar so it really gets down to customer service as the selling leverage. Retailers are increasingly selling services rather than any specific hardware. The future of independent retailing lies in your ability to serve specific markets exceptionally well.

Retailing is an incredibly unique opportunity because, as with an attorney or accountant, you get to see a wide variety of other peoples' businesses. You get invited in and talk to the top people and see incredible situations you would never see if you were selling typewriters or other office items. I have been able to get insight into an exciting array of other businesses and it has been fascinating.

Should you start your own computer store? The questions you should ask first are "What will make my store unique?" and "Where is the market?" It has often been said there are three keys to successful

*IF YOU HAVE ANY DOUBTS ABOUT THE FUTURE OF COMPUTER STORES, PROJECT THESE FIGURES INTO 1985!*

TANDY CORPORATION ANNUAL REPORT 79
($ millions)

| | YEAR ENDING 6/30 | | | | |
|---|---|---|---|---|---|
| | 1979 | 1978 | 1977 | 1976 | 1975 |
| NUMBER OF RETAIL STORES | 7353. | 7071. | 6412. | 5154. | 3865. |
| United States (Radio Shack) | 5913. | 5838. | 5312. | 4195. | 3188. |
| Company | 3600. | 3564. | 32.93 | 2676. | 2118. |
| Franchise | 111. | 114. | 112. | 119. | 126. |
| Dealer | 2086. | 2109. | 1888. | 1396. | 944. |
| Internl Dealers | 71. | 48. | 19. | 4. | — |
| Computer Centers | 42. | 1. | — | — | — |
| Other | 3. | 2. | — | — | — |
| Canada - Radio Shack | 781. | 749. | 640. | 523. | 338. |
| Company | 395. | 369. | 322. | 290. | 246. |
| Dealer | 386. | 380. | 318. | 322. | 92. |
| Canada - Tandy Intnl Elct | 596. | 478. | 457. | 434. | 339. |
| Company | 407. | 358. | 348. | 347. | 287. |
| Franchise | 71. | 64. | 64. | 56. | 52. |
| Dealer | 118. | 56. | 45. | 31. | — |
| Japan, Orient - Radio Shack | 63. | 6. | 3. | 2. | — |
| Company | 6. | 5. | 3. | 2. | — |
| Dealer | 57. | 1. | — | — | — |

retailing: location, location and location. This axiom holds true even for computer stores. Notice the locations of key chains like Heath, Radio Shack and The Byte Shops. These companies spend extensive amounts of money researching the area before making a hard location decision.

Retailing can be a life-eater. A retail store is typically open 56 hours a week, and more during holidays. The help you hire is generally inexperienced and you will lose important sales and system leads if you aren't there personally to supervise.

A successful store requires a good service department and a lot of sales stock. A full service store might also consider taking trade-ins, another problem you have to deal with.

Start-up costs for a store today are probably around $250,000. You can do it for less if you are lucky and get a great location overlooked by the hungry retail chains. But the tighter you have to run and the lower your opening inventories, the more you will limit your overall chances for success.

It can be great fun and you can make a good living with even a moderately successful store.

Scott Daley is a bright and energetic guy who has made his choice and wouldn't have it any other way.

# Electronics Distribution

Interview with computer electronics distributor Tom Pine of VITEK, 930 G. Boardwalk, San Marcos, CA 92069, (714-744-8305). Tom Pine is an aggressive, intelligent and seasoned grass-roots computer professional. His career has led him all over the industry. His original education was technical but his flair for people and products soon led him into marketing. After doing everything from circuit design to being a high level executive with a big company, Tom has decided that the independence and action of owning his distributorship best suits his needs.

Tom is an impressive man. He communicates brilliantly and has the no-nonsense demeanor or a seasoned business street fighter. The following are his words, taken directly from our interview tapes:

"I graduated college in '51 as an electronics engineer and have been in the electronics computer business ever since. Interest in new things has led me step-by-step along the path this industry has made just ahead of me. Right out of college I went to work for an aircraft instrument company. We made real kludges for military aircraft. This company spawned the digital voltmeter market.

I worked as an engineer until '63 when I went in with a group of people to start Digital Development Corp., making disc memories. I did marketing for them. It was a natural transition for me because I always enjoyed strategic planning more than the details of designing. I realized marketing was the right niche for me. I enjoyed being on the analytical end and trying to see where all of this would go.

The transition between working for someone and holding the bit yourself is sometimes difficult. You don't have to necessarily be aggressive or belligerent to succeed in a business. In a way, success factors are undefinable. I think a person is born with certain things which guide him in life. Some people have a tremendous potential for self-directiveness from the day they emerge from the womb; others need to learn it.

I'm not a maverick, I just don't like another company to dictate what kind of business I run. There are many retreads in the computer business. People don't get into this business so much because they are mavericks but because they get turned on by the nature of the business itself. It is a technological Hula-Hoop and is exciting. A lot of people are drawn to this business because of its intrinsic excitement.

Originally most of the people doing this were young — in their early twenties. They were the real driving forces in the business. Most of them were technically-oriented—programmers, and so on. They saw the opportunity.

*Tom Pine of* **Vitek**

The only entrepreneurial avenue in the computer business was to go out and start a hardware company and then sell it back to the same industry. It was very ingrown. At first the only market for computers was the Census Bureau, then the Military and Government came into the picture. It expanded into industrial and OEM-type users.

The hobbyist market started with mail order boards, then chassis sellers. MITS Altair started, IMSAI came along and copied them and the S-100 was born *de facto*. People started breaking off from there, building 6800-type things.

Most of these early companies would have been successful if they had been managed properly. There were no disc systems to begin with. We relied on cassettes, paper tape and front panel switches to input programming. There weren't that many terminals around. Digital Research was started when Gary Kildall developed a system to handle Intels' developmental systems when they were experimenting with their 8080 chip. It was the only disc operating system and it got sucked right into the market. There was a vacuum there and it took over fast. People started writing their BASIC's around it and CP/M has made history..

The biggest mistake people make is to do something they are not suited for. You must use your common sense and have an understanding of your capabilities. Sometimes you can only learn by spending your life's savings on a business; some people never learn. If you just follow your intuition, things will turn out in the best way.

People who do what they enjoy go further than people who do something for the sake of a long range goal. People who develop an integrated knowledge over a long period of time can bring a high degree of skill in an area at some stage in their life and what will most surely lead to success. *Doing what you want do do and feeling good about yourself is the key.* This person will eventually find the world is full of opportunities.

Enthusiasm comes from enjoyment of what you are doing. You are willing to put more energy into what you enjoy and it won't seem like work. You will have more fun,have more pride and fulfillment if you are doing a job you enjoy. Probabilities are highly in favor of a person who does what he likes and who develops his skills and experience in one area until he reaches a critical stage in his life where success comes and speaks his name.

My entrepreneurial stage came about 1960. I worked with a group of people to develop digital voltmeters. It never went much beyond the chalk board stage. We were too naive to really get it going. Electro Instruments and Non-Linear Systems got started on DVM's and the industry really took off. Wavetek and Digital Development came along soon after a new industry was born.

I got started in what I thought was the last job I would ever have. I worked for Digtal Development Corporation with a group of people I had known in college. The company had the best disc on the market but the owners lost control of the company to outside investors. Things developed in a way I didn't like so soon I was an entrepreneur. I went with Terminal Data in LA developing COM cameras. The COM business lost out to magnetic disc media. It was a liberal education. The engineering business, in general, suffered a major setback with the cessation of major NASA programs. The whole world slowed down.

I then went to the LA area and worked for Electronic Memories, becoming involved with the magnetic tape business. I started with a mechanical engineer, working a design which evolved into a really good daisy-wheel printer. I spent most of the time in those days doing marketing consulting for companies like Signetics and Intel Data Disc, Electronic Memories *et al.*

I enjoyed consulting for a while but found it hectic. You work your butt off getting a job while you are still on assignment with the last company. You are humping all day and often far into the night preparing reports. Often my wife had been typing a final report at three in the morning while I showered so I could get to the plane in time to arrive and present the thing.

It was a good living and during the time I helped in the development of a daisy-wheel printer.It eventually became one of the major printers. We licensed it, helped get it produced and marketed, and we went on to the next project.

How do I see the market and its segments? I don't view the market in segments because segmentation doesn't bring anything to the bottom line. It doesn't do me any good to sort out the different markets. All I need to do is follow the growth. I need perspective of knowing what is good and better from a product standpoint. But application is intuitive.

If you get into a company situation a systemic segmentation approach may become relevant. You need to lay down a business plan of action and formal market segment analysis may be appropriate here. Start-ups now typically involve a lot more money than a few years back and so require quite a bit of formal study.

Many times start-up money is blown at the front end. By definition, everyone who goes down the tubes was mismanaged. That's wonderful. That's like saying the sun comes up in the morning. We already know that but it doesn't help anybody.

In a business sense this is where you go from blue sky to the practical aspect. It's what you do every day that really counts. You are pulled in so many directions as an entrepreneur it is hard to keep your bearings unless you start a big organization with large funding. The problem then, is you are doing a lot of giving-up in the beginning. You are more an organizer than an entrepreneur. A lot of pressures are placed on you in this situation.

You have to be a certain type of personality to start a company, plan it, and make it grow. I'm not talking about a bootstrapping operation like I'm doing now. I'm talking about one where you go out and get a lot of capital to begin with. You need the right blend of people for this sort of start-up and a good management group, too. The man who puts all that together is not necessarily the best guy to run the thing and so you need someone who is a tech specialist, a financial specialist, a marketing specialist.

How do you manage technology without being a technician? There are only so many hours in a day and there is only so much that is humanly possible to accomplish. It's obvious some human beings are much more productive than others. I don't know how many people are involved in all the technological revolutions going on now but it has got to be a fraction of a percentage of the population. Almost all the good ideas emanate from a very few individuals. Only a few people point things in a direction for change. There are some retreads in the computer business but it's because people have learned they don't have to stay at the same old job. It's a matter of education and awareness. We live in an age where people know more and expect more of their lives.

The big companies have planning to guide them. Small operators characteristically say the big companies are lethargic and can't change to meet the times. I think on the other side of this: It is amazing that anyone could mobilize all these amazing numbers of people to accomplish a complex and synchronous task.

People generally fail to see that huge companies have a vested interest in maintaining the *status quo* of the market. Unless they are pushed they aren't going to obsolete their present systems. They will try to amortize their research, development and overheads over the longest time possible. They lease products to make money on that use of their funds. Leasing and rentals are much more productive for them. They would rather loan you the thing and have you make payments on it than sell it to you.

Since IBM spends over a billion dollars a year for R&D they can keep up or ahead if they want. So what if the daisy-wheel printer is better? They have a huge investment in the golfball type selectric machines. It is all a matter of calculation. They have people who daily go through the decision to introduce a product or hold it back. It is all a financial decision based on the numeric summaries of these sophisticated analyses. None of the smaller companies are so well organized. Now that IBM has entered the personal computer market there is a driving force.

Remember, companies with the power of IBM create markets. When I say market creation let me explain: We know there is a need for an item. Nobody knows how big the need is. So one company plays it by ear and builds incrementally more and feels the market out that way. Someone else says, "If I go in and build one for half as much, which has twice the power, the market will be elastic as hell and respond to this product." So they go ahead and build the Apple computer.

There isn't one person in the world who could have told you Apple was going to be a big success. They just did it! They set their sights on something and said we are going to sell X number of Apples and we're going to make it happen by providing a better machine at a lower price. [By price elasticity, Tom is speaking of the idea that a market expands if the price is lower.]

The Apple people were the first ones who showed what could be done with this market. It was growing but still wasn't of the magnitude to attract IBM into the business.

Apple had some luck. They took a tremendous risk, and started a whole market. Now you'll find the market will expand tremendously with the entrance of Xerox and IBM because their names are well known and just the fact they are there will create sales. People trust these companies and will show it by buying the products they offer.

I got into marketing because I enjoyed strategic thinking more than the details of designing. I had few actual business classes. Marketing was a nice niche for me between the engineering world and the people world.

All along I was thinking of becoming an entrepreneur. Typically engineers in their early thirties start thinking of making more money and being on their own, getting out of the rat race and getting into another rat race.

This bridge is critical. It is more in the individuals' personalities then their technical training. Many people can work well in larger companies. In fact, we get training that says it's not ok to just be happy working for someone. We are all motivated by fame, greed and achievement.

At one point I formulated a joint venture to start Vista Computer Company, which is still quite successful. It had to be sold at a certain point because the new owners weren't supporting it. They were supposed to provide the engineering and parts. We started building small disc memories for computers and disc drives with CP/M. We were about the fourth licensee of CP/M. We took a blanket license so we had total freedom to supply it with our system. Digital Research had about four people then.

We had CP/M a drive and a controller. It was doing about a million dollars worth of business but Randall Data Systems got into financial difficulties and we didn't get any product. My revenue dropped off because I couldn't ship and we needed to continue to develop new products. So I dropped the project and found a job as a marketing VP for Technical Design Labs, one of the leading design firms whose name was later changed to Xitan. They ran into financial difficulties and couldn't make it. Same story as IMSAI—cash flow problems ate them up because they hadn't planned their finances properly.

At that point I decided to do my own thing completely. I told myself there is no point in trying to develop a hardware product unless you have a lot of money. The risk profile of a hardware manufacturing start-up is too high.

The risk of choosing a product a bigger company is going to come out with at the same time is high. This situation results in a collosal collision where the smallest entity looses.

I decided to become a distributor. I had set up distributorships for TDL and Vista so I knew the dealers, the market place and what was going on. So I scouted around and found a product to get going on and started building on that. I call this business Vitek. We carry Epson, Microperipherals, NEC, 3-M, Sincom. We sell cables, modems and accessories. I have been with this company since August '79. We really started shipping six months later due to slow shipment by backlogged manufacturers. This industry has problems of discontinuity and a coming shakeout of marginal distributors. But you can't get away from that—it is built into the industry. The whole industry isn't like that but it is getting that way. Every market runs its cycle. Right now there is a shortage of product. We are in the early stages of market penetration but when you get to 1986 this will change. Production capacity will overrun the market. You will find people wanting to sell inventory very cheaply.

A real shakeout is coming. There is competition now but most of it is what I call stupid competition. Some distributors work on as little as 8% margin. If a price is advertised at a general level there is no way you can sell it for more. The biggest offenders are the ones that are hollering because prices are low. "We have to stop this price cutting," but the loudest complainers are giving the biggest discounts. Greed is the driving force. People are naturally competitive and will get anxious about not moving enough product so they drop prices. The others follow. Another bad day comes along so the dealer drops his price a bit more. The price steadily jogs down in this way. There are certain dealers who give service—they can hold a price.

There are a lot of different philosophies of doing business. Some people feel more comfortable with the security of a franchise or a dealership closely supervised by the manufacturer. They are depending on the other guy to protect and guide them.

Who is the right person to start a business in this industry? Everybody! *There is a time in the tide of human affairs when things just work. Other times you can go out and bend your pick. This is a time when new businesses are sucked into the vacuum of this industry.* The LSI chip really invigorated this business.

My business plans are, for starters, to survive. We have been profitable from the first and I want it to stay that way. I have a partner who I have known for years and trust totally. He helps with the financial aspects of the business. I handle the marketing and promotion and it works fine.

When starting a business it's important to identify the areas where you can stub your toe. Mine is finance so I got a partner who has strength in that area. Inventory management and cash flow are critical in this business. Our inventory turn is currently 18 times a year. That is high and indicates the problem we have with slow deliveries. Printers especially are hard to keep in stock lately.

My philosophy is not to take risks but to remain flexible and dance with the market. The risks are not too bad right now but there is always a chance of getting stuck with inventory. Commitments often have to be made a long time in advance. It doesn't take much bad inventory to screw up your profit margin. We do well on small items, like modems and supplies. A lot of discounting of big ticket stuff is based on the support we get from better margins in the smaller stuff. But it is a mistake to turn equipment for 8% markup. It doesn't make long-term sense.

Here is an example of what can happen in this business: NEC has a green screen monitor that has a list price of about $280. Dealer price is about $185. There is about a 30% margin on that item. The catalog price is about $239. We could sell tons of those at these prices. But it all turned around in one month. Zenith came out with a new green screen monitor that sells at $149. Dealer price is a hundred bucks! Distributors make ten or fifteen bucks on the thing. It matches an Apple better and works every bit as well. I can't find any reason not to buy it vs. the more expensive one.

We had only a few NEC units in stock so it didn't hurt us. One distributor I know has 750 in stock. He was moving about 500 a month and his volume dropped to fewer than a hundred a month. The dealer price has now been dropped by NEC to a hundred dollars and he has all that inventory he bought at $185.

This pattern will repeat as more giant companies enter the market geared up to get the market. They want to get the business any way they can. We are now still looking at the grass roots market. There are 200 million people and maybe 50 million families in this country. We might be talking about a market in tens of millions of personal computers.

The big growth of the personal computer market will come out in '85 and '90. The big growth in the early 80's will be in the business sector.

The hobbyist market is not what will fuel the home market. People will be using computers for personal tasks—as an extension of their own minds.

Graphics, games and modeling will be big. There is a vast business market out there. There is a far greater market out there for home units. Businesses are buying computers now because they can afford the things. The hardware will be the main cost, and as the big companies come into high production the prices of hardware will drop sharply. Enter the home market. It's just a matter of mass production.

Electron beam and X-ray lithography will vastly increase the amount that can be put on a chip. There is no indication that the level of integration of a chip and magnetic recording density has slowed down. The tools we have to work with are becoming incredibly advanced. The better our tools the better the product. Metrology—the ability to measure the microcosm gets greater and greater. It all helps us build better computers. Remember, 100 years ago they thought the patent office should be closed because everything had been invented.

The computer business is a tremendous opportunity because it is a pervasive, unlimited application. It is not a thing people will shortly tire of. Computers are extremely useful and provide unlimited entertainment. It is also tremendously interactive with respect to stimulation of the human brain. There are people to sit in front of the tube and feel like they are relating to another person. The computer is an electronic extension of the human intellect.

There are certainly more uses for computers unthought of than are already being utilized. The opportunity for programming is unlimited.

The most fruitful thing you could do is to write a new computer game for the Apple. You would be an overnight millionaire! One of the most popular accounting programs (VISICALC) has been outsold by a factor of several hundred by a group of Apple games.

The future is in small, personalized computers. We are making a transition from the computer as a technical item to a computer as a tool, like a toaster. The software at present is not perfected to where you can relate to the computer as a person. There are two catch words in the industry now: Ergonomic (human engineered) and "user friendly." That implies that the software relates to you in a human way. There is a tremendous effort in the industry to improve the software so anybody can sit down and interact with the computer. Pretty soon you will be able to use the machines very easily. User friendliness will break the barriers of intimidation that are holding up the market now.

I'm more excited about the computer business than ever before. I'm happy to be alive and a witness to the incredible changes the computer is making in our world.

*Computer equipment rental allows someone to use a computer and peripheral equipment before making a purchase commitment.*

## Chapter Five

# MARKETS FOR THE FUTURE

The microcomputer market is obviously going crazy. There are heated arguments about which sector of the business will show the most growth, but each side is talking in orders of magnitude. By any measure the industry is destined for expansion.

What does that mean to the small operator? Most markets are made by large firms with the power to create markets by advertising and production. Won't they get all the business? Not even close. Each foreward bound throws off hundreds or even thousands of markets which are beneath the gaze of the mighty but can make you successful beyond imagination. Each leap of the major market creates huge numbers of opportunities perfectly suited to you.

The established companies are busy with their own problems and have no time or motivation to take advantage of all the developments in the industry.

When you are just starting your speed and ability to adapt to change puts you in a perfect position to select the way you will make your fortune in the microcomputer business.

I learned the other day why ants can successfully raid bee hives. The ants are so skinny the bees can't catch hold of them—so they can't throw them out of the hive! Bees can't hurt ants because they can't aim their stinger accurately enough to impale them. The result is bees suffer constant attrition from marauding ants. As it is in the bee hives, so it is also in the microcomputer business! As long as you and your company are lean and mean you will be able to profit and prosper in this market.

The following is a description of only a few opportunities that exist currently:

*Temporary help agencies specializing in computer oriented personnel are an idea we will hear more of in the future.*

## Information Business

On-line terminal access information utilities and Information Brokers are showing up to meet the demands of a world in search of more information. There is so much being published that one person, even highly specialized, cannot keep track of it all. This creates the information brokerage market.

Information brokerages, home and educational needs to access information, news, special programs, electronic mail facilities, and even specialized learning programs like "French Language Drill" are rising to meet a growing demand.

The number and size of data bases are increasing rapidly. There are currently more than 300 serving almost every conceivable information retrieval need. Every conceivable? How about starting a Science Fiction reference data base, cataloging subjects and references that have appeared in Science Fiction novels and stories? All you need is a phone line, modem, processor, a simple retrieval and billing program and a large memory/recall capacity. You could charge a yearly fee to belong and a fee for on-line time. How many writers, researchers, futurists, consultants and professional forecasters would want to have access to such a rich source of data, ideas and information?

A gap analysis aimed at uncovering unfilled data base needs would be mighty interesting indeed.

## Infomart

Fred Bellomy is the founder of Infomart—probably the first "information brokerage" business in the country. He is a man who insists on living life as he defines it; he has a business that allows him to work his own hours at his own pace.

Fred lives in an apartment which provides good security for his now elaborate computer system and divides his time between his work, running, meditating and enjoying exceedingly lovely companionship. His latest "hobby" is a color graphics machine which he prods and tinkers with for hours on end.

Fred originally worked as a government physicist developing items he prefers to forget. He couldn't stand it so he quit and took a job at the University of California at Santa Barbara in the library as a systems mechanic. He learned something about computers in his government work and extended his knowledge and interest while computerizing the UCSB library.

Fred is a curious and energetic fellow so he borrowed an old

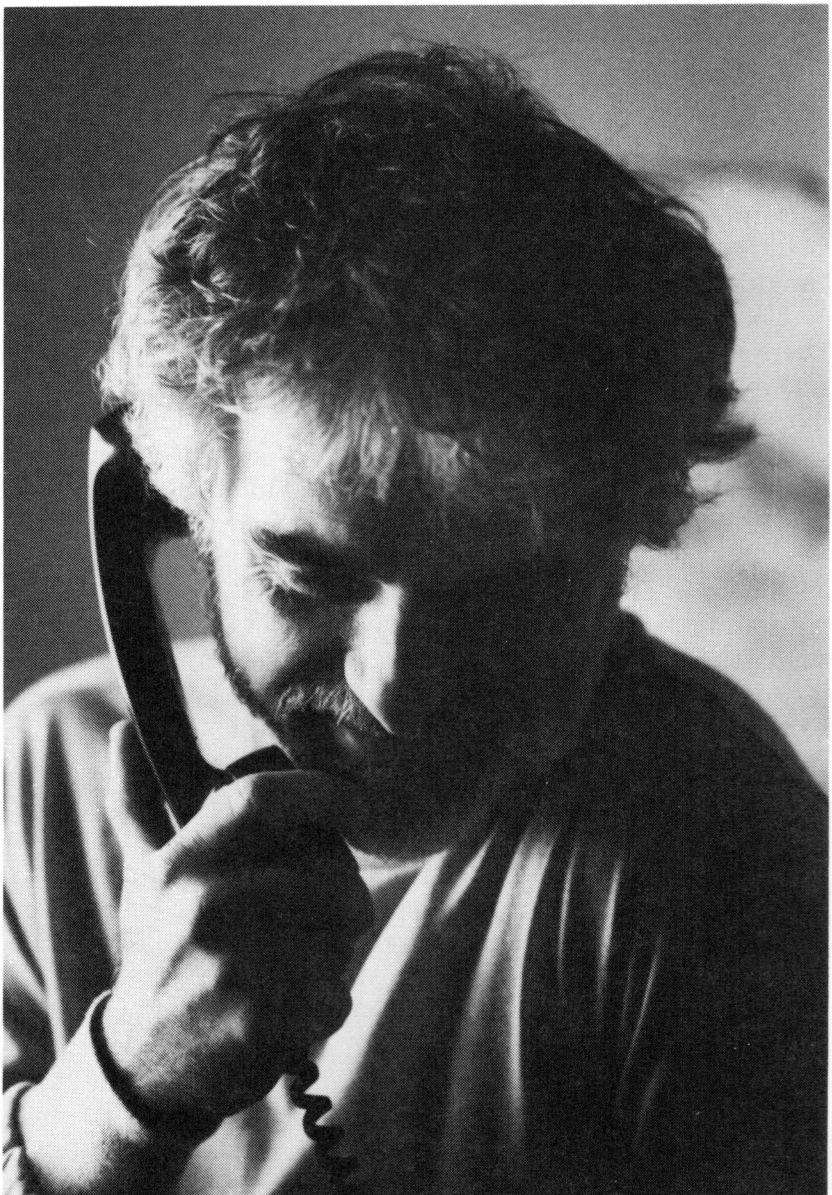

*Fred Bellomy of* **Infomart.**

klunker terminal from one of the professors. This enabled him to take work home. He learned to do searches of the very few data bases then on-line and was so pressed for this service he began to charge a fee for it.

Then he took a serious step — spent a hundred bucks on a used Itel 1121 (300 baud max). A year later he bought a used CRT.

Fred Bellomy:

Every time I had extra money I would buy another piece for the system. My job with the University was not that exacting—long serial lists, flow charts, forms design and stuff like that. So I began to spend more time and money on the information retrieval idea.

I evolved into what I do now. There are several names for it: information broker, information-on-demand specialist and so on.

There were others providing information services but no one had conceptualized putting many services in one place. That's the idea I homed in on.

I read a magazine article one day — the author was blue-skying about the future and said, "One day we will have information brokers who access multiple data bases." I was already doing that—so I began calling myself an information broker.

One problem in this business is every search service has their own program. All you have to do is sit down at your terminal and use the service, but the problem is they use different prompts. In one system they use a period for the Boolean operator; another place they use an asterisk or a plus. I fixed my system so it would make these conversions for me. That way I can rely on a standardized set of commands and my program does the conversion.

I started in '73 when there were relatively few data bases. Now there are more than 300 data bases to choose from. (Actually I only use 30-40 of them regularly.) It was hard to get customers at first because the idea was so new. As I began to complete jobs I started getting referrals. Now I consciously adjust the business to the volume level I'm comfortable with. The bulk of my work is for medium-sized companies, medical engineering firms, consulting companies and a growing number of writers. In fact, I do searches for every medical device manufacturer in this area.

It is clear this kind of cottage industry is on the increase. More people are working at home, not only as entrepreneurs but also for companies that hire them to work in their home. Here I have an office that doesn't cost any company a thing. Office space is an expensive overhead, supported by secretaries, people to watch the facility, clean it and so on. If you put an office in your house you not only get income tax benefits but you get convenience.

A person seems to go through a cycle with a home business. There is a period when you can't bear to get up in the morning. Yet there were times when I wanted to live with it day and night, when I could hardly wait to get through dinner so I could get back to it. Sometimes I would sleep at the desk. When I first started there was a period of confusion—the business started and stopped and in-between I didn't know exactly what to do. Advertise? More equipment? Confusion. As it got bigger and bigger adding more clients, some of the worries disappeared and I began thinking "well now it's possible. What can I do with this technology?" This became the focus of most of my activity for practically the whole time I've been in business. What's possible with this technology? I enjoy this work and the minute I don't enjoy it I'll stop it. For years I took in very little money, I was lucky to break even. My business is now producing income so there is a new set of ideas to deal with.

I run my business as a hobby and seldom do what I don't want to do. I keep commitments but am careful about what I take on. I used to call clients every six months. I even kept a log of the calls. I don't do that now. When I want more work I call a few clients and usually rustle up enough business to meet my needs.

I now have a superb system for the kind of work I do. I got it by doing a consulting job. I bought two systems for a client and got to keep one for my fee.

One problem of keeping your job while starting a business is you don't have the energy to do all of those things you know you should do to make the business go. I was laid-off by the University so I had unemployment insurance to help me through the thin time. It is supposed to be a bridge and that's exactly what I used it for.

You can go into business while you are on unemployment. You have to report all income over and above expenses. This is deducted from your weekly payment, but it extends the time you get the benefits. So you still get the same amount which is set aside for your account by the unemployment people.

Unemployment insurance is not welfare; it's *insurance* and it can provide an important bridge to a new career.

Fred is a pioneer in a field which represents the new age: The age which is beginning to permeate every aspect of our lives. We have evolved through the ages of stone, bronze, and iron. We are now on the doorstep of the Age of Information.

The information industry is in its infancy and the businesses designed to serve information needs are in the early stages of their development cycle. Two successful information utilities, *The Source* and *Compuserve,* provide on-line services on a hobby-level. Many of their services aren't comparable to commercially oriented services such as Systems Development Corporation, Lockheed's *Dialog* or BRS in New York. These giants are sweeping the serious data seeker market and are growing daily.

There are, at the time of this writing, about twenty bibliographic services and several hundred non-bibliographic data bases waiting to be accessed.

## Reconditioning Used Equipment

When the automobile market got started everyone wanted one and they were only available new. Henry Ford brought the price of his Model T down to 70 days' wages for the average working man and an infant industry spring into ferocity.

More automobiles showed a restless population new freedoms, and soon everyone wanted one. People who had an older one wanted a new one and those with none at all wanted to buy their way into the game. Dealers found they could more easily sell new ones if they were willing to accept a trade-in. The trade-ins could easily be sold to willing buyers of lesser means. The Used-Car Lot was born!

Will the same cycle happen in the computer business? Will more people buy computers, fall in love with them, and want to trade up? Perhaps as people learn more about computer systems they will be increasingly willing to buy a guaranteed, reconditioned, last seasons' model.

A Used Computer Lot operator could buy trade-ins from dealers who have accepted them to make a sale of newer or more advanced equipment. Businesses too will be a source of used equipment as they upgrade their DP capability. Community newspapers in the Sunnyvale-San Jose metropolis have extensive Used Computer columns in the classified ad section and the same trend is showing up in more community papers every day.

Government and industrial surplus sales include a growing amount of computing equipment. Items can be purchased at these auctions or closed-bid sales for pennies on the dollar or even less.

The problem with this kind of business would not be obtaining reconditionable late model equipment at a good price. The problem as I see it would be to showcase the equipment so your customers would feel confidence in the equipment and its warranty and be willing to pay you 70-80% of new price for the equipment.

One thing in your favor would be that most computer stores don't display much equipment. New equipment computer stores typically display one of each and carry only a few lines. The stores look rather empty.

But not so with a Used Computer Lot. This kind of store would have rows of new-looking machines on display, set up as systems and functioning perfectly. The sight of plentiful merchandise and bright flashing lights makes customers want to buy. They may not only buy, but they can take the system with them — instant gratification of computer fever. "You can't sell from an empty wagon" was coined by an itinerant Snake Oil salesman. He knew what he was talking about.

Many used equipment dealers work on this basis: They pay a maximum 30% of new price for equipment. They spend a maximum of 20% for "reconditioning" — often limited to replacing certain wear parts and polishing up. They sell the equipment for 70-85% of new price, depending on factors of the market (age, use and demand).

These numbers are workable! The reconditioned, previously owned market may not be an item this year—but as the number of systems grows and consumer familiarity softens the ice, a Used Computer Lot concept will become a reality and will also make the fortune of many an enterprising adventurer.

## Maintenance, Disc and Head Cleaning

Want steady work,high pay and a guaranteed future? You might consider providing light maintenance, disc and head cleaning services.

Here's the kicker: There are many new hardware makers who can't afford to have a factory payrolled repair service in most areas. If you are reliable and can fix their equipment the manuacturer would be overjoyed to have you cover a geographic territory and be their "Factory Authorized Service Representative." Many manufacturers will train you at the factory so you will be able to provide first class service on their particular product.

Contact the service manager at the companies you are interested in. If you have an answering service (better than a machine because the customer gets the same treatment when they call the doctor), it gives the customer the feeling they will get fast professional response to their emergencies. If you are an efficient technician and perform as agreed, other companies will hear of you and you'll have to stand them of with a fly swatter.

Rates? $40-60/hour if you're not sure of yourself or need the business. $50-75/hour if you are hot and busy.

You might discuss getting a portion of the monthly service

contract revenues, called "piece of the action". In this way you are in the insurance business on the side.

If the customer pays $100/month for his maintenance contract you might reasonably ask or $60-75 of that. It can work out nicely if you have a hundred or so of these sweet deals. Be careful that you can service everyone you accept on contract. Insurance which collects premiums but pays off slowly makes customers and the factory service manager crazy!

You can't really do field service work until you are completely away from your 9-5 job. When a system goes down, the user wants it fixed yesterday!

There are several places you can get help starting out:

NRF Schools offer a reference and home study course. 3939 Wisconsin Avenue, Washington, DC 20016.

Cleveland Institute of Electronics, 1776 East 17th Street, Cleveland, OH 44114. Offers a complete home study repair course.

Hewlett-Packard, 1501 Page Mill Road, Palo Alto, CA 94304, (415) 857-1501 offers some of *the best* courses and equipment available, also the most expensive.

Memspec Computer Systems sells the Orion — the best and lowest priced Asynchronous Analyzer on the market. 2445 Treasure Drive, Santa Barbara, CA 93105, (805) 687-5680.

Computer-Link Corporation, 40 Ray Avenue, Burlington, MA 01803, (617) 272-7400 sells a line of tape and head cleaning equipment and suppliers. They have excellent booklets called *Magnetic Tape Management* and *Disk Pack Cartridge Management* and will send it free for the asking.

Texwipe, P.O. Box 575, Upper Saddle River, NJ 07458, (201) 327-5577 sells a complete line of disc and tape maintenance supplies. They will send you a generous sample pak if you ask them nicely.

## Voicetek Interview

Voicetek Speech Recognition and Voice Response Systems, P.O. Box 388, Goleta, CA 93017, sells a speech recognition box for personal computers.

Voicetek's founder, Dr. Bill Georgiou, is one of the foremost experts in this state-of-the-art field. His unit is able to recognize a specific person's voice and respond with any voice you program in. His unit represents the leading edge of this complicated technology and a large part of his sales are to other researchers who want to see what Bill has done and how he goes about doing it.

Bill Georgiou is the kind of person who sets his sights on a project and goes straight for it until the goal is met. He went to high school in Greece and decided to become a computer engineer. He came to this country and went straight through to get

*Dr. Bill Georgiou of Voicetek demonstrates his incredible* **Cognivox** *voice recognition/synthesis system.*

*Voicetek's* **Cognivox**

a BS, MA and a Ph.D. in computer engineering. Now his sights are set on developing voice recognition and speech synthesis technology to its highest possible state.

Bill says his system is capable of much that is unappreciated. He says the limiting factor on sales of his SR/VS synthesis system is the newness of the concept. "People don't know the capabilities of a system like this and so don't have a clear idea of its applications. Also the technology has limitations in that you can't interact on a personal level, as with a human being."

Bill plans to expand his business by expanding the capabilities of the unit he already sells. With the present unit the user can write a program to interface with it and can use a BASIC statement to call the functional voice or the function of speech recognition. He is planning to alter the speech recognizer so it will operate in parallel with the keyboard. With the new set-up you will have the option to type the words or say them to the machine. The program will operate off-the-shelf. All you will have to do is plug it in and start talking or typing.

Bill Georgiou:

A useful system has to recognize and create speech. Let's say you are measuring something, your hands are busy and you want to put the data into your computer. Your eyes would be watching your hands.It is not practical to turn your head around and look at the display screen to get the next prompt. Let's say you are using test equipment—the computer guides you through the routine. It's like the repair scene in *2001.* The computer calls out the prompts for each step of the test sequence.

These systems exist now. Computer Systems Test Programs exist that guide you through the test point-by-point. In this case there could be a special SR/VS system creating a conversation between the computer and test operator.

We have a gadget that hooks up to a microprocessor and functions as a voice output multitester. In many situations you have to perform tests between racks of equipment or in other places where you can't see the readout very clearly. In a case like this voice readout would be very helpful.

To operate the system you first look at the menu on the screen. You then input your own vocabulary. It uses the voice of the user for voice response. If it is going to sound good it has to be the voice of the user. The Texas Instruments Speak and Spell®, the National Digitalker® has a Texas accent because it was programmed by a Texan. These techniques are not voice synthesis.

Voice synthesis is a specialized area which will loose out to our recall and playback methods. We simply don't know enough about speech to synthesize it and get a quality product.

The difference between our unit and a tape recorder is random access. This unit can instantaneously access any word in the memory. But since it is not a tape recorder the memory is limited. The data rate is the thing we are trying to reduce. You can have a high quality output if you don't have the restriction of data rate. Digital audio is much better than conventional hi-fi. The data rate on that is ridiculously high—800 times more than this unit.

Speech recognition is the correct term for what this unit can do. Voice refers to speech that has glottal excitation like 'uhhhh' or 'ahhhh', or sibilants like 'ssssssss'. There are many nuances that have been butchered by lack of specific understanding of the speech and voice process. Voice sounds better than speech because it is how we really communicate. When we talk we run words together and you still understand it. The computer in this system has to be trained to the user and the words have to be said in isolation. This is a state-of-the-art limitation and it is very serious. With our current technology you would have to train the computer in a voice typewriter system to recognize 20,000 words *of the operator.* This is obviously unrealistic.

Some applications then are not possible at this stage of our voice input research. However, there are a great number of applications where the vocabulary is limited. For instance, in a word processing system you have different commands which could be voice actuated. You could then enter a limited number of actual text with the keys. You could say "line 1, page 110"; the screen scrolls to that line and you key in your correction. If you are looking through a microscope counting cells, the type of cells and their occurrence could be input by voice. What we are going to see is computers trained to the voice of the user. The voice training method gives you full control of the vocabulary. With the other systems you get whatever the factory gives you. This system gives you diversity and flexibility. My machine is currently limited to a 32-word vocabulary. There are many applications where this is sufficient.

The competition in this business is fierce. It is a game of getting the attention of the users without bringing competition into our arena. We have special procedures to provide security of our design. As you know, patents have many limitations, among which are costs involved for attorney fees to protect your patent. Large companies can muscle you out of your design rights by spending more than you on the legal battle. This whole area is not only new but is interdisciplinary. These facts give us some protection. The best protection is a low profile and certain security measures inthe product itself.

Voice quality is a problem with all vs units including ours. These units have a small speaker and if there is any problem with the communication (i.e., being out of context or difficult to understand), then there are recognition problems. Context helps communication because of your expectations. If you have to search to find what was said in the beginning you can't narrow it down. If you have ever listened to the radios on a small airplane you will know what I mean. When you first listen it all sounds like static. But when you are familiar with what is being said it becomes easy to understand. Also there is motivation—your life may depend upon understanding what the tower controller is saying. If there is an expectation of what will be said computer speech is easier to understand.

If you had asked me five years ago if this could be done I would have said "no way." I was at a conference listening to someone who didn't know anything about computer speech. His demonstration gave me the clue to developing this unit. They stumbled upon a great idea but didn't know it.

I was looking for somewhere to start to solve this problem and I ran across this demonstration. A little clue opened a window for me and this business started.

All of this is leading edge technology. The hardware is not so complex but we are really selling our research and programming to achieve these functions.

Electronic patents are a matter of money. If I have a patent and someone with financial backing wants to challenge it he gets my patent. A patent is not such a good idea in a fast moving industry like this.

The thing we need to do to expand this business is to sit down and write a bunch of articles—go through a user education phase. The whole computer industry is facing this same problem, but it is even more acute in this particular area because it is so new and highly technical.

Many people who write articles are pushing their own theories. I don't exclude myself from this bias. This technology has limitations and many writers don't like to talk about them in the popular articles. The limitations are not so great that you can't find many interesting and useful applications for voice synthesis and recognition. It is not necessary to misrepresent the capabilities of these systems to create reader interest and even action. There has been some bad publicity generated from exaggerated claims and omissions in articles about the subject.

A lot of customers have been burned by hard sell techniques with regard to these systems. This creates an unhealthy skepticism which is hard to overcome. Education is the only way to get things on the right track for this industry.

Half of our customers are big companies. They buy the units in order to investigate speech recognition. IBM, LITTON and a lot of other technology-dependent large companies are paying attention to the developments in this field. Our unit is the best investment a company wanting to go into the speech recognition area could make. They can buy our unit and check it out to see if it will work for their application before they send the money for more expensive development or hardware.

## References

**American Systems Inc.,** 123 Water Street, Watertown, MA 02172, 617/923-1850

**Periphonics Corporation,** Airport International Plaza, Bohemia, NY 11716, 516/567-1000

**Transcom Inc.** (alpha terminals), 580 Spring Street, Windoor Locks, CT 06096, 203/623-2481

**Federal Screw/VOTRAX,** 500 Stephensen Hwy., Ste 102, Troy, MI 48084, 313/588-2050

**Carterfone Communications Corp.,** 2639 Walnut Hill Lane (Receivers), Dallas, TX 75229, 214/328-5110

*Voice News* is a speech recognition/voice synthesis newsletter published by Stoneridge Technical Services, P.O. Box 1891, Rockville, MD 20850, 301/424-0114.

**Street Electronics Corporation,** 3152 E. La Palma Avenue, Anaheim, CA 92806, 714/632-9950 sells the Echo-Series™ speech synthesizers.

M.I.-8, 822 East County Road 30, Fort Collins, CO 80525. (303) 669-4116. Ted Benglen. Literally a cottage manufacturer of peripherals for Health/Zenith H8/H89 computers. Their line includes voice synthesizers. This company might have more general interest for your book.

Phonic Ear (was H C Electronics), a division of Universal Health, 250 Camino Alto, Mill Valley, CA 94941. (415) 383-4000. Anna Hoffman, market research analyst

This company markets a Votrax-manufactured speech prosthesis for the verbally impaired. They are developing their own designs.

Street Electronics Corporation, 3152 East La Palma Avenue, Suite C, Anaheim, CA 92806. (714) 532-9950. Andrew Clare.
Has a growing line of synthesizer products.

Weitek Corporation, 3255 Scott Boulevard, Building 2B, Santa Clara, CA 95050. (408) 727-6625. Godfrey Fong, v.p. operations.
A one-year old IC design house that has a one-chip speech recognizer and more products on the way.

Covox Company, P.O. Box 2341, Santa Maria, CA 93455. (805) 937-9545/928-4818. Dr. John Stewart or Brad Stewart.
A father and son team that has a unique approach to voice recognition. I believe that their techniques will be very relevant in future technology.

Data Voice Corporation, 2 North LaSalle Street, Suite 1900, Chicago, IL 60602. (312) 327-8488. Rick Arons or Rick Miller.
A recent start-up marketing low cost board-level synthesizers.

Excalibur Technologies Corporation, 80 Rio Grande Blvd. N.W., Albuquerque, NM 87104. Jim Blackman, president.
This small public corporation has developed an executive "power station" (i.e., work-station), with voice recognition capability. They are one of the many firms putting voice to practical use.

Maryland Computer Services Incorporated, 502 Rock Spring Avenue, Belair, MD 21014. (301) 838-8888. Mike Mason.
A manufacturer of computer terminals with voice synthesis, primary for blind users.

Mimic, Incorporated, P.O. Box 921, Acton, MA 01720. (617) 263-2101. Bob Dodge or Jim Anderson.
Anderson has patented a simple, unique speech encoding scheme that can beused for synthesis and recognition. He also has some interesting ideas about the future of speech.

Alford and Associates, P.O. Box 6743, Richmond, VA 23230 sells a phonetic Speech Synthesizer for the S-50 and S-50C buss.

Heuristics, 1285 Hammerswood Avenue, Sunnyvale, CA 94086 sells a line of speech recognition products.

If you're interested in finding out more about computer speech some of the following articles may be helpful:

Circuits with Ears; Speech-Recognition Systems Let You Speek to Your Computer. Here's a Look at What They're All About.
Weinstein, Martin Bradley
Radio-Electronics v52 p61(4) June 1981
Descriptors: automatic speech recognition—equipment and supplies

Personal Computers Accept Oral Input
Neff, Robert
Electronics v54 p78(2) June 16, 1981
Descriptors: Sanyo SSR-16 (computer) — design and construction; Nippon Electric PC-8012-03 (computer) — design and construction; minicomputers — technological innovations; computers—technological innovations; automatic speech recognition—industrial applications

Voice Controls Image Processor
Waller, Larry
Electronics v54 p60(1) May 5, 1981
Descriptors: Comtal Corp. — technological innovations; image processing — technological innovations; automatic speech recognition—industrial applications.

Personal Computers Accept Oral Input
Neff, Robert
Electronics v54 p78(2) June 16, 1981
Descriptors: Sanyo SSR-16 (computer) — design and construction; Nippon Electric PC-8012-03 (computer) — design and construction; minicomputers — technological innovations; automatic speech recognition—industrial applications

Voice Control System Tests Scheduled
Klass, Philip J.
Aviation Week v114 p83(5) May 11, 1981
Descriptors: Lear Siegler Inc.—technological innovations; fighter planes—equipment and supplies; airplanes, military—equipment and supplies; Massachusetts Institute of Technology—research, United States; Federal Aviation Administration—research speech processing systems — military use; automatic speech recognition — military use

Talking Wheelchair
USA Today v109 p15(1) April 1981
Descriptors: handicapped — aids and devices; wheelchairs — innovations; speech, disorders of—aids and devices; automatic speech recognition—innovations.

Speech Recognition by Computer
Levinson, Stephen E.; Libermarn, Mark Y.
Scientific American v244 p64(11) April 1981
Descriptors: automatic speech recognition — technological innovations; speech processing systems — technical innovations; computer input-output equipment — technological innovations

Multiboard Systems Shrink to Chip Sets
Costlow, Terry
Electronics v54 -42(1) March 24, 1981
Descriptors: automatic speech recognition — technical innovations; Auricle Inc. — technological innovations; Interstate Electronics Corp.—technological innovations

Listening Chip Trims Voice-Command Costs
Patterson, William Pat

Industry Week v208 p77(2) Feb. 9, 1981
Descriptors: Interstate Electronics Corp.—manufactuers; A-T-O Inc.—manufactures; automatic speech recognition—technological innovations; speech processing systems —technological innovations; microelectronics—technological innovations

Computer Speech: An Update (Editorial)
Dahmke, Mark C.
Byte v6 p6(4) Feb. 1981
Descriptors: speech processing systems — technological innovations; automatic speech recognition—technological innovations; microelectronics—technological innovations;

Unit Identifiers Words in Run-On Speech
Smith, Kevin
Electronics v54 p82(1) Feb. 24, 1981
Descriptors: speech processing systems — technological innovations; automatic speech recognition — technological innovations; Great Britain, National Physical Laboratory—technological innovations

Just a Phone Call Will Transfer Funds
Hamilton, Pamela
Electronics v54 p53(1) Jan. 27, 1981
Descriptors: Threshold Technology Inc.—technological innovations; automatic speech recognition—technological innovations; First National Bank of Chicago—electronic equipment; electronic funds transfer—technological innovations

NEXT: Typewriters That Listen To You
Nation's Business v 68 p28(1) Nov. 1980
Descriptors: automatic speech recognition—aids and devices; voiceprints—aids and devices

Small Talk (Talking Computers)
Scientific American v243 p82(3) Oct. 1980
Descriptors: speech synthesis—technological innovations; automatic speech recognition—technological innovations

Martin: Backer of Voice Recognition
Hamilton, Pamela
Electronics v53 p202(1) Oct. 23, 1980
Descriptors: Threshold Technology Inc.—presidents; automatic speech recognition—apparatus

Talk and Type (Computerized Speech-Recognition System)
Colligan, Douglas
Omni v2 p38(2) Sept. 1980
Descriptors: speech processing systems — technological innovations; automatic speech recognition—technological innovations

PBX Takes Text and Voice Messages; Some Operations Need No Operator
Marshall, Martin
Electronics v53 p53(2) Aug. 28, 1980
Descriptors: computer programs—technological innovations; computer storage devices—technological innovations; automatic speech recognition—technological innovations; speech processing systems—technological innovations

Me Tarzan, You IBM System-370 Model 168 (Computer Speech Recognition)

Science News v117 p244(2) April 19, 1980
Descriptors: automatic speech recognition—research; recognition systems—research

Smart Machines Learn to See, Talk, Listen, Even 'Think' For Us (Computers with Artificial Intelligence)
Restak, Richard M.
Smithsonian v10 p48(10) March 1980
Descriptors: artificial intelligence — research; perceptions — research; automatic speech recognition—research; heuristic programming—research; diagnosis—automation

Voice Data Systems Progress
Aviation Week v112 p205(1) March 3, 1980
Descriptors: automatic speech recognition—research; rare animals preservation

Ears for the OEM Market
Myers, Edith
Datamation v25 p70(2) Dec. 1979
Descriptors: automatic speech recognition — technological innovations; Interstate Electronics Corp. — technological innovations; speech processing systems — technological innovations

Machines Respond to Oral Commands
Rohan, Thomas M.
Industry Week v203 p85(2) Oct. 1, 1979
Descriptors: automatic speech recognition—technological innovations; wheelchairs—technological innovations

Voice Prints May Teach Deaf to Talk
Design News v35 p115(2) Aug. 20, 1979
Descriptors: automatic speech recognition — scientific applications; voiceprints — scientific applications; deaf — means of communication; Massachusetts Institute of Technology—research; speech—study and teaching

Phone Answerer Takes Anybody'sCalls
Durniak, Anthony; Hamilton, Pamela
Electronics v52 p55(1) May 24, 1979
Descriptors: computer input-output equipment—technological innovations; automatic speech recognition — technological innovations; speech processing systems — technological innovations; telephone—technological innovations

Speech Is Another Microelectronics Conquest
Science v203 p635(1) Feb. 16, 1979
Descriptors: speech processing systems—technological innovations; speech synthesis — technological innovations; automatic speech recognition — technological innovations; Texas Instruments Inc. — technological innovations; microelectronics — technological innovations

More People Are Talking to Computers as Speech Recognition Enters the Real World
Robinson, Arthur L.
Science v203 p634(3) Feb. 16, 1979
Descriptors: computers—technological innovations; automatic speech recognition—technological innovations; speech processing systems—technological innovations

Voice Recognition Moves Along (Speech Processing)
Posa, John G.

Electronics v52 p84(3) March 1, 1979
Descriptors: speech processing systems—research; automatic speech recognition—research; Bell Laboratories—research; recognition systems—identification; automatic speech recognition—research

Speech Recognition for a Personal Computer System
Boddie, James R.
Byte v2 p64(7) July 1977

Recognition for Heuristics Speech Lab
Byte v2 p50(1) Sept. 1977
Descriptors: automatic speech recognition—evaluation

The following list of microcomputer business refeences may be useful to you:

IBM is homeward bound. (Entry into personal computer market)
Taylor, Alexander L., III
Time v118 p54(2) Aug. 24, 1981
Descriptions: computers—home use; International Business Machines Corp.—marketing

A Computer Program for Retirees
Modern Maturity v24 p10(1) Aug.-Sept. 1981
Descriptions: ACS American Inc.—personnel management; age and employment—case studies; home labor—innovations

IBM elects to buy software outside.
Johnson, R. Colin
Electronics v54 p50(3) Aug. 5, 1981
Descriptions: IBM Personal Computer (computer)—computer programs; computers—home use; International Business Machines Corp.—manufactures

IBM joins the race in personal computers.
Business Week p38(1) Aug. 24, 1971
Descriptions: computer industry—marketing; International Business Machines Corp.—Marketing; computers—home use

Putting your new computer to work
Perry, Robert L.
Mechanix Illustrated v77 p47(3) Aug. 1981
Illustration; photograph
Descriptions: computers—home use

Home Computers: Make The System Work for You
Kolb, Charles M.; Fazio, Gladys J.
Country Gentleman v132 p28(2) Summer 1981
Descriptions: minicomputers—purchasing; computers—purchasing

Personal Computers: Versatility Plus (Special Advertising Section)
Electronics v54 p1116(2) April 21, 1981
34% of Electrical Engineers own or work with personal computers.
Descriptions: minicomputers—usage; electric engineers—aids and devices; computers—home use

Personal Computers: At Home At Work (Special Advertising Section)
Electronics v54 p130(6) April 21, 1981
Descriptions: Minicomputers—industrial applications

Personal Computers: A Brief History (Special Advertising Section)
Electronics v54 p120(4) April 21, 1981
Descriptions: minicomputers—history; computers—home use

The Risky Business of Selling Homegrown Programs
Business Week p74(2) March 9, 1981
Illustration
Descriptions: programming (electronic computers) industries; computer programs—industries

Software Wars Hit Home Computers
Bassak, Gil
Electronics v54 p102(2) Jan. 27, 1981
Descriptions: computers — computer programs; computer programs — marketing; programming (electronic computers—technological innovations; Personal Software Inc. — computer programs; Radio Shack — computer programs; Comodore Business Systems—computer programs

Tuning in to Teleportation
Playboy v28 p185(3) March 1981
Descriptions: businessmen—communication systems; television—technological innovations; computers—home use

New Starters in Silicon Valley
Business Week p67(2) Jan. 26, 1981
Descriptions: computer industry — finance; semiconductors — industries; ZyMOS Corp.—management; Applied Micro Circuits Corp.—management; VLSI Technology Inc. — management; LSI Logic Corp. — management; new busines enterprises — finance

PET Personal Electronic Transactor
Radio-Electronics v51 p51(3) Oct. 1980
Descriptions: computers—home use; Commodore Business Machines—technological innovations

Coping with Crowds; NCC has trimmed its exhibitor waiting list by going to a second parking garage in Anaheim. But this year the air conditioning will work.
McCusker, Tom
Datamation v26 p122(5) May 1980
Illustration
Descriptions: National Computer Conference — 1980; computer industry — conferences and Congresses

Computer, Oil Companies New Black Business Wave
Jew v58 p16(1) May 22, 1980
Descriptions: Afro-American businessmen — surveys; minority business enterprises —surveys

How to Make Money with Computers (Book Reviews)
Datamation v26 p212(1) April 1980
Article Type: Review
Grade: C+
Descriptions: books—reviews, etc.

Computers Go Beyond the Business Office
American School and University v52 p46(5) Sept. 1979
Descriptions: computer-assisted instruction—varieties; computers—educational use

Home Computers for Work and Play
Buckwalter, Len
Mechanix Illustrated v75 p40(3) June 1979
Descriptions: computers—homeuse; toys—techn aims and objectives

A Computer of One's Own
Potter, Ned
New York v12 p59(3) May 7, 1979
Descriptions: computers—home use; electronic apparatus and appliances—home use; budgets, personal—computer programs; microcomputers—home use; International Business Machines Corp.—technological innovations

Home Computers About to be a Big Business
Much, Marilyn
Industry Week v200 p128(2) March 19, 1979
Descriptions: computers—home use; computer industry—growth and development

Is There Magic in a Name? SDS Debuts Again, with New Business Computer (Scientific Data Systems, Inc.)
Electronics v51 p50(2) Oct. 26, 1978
Descriptions: Scientific Data Systems, Inc. — manufactures; computer industry — manufactures; computers — industrial applications; business enterprises — automation

Cheap Labor: The Personal Computer
Berge, Reva
Working Woman v3 p60(2) Oct. 1978
Descriptions: computers—home use

Personal Computers For Small-Business Applications: More and More "Home" Computers are Being Used for Commercial Purposes
Isaacson, Portia
Popular Electronics v14 p53(5) Aug. 1978
Descriptions: microprocessors—industrial applications

Put Your Computers to Work
Roch, Bill
Byte v2 p102(2) Feb. 1977
Descriptions: computers—home use

Coming Full Circle (Product Development) (Column)
Frand, Erwin
Industrial Research v23 p29(1) May 1981
Descriptions: cottage industries — history; home labor — innovations; industry — innovations; factories—automation; transportation—prices

Working At Home on a Computer
Yarmon, Morton
50 Plus v21 p56(2) June 1981
Descriptions: personnel manageent—innovations; computers—home use; occupations—innovations; professions—innovations

Commuting By Computer (Working at Home via Computers)
Newsweek v97 p58(2) May 4, 1981
Descriptions: telecommunications—home use; home labor—technological innovations; computers—home use; personnel management—innovations

Personal Computers: Working Hart At Home (Special Advertising Section)
Electronics v54 p145(3) April 21, 1981
Descriptions: minicomputers—home use

The Potential for Telecommuting (Working at Home on Computer)
Business Week p94(2) Jan. 26, 1981
Descriptions: home labor — innovations; data transmission systems — home use; telecommunication systems—home use; work environment—experiments

Coping with the 'Word-At-Home' Trend (Automation Extends Options and Raises Questions)
Sample, Robert L.
Administrative Management v42 p24(4) Aug. 1981
Descriptions: automation—industrial applications; Control Data Corp.—technological innovations; computers—home use; home labor—technological innovations

Coming Full Circle (Product Development) (Column)
Frand Erwin
Industrial Research v23 p29(1) May 1981
Prohibitive transportation costs indicate computer controlled distributed manufacturing; parallel to pre-industrial revolution cottage industries.
Descriptions: cottage industries — history; home labor — innovations; industry — innovations; factories—automation; transportation—prices

Very Small Computers (New Business Opportunities)
McCusker, Tom
Datamation v24 p56(3) Oct. 1978
Descriptions: Pertec Computer Corp.—manufactures; computer industry—manufactures

## Chapter Six

# FRANCHISING: THE GOOD, THE BAD, AND THE UGLY

Computer business schemes lend themselves nicely to the franchise concept because of the high degree of skill and expertise involved. There are many kinds of computer related franchises—a long list is given in the back of this chapter. Most of them revolve around computer augmented performance of some service. Since the computer lends itself so well to a great many service related businesses, we can expect to see more and more franchised operations of this nature in the future.

A visible and very successful computer franchise concept is the retail computer store. Computerland® was started in September, 1976. At that time franchising was relatively new in the industry. Computerland came along with the idea of providing a known and advertised name, professional market plans and experienced help in setting up and managing a store in return for an initial fee and ongoing royalties.

Bill Millard is the founder of Computerland. One of the people we interviewed for another part of this book told us Bill Millard was the founder of IMSAI, a pioneer in the S-100 Bus business. Our interviewee said IMSAI was going down the tubes at about the same time Computerland was started, but the PR guy at Computerland didn't seem to know much about it. In any case, Mr. Millard undoubtedly learned a lot from his IMSAI experience because the Computerland operation seems to be flying along quite nicely.

To buy a franchise you need some kind of business and at

least $45,000. For your money you get a territory, a name and some help in starting and managing the store. Part of Computerland's deal is to pay $1500 of the sign cost—this is probably so they can regulate the sign design to achieve interstore image uniformity. They also help design the store, provide graphics and help you throw a whiz-bang Grand Opening to get things rolling.

A big city store requires between 150 and 225 kilobucks to make it fly. They recommend 60K for inventory, 25K in working capital and 25K for leasehold improvements to start a store in a major city.

When computerland started in '76 they looked for franchisors who had a computer background. In '78 they adjusted this policy and began looking for franchisees with a solid business background, not necessarily in computers. As they put it, they look for "young aggressive business people who have a vision of the computer future."

Their stores are successful! They have, to date, never lost a store for financial reasons. They have noted, however, those stores whose operators have a good business background do better. They say competition hasn't been a big problem and that the biggies help create the market!

The Computerland stores carry the new IBM personal computer and Apple. They have no exclusives because they feel this arrangement unfairly ties down the vendor and also commits too much to the exclusive product. Stores are allowed to purchase outside of the corporate office. Their control consists in helping to open stores and follow-on management and accounting guidance. The stores generally police themselves. If I make an investment of that magnitude, I would be really interested that the other same name stores did things right.

Computerland has very conservative plans for the next five years: Keep on doing what they are presently doing, but eventually including plans to start a national TV ad campaign to add more training classes, new products and probably some imported hardware items to the present line.

The present customer mix is as follows:

| | |
|---|---|
| Professional and Business | 60% |
| Home | 20% |
| Education | 20% |

30% of the store's dollar volume is currently software, supplies and print media.

Computerland is planning a new store concept for the near

future: software and supplies franchises. These stores will be small—400-800 square feet—and will be placed in busy malls. A big store currently does around 300K annually in software and supplies. As more users get into the system they will utilize increasing amounts of supplies. The new computer supplies mini-mart concept is expected to be an important part of the industry by the mid 80's.

The test of this concept has been operating in Jericho, NY, and has been a great success. The concept has been taken public on the Over-The-Counter market and is called "Software Unlimited."

Computer hardware stores, the main business, is going greatguns. They currently have more than 20 stores and plan to have 500 by 1985. This means opening 7-8 stores a month for the duration.

Computerland management estimates the limit is one store per 150 thousand population (this means room for 1500 computer stores!).

The company's major problem thus far has been the inevitable stresses of major growth. They have gone from one employee five years ago to currently more than 150. Training, communication and synchronization of effort are understandably difficult to optimize with this growth profile.

This is the story of Computerland as told by Computerland. Perhaps there are more problems than they are willing to discuss and perhaps they are pushing things very hard. But the industry is drawing them along with a great and accelerating rush. If you are interested in finding more about their franchising program contact Don McConnell at corporate headquarters in San Leandro, 415-895-9363.

## Becoming a Franchisor

If you are thinking of setting up a franchise operation (becoming a franchisor) you should first consult the *Federal Trade Commission Rules and Guide Book* for franchisors, then consult your State Corporations Code to get an idea of the rules and regulations you will be dealing with.

Governmental rules dealing with franchising concern themselves with potential wool-pulling of franchisors over the unsuspecting eyes of franchisees.

These rules define two kinds of franchise: "Package and Product Franchises" and "Business Opportunity Ventures." The first category is the familiar fried chicken and hamburger franchise where the franchisor provides a turn-key business operation complete with trademark, supply, and operational control.

The product franchisor provides trademarked goods and some degree of help in return for a fee for the variously limited rights to sell the product.

Many franchise contracts specify that the franchisor will provide "significant assistance" to the franchisee. You can imagine the sort of disputes that have arisen over due performance of this concept.

In California, which is probably the tightest state, the rules regulating franchising are enormous. In case you are interested, it is called the Franchise Investment Law, Title 10, California Administrative Code, Section 310.

If you are still undaunted (and live in California) you can call the State Department of Corporations, Qualification and Regulation Division 213-736-2713 and ask for the Duty Counsel (most states have a similar service).

The Duty Counsel is a lawyer hired by the Corporations Commission to answer the phone and field your questions. If you approach it right they can be incredibly helpful, and it is free.

If at this point you are still thinking about starting a franchise, then find a franchise lawyer and start spending big bucks.

Is the point clear? Being a franchisor is a big deal. Franchisors spend megabucks satisfying bureaucrats who see their role as the protector of franchisees.

But does all this regulation make franchising a good deal? How is franchising from the franchisees' point of view? Lets define a franchise and look at some pros and cons.

Before signing a franchise agreement, as with any contract, be alert for what might go wrong. It is strongly recommended that prospective franchisees see a lawyer, before signing, to explore the contract provisions. The contracts are designed by the franchisors to protect themselves by means of restrictions on the franchisee. As long as the franchisee accepts these controls and maintains a good working relationship with the franchisor, few problems should arise.

There is little protection in the contract if something goes wrong. Once a franchising contract has been signed, there are few legal remedies for franchisees. Some suits have been successfully brought under federal and state anti-trust statutes concerning required suppliers and other franchisor controls. Some

FRANCHISE

A DISTRIBUTION CONTRACT OR "LICENSE" BETWEEN TWO ENTITIES, THE FRANCHISOR AND FRANCHISEE. IT IS NOT AN ADDITIONAL LEGAL FORM; EITHER PARTY CAN BE AN INDIVIDUAL, PARTNERSHIP, OR A CORPORATION.

MOST FRANCHISEES ARE AT A RETAIL OR SERVICE LEVEL. BASICALLY, THE FRANCHISEE INVESTS CAPITAL IN EXCHANGE FOR THE EXPERTISE AND WIDELY-KNOWN PRODUCT IMAGE OF THE FRANCHISOR. OFTEN THE FEE INCLUDES THE COST OF START-UP STOCK.

EXAMPLES OF FRANCHISORS: McDONALD'S REALTY WORLD, GENERAL MOTORS, ROTO-ROOTER, SUNOCO.

states have strong franchise legislation. In addition, the Uniform Commercial Code (a similar set of statutes passed in each state which regulates commercial dealings) contains two concepts that can support franchisee actions against franchisors: "unconscionable contracts" and "good faith dealings." These points should be discussed with a lawyer experienced in franchise law.

However, litigation is an expensive process, and the above statutes are recent developments that contradict the traditional notion that a contract is binding, no matter how harsh its application. In court, this traditional concept of a binding contract often prevails.

Whatever your decision regarding becoming a franchisee or franchisor, two things are clear. The first revelation is many computer concepts lend themselves readily to the franchisee concept. The second is that offer or acceptance of a franchise proposal should be approached carefully.

## THE ADVANTAGES AND DISADVANTAGES:

### EXAMPLES OF SOME OF THE CONTRACTED ARRANGEMENTS BETWEEN FRANCHISEES AND FRANCHISORS

*THE GOOD*

- The established reputation of the franchisor helps bring in business.
- The franchisor can offer a proven marketing strategy, including advertising, sales items at reduced prices, and sales incentives.
- Training and guidance may be provided to get the business going, as in setting up the store, ordering and bookkeeping, and regular training meetings.
- Proven products and methods supplied by the franchisor can help bring in business.
- Accounting and record keeping systems may be provided.
- Financial assistance is sometimes provided in the form of credit, lower interest loans, or insurance available through the volume buying power of the franchisor.

*THE BAD*

- Franchisees must buy from designated or approved suppliers.
- In addition to the original investment, the franchisee must pay the franchisor a percentage of gross sales (not just a percentage of the profits).
- The franchisor may choose not to renew the contract each time it expires (often yearly).
- In addition, the contract may be terminated by the franchisor for any of numerous reasons stated in the contract, thus allowing termination virtually at the will of the franchisor.
- If the contract is revoked, the franchisor will pay the franchisee for equipment, supplies, and stock on hand, an amount often much less than the franchisee's total investment.
- If the contract is revoked, the franchisee cannot open a similar business in the same area ("anti-competition clause").

# References

*Franchising and Business Opportunities,* Federal Trade Commission, USGPO Stock #018-000-00254-0.

*Franchising in the Economy,* U.S. Department of Commerce, Bureau of Industrial Economics, USGPO, 1981, #340-997/362.

Some computer related franchises:

## ACCOUNTING AND TAX SERVICES

Axion Tax & Accounting Service
6575 East 22 St., Tucson, Arizona 85710
Income tax, accounting and tax service. Investment: $1,000 up.

Binex Automated Business Systems, Inc.
1787 Tribute Road, Sacramento, California 95815
Computerized services for small and medium sized businesses. Financial reports, general ledgers, taxes, accounts receivable and payable, job costing, etc. Investment: $7,500.

H & R Block, Inc.
4410 Main Street, Kansas City, Missouri 64111
Preparation of individual tax returns. Available in cities of 15,000 population. Training supplied. A refundable franchise deposit of from $300 to $500 is required.

R & G Brenner Income Tax Centers
435 Lexington Avenue, New York, New York 10017
Income tax preparation service.

Comprehensive Accounting Corp.
2111 Comprehensive Drive, Aurora, Illinois 60507
Monthly bookkeeping, accounting and tax service for small and medium-sized businesses. Investment: $15,000.

Continental Tax Service
14507 W. Warren, Dearborn, Michigan 48126
Individual state and federal income tax preparation service.

Econotax, Inc.
1211 Ellis Avenue, Jackson, Mississippi 39209
Tax planning, accounting and income tax preparation service. Investment: $3,000.

Incotax Systems, Inc.
223 Datura St., West Palm Beach, Florida 33401
Tax service and income tax preparation. Investment: $15,000.

Reliable Business Systems, Inc.
19 Ransom Road, Newton, Massachusetts 02159
Publishes *The Reliable Business and Tax Service System.* Offers a bookkeeping system together with an advisory service and end of year Federal and State tax return preparation. Investment: $8,950.

Safeguard Business Systems
470 Maryland Drive, Fort Washington, Pennsylvania 19034
Accounting systems for modern business. Working capital provided by Company. Franchisee provides own operating money.

Tax Man, Inc.
639 Massachusetts Avenue, Cambridge, Massachusetts 02139
Income tax service. Investment: $5,000.

## BUSINESS SERVICES

Audit Controls, Inc.
87 NE 44 Street, Fort Lauderdale, Florida 33334
Distributorship for collection letter service. Investment: $150.00.

Best Resume Service
625 Stanwix Street, Pittsburgh, Pennsylvania 15222
Resume and job search services to individuals and business. Investment: $5,000-$25,000.

Business Consultants of America
P.O. Box 4098, Waterbury, Connecticut 06714
Small business consulting franchise. Investment: $8.500 plus $5,000 working capital.

Business Data Services, Inc.
1775 Lelia Drive, Jackson, Mississippi 39216
Business advisory service featuring computerized accounting and tax preparation. Investment: $14,500.

Business Exchange, Inc.
4716 Vineland Avenue, North Hollywood, California 91602
Barter service for business owners that utilize a computerized trade check accounting system. Franchisees receive a percentage of each trade check used in their area. Investment: $19,900.

Butler Learning Systems
1325 W. Dorothy Lane, Dayton, Ohio 45409
Executive training through audio-visual systems. Investment: $9,000.

Commercial Services Co.
2699 Lee Road, Winter Park, Florida 32789
Service to medium and small businesses offering accounting, bookkeeping and tax services. Investment: $$18,000.

Computer Capital Corporation
6922 Hollywood Boulevard, Los Angeles, California 90028
Service that matches firms seeking capital with investment sources. Investment: $10,000 to $40,000.

Computer Servicenters, Inc.
714 North State Street, Jackson, Mississippi 39202
Provides doctors, dentists and veterinarians with computerized billing, control systems and administrative information. Investment: $12,000.

Corporate Finance Associates
22 Perimeter Park Drive, Atlanta, Georgia 30341
Financial consulting business also dealing with mergers and acquisitions. Investment: $25,000.

Data Research, Inc.
1818 Gilbreth Road, Burlingame, California 94010
Dealer/Distributorship program offering a computer, terminal, data processing services and systems to small and medium-sized firms. Investment: $50,000 up.

Edwin K. Williams & Co.
5324 Ekwill Street, Santa Barbara, California 93111
Financial consulting and bookkeeping services for service stations and petroleum wholesalers. Also the E-Z Keep Systems division that services all small businesses. Investment: $8,000 to $25,000.

General Business Services, Inc.
51 Monroe Street, Rockville, Maryland 20850
Financial management services for small independent businesses including record keeping and tax services. Investment: $18,000.

Getting to Know You International Ltd.
9 Chelsea Place, Great Neck, New York 11022
Newcomer welcome service sponsored by retailers and professionals. Franchisee sends a personal phone directory free to new homeowners. Sponsors underwrite all costs. Investment: $16,000 plus $10,000 operating capital.

J. P. Dolan Associates, Inc.
P.O. Box 125, Glenolden, Pennsylvania 19036
Communications consulting service to businesses for the purpose of improving telephonic communications, reducing costs and obtaining refunds in case of overcharges. Investment: $15,000.

The Home Office, Inc.
500 Airport Blvd., Burlingame, California 94010
Offers office and desk space, secretarial services, and use of office machines. Investment: $20,000.

Marcoin, Inc.
1924 Cliff Valley Way, N.E., Atlanta, Georgia 30329
Business management and counseling service for small businesses, turnkey computer program. Investment: $18,000-$25,000.

Medipower, Div. of The MacKenzie Corp.
P.O. Box 613, Bellaire, Texas 77401
Computer services to the medical profession. Investment: $1,000.

National Housing Inspections
1817 North Hills Boulevard, Knoxville, Tennessee 37917
Complete inspection service for the potential home buyer. Investment: $750.00.

Sandy Hook Scientific Inc.
Columbia, North Carolina 27925
Small business consulting and/or programming service utilizing small computers, service bureaus or manual approaches. Investment: $5,000.

Simplified Business Services, Inc.
100 Presidential Blvd., Bala Cynwyd, Pennsylvania 19004.
Business management control package for small business, incluing income tax preparation, consultation. Investment: under $2,500.

Small Business Advisors, Inc.—Whithill Systems
12 Franklin Place, Woodmere, New York 11598
Business advisory service to independent businessmen. Provides record systems, interim tax advisory and preparation, data processing and collection services. Investment: $14,500.

Systemedics, Inc.
Box 2000, Princeton, New Jersey 08540
Computerized accounts receivable and record systems for medical and dental practices. Investment: $10,000-$15,000.

Telecheck Services, Inc.
1611 South Federal Boulevard, Denver, Colorado 80219
Computerized check verification and other immediate information service. Investment: $$200,000.

Typing Tigers
P.O. Box 613, Bellaire, Texas 77401
Secretarial, telephone answering, mailing, temporary employee service, computer services, office supplies and equipment. Investment: varies.

## RETAIL STORES

Computerland Corporation
14400 Catalina Street, San Leandro, California 95477
Retail sales of personal computers and related systems. Investment: $160,000-$225,000.

The Electronics Boutique
811 Church Road, Cherry Hill, New Jersey 08002
Electronic consumer goods retail store situated in enclosed mall locations. Investment: $40,000.

Lafayette Electronics Sales, Inc.
P.O. Box L, Syosset, New York 11791
Retail stores selling consumer and hobbyist electronic equipment. Investment: $50,000-$75,000.

## SCHOOLS

Automation Institute of America
760 Market Street, San Francisco, California 94102
Data processing center for computer programmer and data systems educational training. Investment: $50,000.

IBM Franchise Program
1000 NW 51st Street, P.O. Box 1328, Boca Raton, Florida 33432
(305) 998-2000, ext 3259, Jim D'Arezzo.

# ADDITIONAL FRANCHISING REFERENCES

Bus Week 81/04/06
Software supermarket stocks more than 600 programs for top-selling microcomputers. Programs Unlimited (Westbury, NY) is the first store in a planned chain owned by Cut & Curl Inc., an international franchiser of hair salons. Within three months, two additional units will be opened in New York and New Jersey. Plans call for 100 stores to be operating nationally by 1983. The programs, prescreened by local user groups and store management, are supplied by 80 software producers. Prices range from $10 for simple word games to $1,200 for a sophisticated inventory control package.

Comp Wkly 81/04/02
LSI Computers (Woking, England), a microcomputer company, will set up 20-30 franchises in the UK to sell its systems M-One and M-Two small business computers. LSI will continue to operate its own installation, after sales, service and software development.

Comp Talk 80/10/22
UK retail shops will sell the majority of an estimated 600,000-750,000 microcomputers, worth 400 mil/yr, in the UK by mid-1985, according to a report by International Management & Computer Systems Security. Small retail shops are advised to establish cooperative purchasing deals with similar shops, to combat big chains and franchise dealers able to obtain large discounts on bulk buying of hardware.

Chain Store 79/03
Microcomputer sales could reach $3.5 bil in 1982, and the new category of computer chain stores represents an exciting challenge. The hobbyist portion of the microcomputer market is becoming saturated and will fall off by 1982. However, the small business sector will increase from $100 mil in 1978 to some $1 bil by 1982, according to Creative Strategies Interational. Tandy Corp., one of the leaders with $1 bil in consumer electronic retail sales in 1978, has opened its first Radio Shack Computer Center, with 50 such stores planned by year end. (Radio Shack also sells its TRS-80 in its regular outlets.) Computerland, a San Leandro, California based franchise chain, hopes to double its present 70-store total by the end of 1979. Digital Equipment Corp., the minicomputer hardware manufacturer, is testing computer retailing to business in Manchester, NH, and Boston. DEC's prime market is professsionals and small businesses seeking complete commercial data systems at the low end of the market. Computer stores fit between department stores and manufacturers. They offer full lines of central processing units and peripherals, as well as educational and other support services. The problem with selling little computers is salesperson training, which accounts for department stores' poor showing. Impulse buying is virtually nil, and product demonstration and user support are crucial. One problem that may plague the industry is the slowing economy, but this also could be a benefit. If small businesses are forced to find new ways to cut costs, having their own computer will begin to look more attractive. Many aspects of computer merchandising are examined.

Fortune 78/04/24
Computerland heads for success in microcomputer franchising by selling to small insurance offices, one-person consulting ventures, retailers and other small businesses. To date computer power has been too expensive or too large to be an effective tool for small enterprise; the new generation of micros brings automation to a more appropriate scale. The other major market is computer hobbyists, whose independent brainpower is providing much of the software for the new machines. One of the factors in computer retailing is the 'parakeet syndrome'—upgrading, with real opportunities to be found in still expensive peripherals. Despite start-up charges estimated at $100,000, Computerland's initial franchise outlet in Morristown, NJ, recorded operat-

ing profits of $75,000 on sales exceeding $250,000 in its first year (1977), which its owner attributes to the parakeet syndrome. Computerland Corp. (San Leandro, California), the only franchiser in the field, markets such products as the Imsai and Apple II personal computers and a computerized chess game for hobbyists and game players, but the rest of its stores are devoted to small systems for business priced at $6,000-$10,000 and offering the same computing power as million-dollar machines in the 1950s. Computerland, growing faster than McDonald's hamburger franchises did in their early years, is the clear leader in compter retailing, its main competition being from manufacturers like Pertec Computer, Texas Instruments and even IBM. Another retailer is a loosely associated chain: Byte Shops. Article reviews Computerland's franchise system and the products in the expanding personal computer market.

Mart 77/09/01
Sears and Radio Shack set home computer systems for retail sales debut. Sears, Roebuck & Co. will test market a personal computer late this fall. Sears expects the first customers to be hobbyists, computer students or buffs and small business entrepreneurs. No further details are being released at this time. Tandy Corp.'s Radio Shack chain, meanwhile, introduced its first entry into the expanding microcomputer market in August 1977, the TRS-80 Microcomputer System. The unit will be available worldwide late in September in company-operated franchise and dealer stores. The microcomputer alone with a regulated power supply will retail for $400; the complete system with 12-in video display monitor and data cassette recorder, for $600. The TRS-80 is not a kit, and will be retailed fully wired, tested and ready to plug in. A variety of software on cassettes for business, educational and personal applications also will be avai!able. Radio Shack also expects its initial market to be the hobbyists, then business people within the first six months, and an enormous home market within two years. B. Simpson, Pittsfield, Mass., store manager, commented, "In the next couple of years, you'll find as many microcomputers in homes as you'll find cameras and calculators." Simpson also feels that microcomputers will eventually be available for under $100. Sales target for the TRS-80 is at least one sale per week within the next year to 18 months.

Chain Store 79/03
Microcomputer sales could reach $3.5 bil in 1982, and the new category of computer chain stores represents an exciting challenge. The hobbyist portion of the microcomputer market is becomming saturated and will fall off by 1982. However, the small business sector will increase from $100 mil in 1978 to some $1 bil by 1982, according to Creative Strategies International. Tandy Corp., one of the leaders with $1 bil in consumer electronic retail sales in 1978, has opened its first Radio Shack Computer Center, with 50 such stores planned by year end. (Radio Shack also sells its TRS-80 in its regular outlets.) Computerland, a San Leandro, California based franchise chain, hopes to double its present 70-store total by the end of 1979. Digital Equipment Corp., the minicomputer hardware manufacturer, is testing computer retailing to business in Manchester, NH, and Boston. DEC's prime market is professionals and small businesses seeking complete commercial data systems at the low end of the market. Computer stores fit between department stores and manufacturers. They offer full lines of central processing units and peripherals, as well as educational and other support services. The problem with selling little computers is salesperson training, which accounts for department stores' poor showing. Impulse buying is virtually nil, and product demonstration and user support are crucial. One problem that may plague the industry is the slowing economy, but this also could be a benefit. If small businesses are forced to find new ways to cut costs, having their own computer will begin to look more attractive. Many aspects of computer merchandising are examined.

Mis Week 81/08/26
Stockwatch Southeast (Florida) is offering stock data links to home computers. It purchases data links from various stock exchanges and sends them to clients via long-distance telephone lines to their home computers. Investors can get quotations from 4 stock exchanges with a 10-15 minute delay. The firm is a franchise of National Stockwatch Inc. (Albuquerque, New Mexico).

Computing 81/04/30
UK estate agents will use computers to improve their services and prevent the growth of American real estate franchising organizations in the UK. Some 14 estate agents in Sussex will start up on online time-sharing system in 8/81, with all the agents' property registers on a central Systime machine. The agent first instructed to sell the property will receive 60% of the sale commission. The 12 companies involved in a SW London computerized scheme will store their individual lists on in-house Alpha Microsystems machines. Shared property will be held on a central Systime computer, and commission will be split equally between the instructing and selling agent.

Rent All 8104
Only 20% of equipment rental shops will remain independent in 1990, vs 80% in 1980, predicts D. Heffernan, delegate from Jartran Corp. at the recent American Rental Assn. Convention in Las Vegas, Nevada. Fellow delegate J. I. McKinney, whose 21-store chain has greatly increased operating efficiency to the point where six new rental stores can be built later in 1981 with the help of a computer-designed inventory, says independents who successfully apply new technology will be able to stand up to franchise operations while those who do not will crumble.The future of the rental industry as seen by these and other practitioners is reviewed in Bob Elmen's Rental Economics column in Rent All.

Output 81/05
The Headquarters Co. offers a full range of EDP services through its nationwide 'executive center' franchise at a price even the smallest business can afford. Each of the company's (San Francisco, California) centers, which now number 14, occupies 10,000-20,000 sq ft of leased prime central business district office space. Headquarters clients can rent one or more of the about 35 executive offices in the center, where text editing equipment, telecopier systems and telex terminals are at their disposal. The terms of rental are totally flexible, allowing clients who need only one day/month of use to pay no more than is necessary. Headquarters will soon be installing modem-equipped communicating word processors which, in addition to giving its clients even more options, lays the groundwork for the establishment of a complete electronic mail network. Regional sales executives wanting the same EDP capabilities found at the corpoporate headquarters are prime users of Headquarter's executive centers. One satisfied customer, Atari Inc. (Sunnyvale, Califoria) East Coast accounts executive J. Hayes says, "Through Headquarters, I have access to the same kind of high-powered, sophisticated equipment my home base has (been) . . . paying less than what it would cost for me to have an office or full-time secretary."

Comp Talk 80/01/16
The world's largest computer shops chain, Computerland (US), is ready to set up in the UK, now that the Byte Shop/Computerland chain (UK) has agreed that only the US based company will trade under the Computerland name in the UK. Computerland expects to have 20-25 shops in Europe by 12/80, vs 5 in 1978. The company operates a franchise set-up with 105 shops worldwide, providing products, back-up and expertise for the franchiser. The company may set-up a co-operatively owned software house to convert its US-type package program for use in Europe. In 1979, 80% of systems were sold to business users, vs hobbyists.

Sales Mgmt 78/01
Electronic Realty Associates sets the pace in the burgeoning franchised real estate field. In 1977, ERA (Overland Park, KY) introduced a comprehensive sales training course, produced sophisticated TV commercials, and became a corporate sponsor of the Jerry Lewis Muscular Dystrophy Telethon. Amidst its other marketing innovations is ERA's 'Buyers' Protection Plan,' a 'Sellers' Protection Plan,' and the 'Moving Machine,' a computerized telephoto transmission device that sends pictures of available homes to buyers across the country. For the use of these services and the ERA logo on house signs and related materials, brokers pay a one-time fee (now about $6,000) and monthly charges ranging from $200-$850, depending on the territory and number of offices. ERA doubled its franchises to 1,600 and forecasts its FY 1978 sales volume to double 1977's record $6.2 mil, while profits should triple 1977's $340,000 (also a company record). Its strong contribution to the indstry won ERA a 1977 Sales & Marketing Management Magazine Distinguished Award.

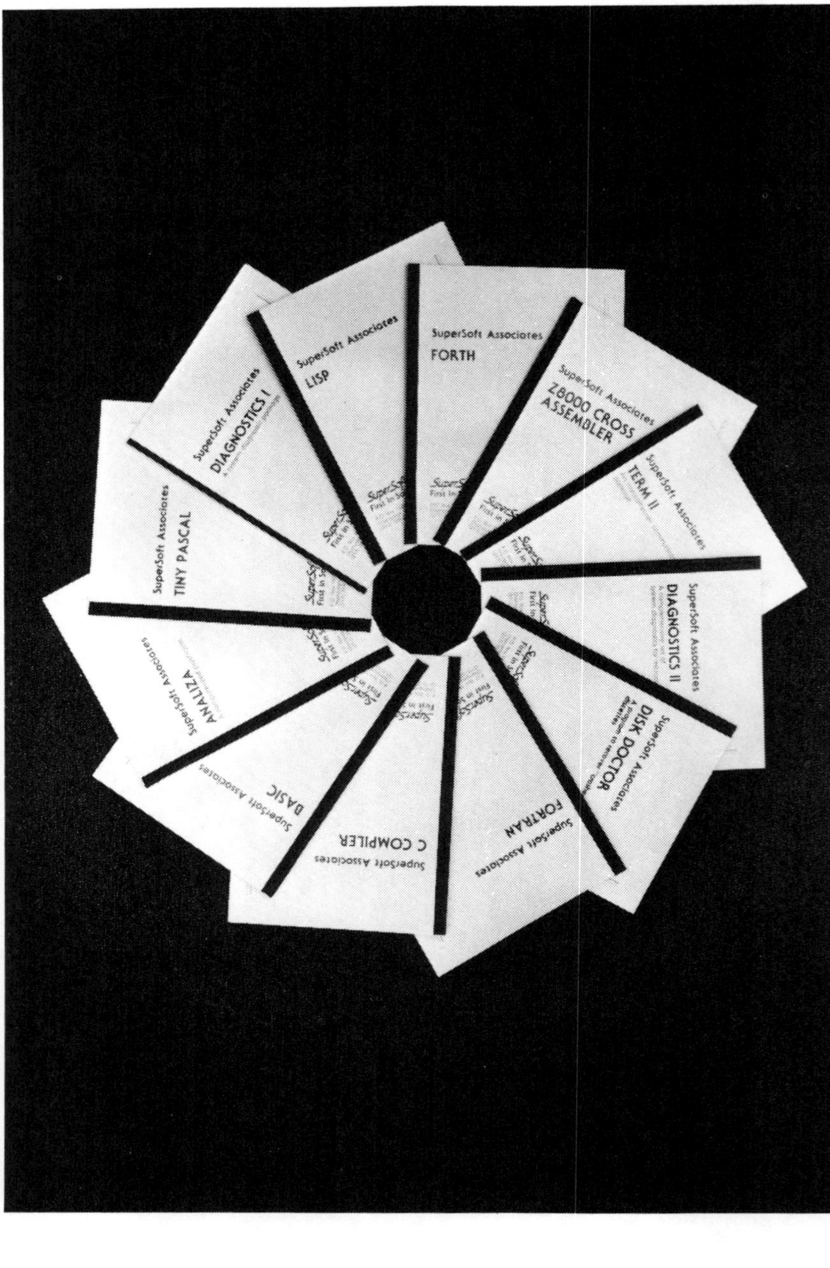


Reprinted by permission of Supersoft Associates.

## Chapter Seven

# SOFTWARE: THE BIGGEST FUTURE OF ALL

Software is the fastest growing segment of the computer industry. The sales of independent software vendors are expected to grow at a compound rate of somewhere between 25% and 40% through 1985.

Software is the market many computer maniacs turn to when trying to justify laying out money for a microsystem. It's safe to say most hobbyists learn some level of programming and immediately daydream of writing programs for the masses. How realistic are these dreams?

It's clear the market for software will be growing exponentially through the mid 80's. This market will be fueled by needs for shelf programs and customized, spoon-fed systems to interface with semi-dedicated operating personnel. Games for all levels are becoming a major factor in the market and will do better and better as a generation of kids raised in Atari-equipped quarter arcades begin to buy computers of their own. A lot of programmers and publishers are going to have a very good decade.

As more people buy computers as a specific tool for a specific function they will want to buy specialized application hardware to carry out the tasks. In the late seventies people tended to buy a processor and adapt it to their needs.In the eighties people will buy computer systems as a solution to a problem. This sums up to a rapidly increasing packaged program sales.

There are many ways to get in on the packaged program bonanza. One way is to act as an independent author and sell your program on a royalty basis to an established software publishing house like *Supersoft*. How much you get and when you get it isn't subject to a strict formula. You must negotiate your deal. The terms ultimately depend on how good your program is and how the publisher views the potential market.

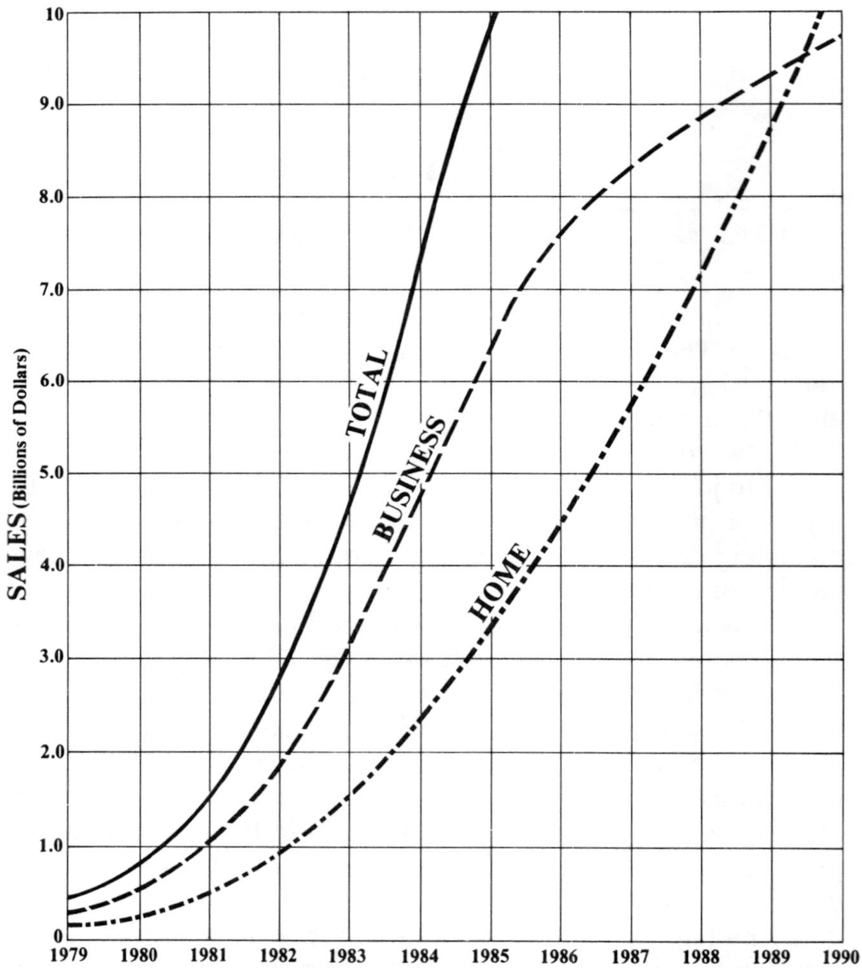


**MICROCOMPUTER SOFTWARE MARKET**

**PRINTED COURTESY GRAYHALL RESEARCH AGENCY**

*Here is a candid shot taken at a trade show in the Los Angeles Convention Center. The software business is growing incredibly rapidly and is segmenting into clear distribution channels. There are so many software vendors for so many systems that distribution will inevitably go in the direction shown by the book publishing business. Wholesale distributors will play an increasingly important role. They can carry enough lines so that their average sale is high enough to justify specialized sales efforts. Distributors also take the burden of collecting a small amount of money from a large number of customers off of the Independent Software Vendor.*

The second stage of the publisher-author relatonship is when your programs are selling nicely and everyone is more or less happy. This is the time when the publisher might come to you with things he wants you to develop. You do your work at home, get advance royalties and progress payments which are deducted from your earned royalties as the program starts to generate revenue. To create this situation you have to develop a relationship of confidence and respect with the publisher. He has to have confidence in your programming talents and your ability to get on with the job. You have to have the confidence that he won't perform a royaltydectomy on you if your program starts to generate really big bucks.

I know of a programmer who lives in a log cabin in the Michigan woods with his dog and a microcomputer system. He spends a few hours a day creating for his publisher and the rest of the time splitting logs and wandering in the woods with his dog. His only expenses are the electric bill, dog chow and band-aids.

Another way to get into the software business is to create, debug, document, mass-produce, support, market and ship your product yourself. This is the way many successful entrepreneurs started and it can still be done.

Don't get the idea there is greater freedom in this do-it-all-yourself approach. The responsibility of maintaining each level of the business is great and can create grinding pressure on you. If you allow *any* functional area to default, the business will be hurt. It is a lot of work and a great risk but the rewards can be great.

## Product Selection

Most people learn something about programming and software development when they get their first microcomputer system. "Why not do this for the unwashed masses of poor computer owners who can't figure it out for themselves? After all, I spent all this money on a system and isn't it a great idea to make up a diskette, toss it into a baggie and buy a rake to pile up the money?"

No doubt it has happened somewhat like that but it might be best to think the whole thing through before going to the A&P for a package of Zip-Lock Baggies. Here is a list to consider before asking your spouse for the car keys:

1. Who buys prepackaged programs?
2. What kind of programs do they buy?

3. What is already filling that need?
4. What program area is presently unsatisfied or inadequately covered?
5. Do I have the capabilities and equipment to produce the needed software?
6. How am I going to sell the product?
7. How am I going to package it?
8. How am I going to protect it?
9. Am I going into the program business or is this a one-shot deal?

Read carefully between the lines in the "Software Barons" interviews and you will see how these incredibly successful entrepreneurs answer these questions for themselves. The secrets of their success lie largely in their unique innovation and energetic answers.

## Specialization

At the present stage of the market the best approach is to specialize in a particular operating or hardware system which is generally thought to be beneath the volume requirements of the established software houses. Small but profitable markets are continually created by the introduction of new equipment and technology.

Spend as much time on documentation and packaging as you do developing the program. By having excellent and careful documentation you will emerge as a polished diamond among much cruder stones. In the big houses the task of documentation is typically considered a dirty-work job so it is assigned to the lowest person in the pecking order. The job is often done poorly as a result and the current quality level of software documentation and instruction manuals proves the point. If you give the printed part of your product equal importance your programs will sell better and longer.

Also very few program grinders pay enough attention to the "shelf appeal" of their product. Your product must have eye appeal and look professional to be sold. In fact, it matters less that it might be the best program ever devised — it has to be noticed, purchased and successfully used to be any good at all.

Never forget every business, from the most humble to the biggest, is show biz! That's why baseball teams wear handlebar moustaches, the kids working at McDonalds wear cute paper caps, and hardware makers have specialists lay out panels and

*Guess why there are so many computer games? A good game written for an* **Apple** *or* **TRS-80 could sell hundreds of times more units than a really great accounting system.**

packaging. Our whole culture is based on show and there is damn little you or I can do to reverse the effects of a lifetime of conditioning. Get the point?

Rexham Packaging Company makes a line of point-of-sale board header bags to display your program package. You can contact them at Rexham, Fashion Packaging Division, Box 40007, Charlotte, NC, 704-899-7262.

## The Software Barons

How do the big software companies do it? I interviewed two of the most successful software companies in the business and from each I heard a story beginning with a simple idea and progressing to great success. In each case they started small, lean and mean.

## Digital Research

Digital Research is a company on the move. It got its start with essentially a single product: CP/M®, the Control Program for microprocessors. Digital Research has, through product relevance, tireless promotional effort and detailed support of the Independent Software Vendors who write their programs under CP/M, established their operating system as the *de facto* standard of the microprocessor industry.

Digital Research was started by Gary and Dorothy Kildall in 1973. Gary was then teaching computer science at the Naval Postraduate School in Monterey and was doing some systems consulting on the side.

At the same time INTEL was working on their 8080 chip which was soon to create a mega-industry. The engineers at INTEL needed an operating system to make their chip work with the then-new floppy disc technology.

Gary Kildall sat down to write a system equal to this powerful new technology and CP/M was born!

Others in the industry heard how well it worked and began coming to Gary to see if his system could be modified to work with their particular hardware. CP/M was an immediate success. It didn't take much space in memory and hardware manufacturers lined up to get it. As more systems began to use CP/M, software written under it sold better and better and things for Digital Research went from great to fantastic.

I visited Digital Research in the fall of 1981 and my impressions of the place and the people who make up this company were refreshing. They were young, bright, honest and growth oriented. They have the eager assertiveness of successful young intellectuals who have not experienced the trauma of failure. Their star is ascendant, they know it and are going all they can to make the most of it.

Marilyn Darling, the Advertising/Public Relations Manager is a serious and dignified woman in her late twenties. She has an education in computer science and quite a bit of experience in the advertising business.

Marilyn was vacationing in Pacific Grove and became infatuated with the place. Digital Research was the only computer game in town, so she naturally looked there for an opportunity. And what an opportunity it had turned out to be.

She sees a towering future for the microcomputer software market:

> This year the market is more than $500 million; by 1985 it is estimated to be between $3-5 *billion*. I feel the major growth will come from business applications.
>
> User friendliness and the impact of IBM's entry into the microcomputer arena will bring the business out of the hobby level. Incidentally, IBM offers CP/M as an option on their new micro systems.

Marilyn told me legal protection is a concern in the software business. She said Digital Research used to have some bootlegging problems, but it was at no time done on a large scale. The firm evidentally has a sophisticated method of serializing disc paks. In the past they have found people selling disc paks with the serial numbers still in them, but a phone call to the offender has usually been enough to stop the problem.

Polly Sloan is another energetic Digital Research crew member. She was a psychology and sociology major in college, but has evolved into handling legal and contractual matters for the company. She works closely with Digital Research's counsel, Gerry Davis, of the legal firm Schroeder and Davis.

Software is a new and largely untested area of the law and Gerry Davis is evidently one of the few lawyers in the country who is familiar with the issues involved in protecting copyrights on software Polly says he has developed this expertise largely through working with Digital Research. Polly works as liaison between Gerry and the contract and copyright infringement situations of the company. She talks like a lawyer and clearly enjoys her job: "We are litigating in those cases where the issues are clear-cut. Prevailing in these cases we select for active litigation will establish precedent and set benchmarks for the future." I asked her how a software author could protect what he writes. "The Trademark issue is clear-cut and easy; put a TM above the name of your program. This will give you immediate protection."

Bill Smale is another of the Digital Research breed. Bill majored in economics an international relations and got a Master's Degree at the American Graduate School of Management and International Relations. Not surprisingly he specializes in the international aspect of the company's business.

When Bill got his Master's Degree he went to Tokyo, taught English there long enough to become fluent in Japanese and then went to work for the largest software developers in Japan, Computer Services Corporation. He then came to this country and went to work with Digital Research.

I asked him about the kind of competition between the U.S. and Japan that we could expect in the computer business during the 80's.

> "Japanese hardware is very good and the turnover rate (consumer cycle—how long they use a TV set for instance before getting a new one) is very short compared to us. The hardware manufacturers are competitive in Japan so they are used to competition when they come to the U.S. They cannot compete with the U.S. in software development because of the entrepreneurial spirit here. It is really the American strength—the idea you can make a product in your garage and become a success with it. This works perfectly with software development, but it is a little harder in the capital intensive industries."

Bill is currently working with Japanese hardware manufacturers to acquaint them with the benefits of basing their systems on CP/M. He must be doing a good job because 80% of the microcomputer manufacturers in Japan use the system!

## The Boss

Gary Kildall is a low profile boss. He is primarily a programmer and would rather write programs than manage an organization. His wife, Dorothy, runs the daily affairs of the business. This leaves Gary free to follow his primary interests. He can be recognized by his cowboy boots, hat and a big black pickup truck.

By 1983 it is estimated Digital Research will have sold three million CP/M's. At a current retail price of $150/copy this adds up to $600 million. (If you had that much money in a sock you could spend almost two thousand dollars a day for a thousand years before getting to the toe.) Certainly Digital Research doesn't receive full retail for their programs — they sell through distributors and through licensing arrangements with hardware manufacturers—but in any case Digital Research is doing quite well, thank you. Next time you are in Pacific Grove watch for Gary Kildall in his big pickup and see if he is smoking a big cigar.

As you can imagine, Digital Research has few financial problems. They sell what is essentially an intellectual property represented on a magnetic disc and a few pieces of paper. There is little equipment involved and so profit margins are high. Software publishing is similar to book or record publishing in

*The modest and informal atmosphere at Digital Research could be misleading: This company has played an important role in unifying the microcomputer industry.*

that ideas or sounds are the real product and the medium is simply a container.

It is easy to believe Digital Research has had to turn investors away. They have selected three venture capital firms to help them grow straight and strong. Their investors, T. A. Associates, Hambrecht and Quist, Venrock and Pagemill, have had experience with the likes of INTEL and Apple and provide the best planning and directional expertise available. Actually there are many companies involved beyond these three because it is the general practice for VC firms to spread their risks.

Growth, new products and limited vertical integration are a part of Digital Research's future. But I have a feeling the company doesn't know just how powerful they are. They have no formal five-year plan and seem to only vaguely realize they are a big business. Sure to form though, they have even covered this base. There is little doubt their VC investors are going to help them plan and track the business along reasonable and healthy lines.

Digital Research acquired Compiler Systems of Sierra Madre, California in October 1981. Gordon Eubanks of CS wrote C-BASIC, a powerful business-oriented compiler for small systems. I get the clear impression Digital Research bought Compiler Systems to bring Gordon Eubanks aboard! Marilyn Darling says, however, this acquisition was calculated to round out Digital Research's language division.

Digital Research actively helps people produce software under CP/M. They provide seminars, consultive assistance, a newsletter and publish a comprehensive catalog of CP/M compatible software. This all is a part of the company's ISV (Independent Software Vendor) program. ISV is a term coined by Gary Kildall to describe the people who write, produce and market software under CP/M.

One of the considerations Digital Research has when planning product verticality is to be careful not to compete with their ISV's. Digital Research's verticality plan is to become a one-stop shopping center for operating systems and languages and to leave the other levels of programming up to the ISV's.

CP/M has made mass-marketing of software possible and this mass-market has conversely made CP/M the *de facto* microprocessor industry standard. The ISV's and Digital Research have made a happy an prosperous marriage.

Digital Research obviously sees distributed processing as their future. As 16-Bit machines become more available there is

*Marilyn Darling, Public Relations Director of Digital Research.*

*Carment Governdale of Digital Research points out a dense area on the map showing the location of hardware makers who base their systems on CP/M.*

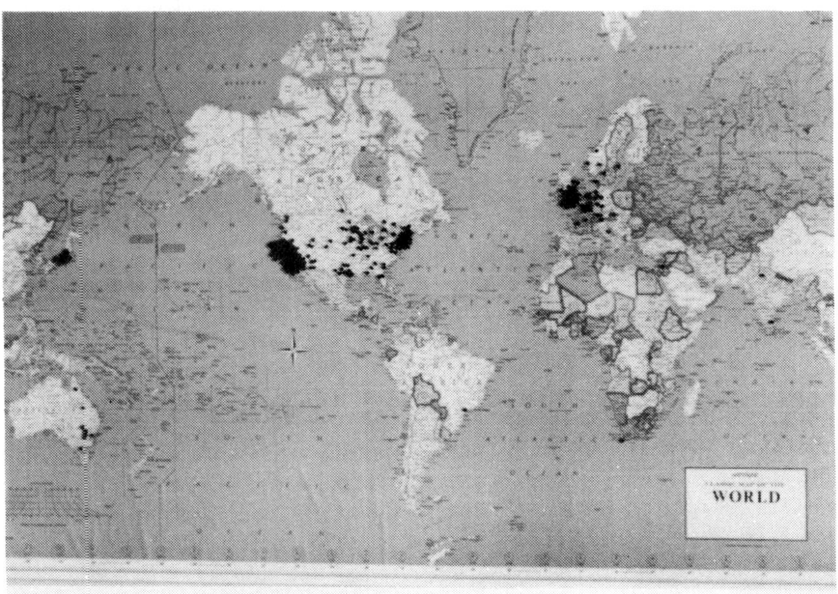


*This map shows the location of hardware manufacturers who base their systems on Digital Research's CP/M. Their efforts to market their operating system have been effective and have contributed to the incredible dynamism of the industry.*

*Bill Smale of Digital Research. Bill is an International Marketing Specialist for Digital Research. Bill speaks fluent Japanese and concentrates a lot of his marketing efforts there. He says Japanese manufacturers are increasingly using CP/M for their operating system.*

*Make a copy of this card and send it to Polly Sloane at* **Digital Research**—*she will send you information about their systems and put you on a mailing list for a continuous stream of interesting information and notices of seminars and meetings sponsored by the company.*

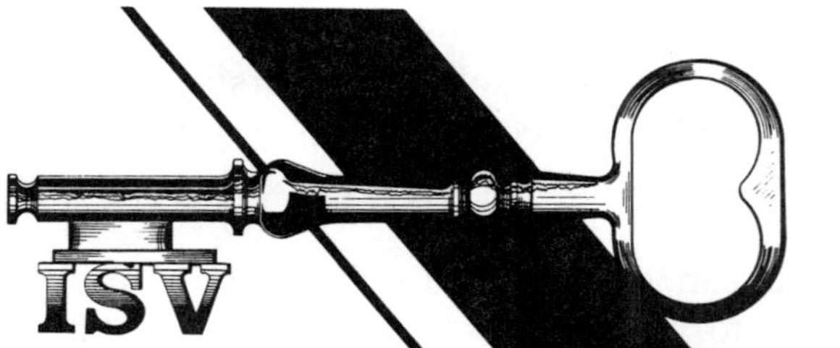


# INDEPENDENT SOFTWARE VENDOR INFORMATION

- ☐ Put me on your ISV mailing list.

I want to:

- ☐ Receive ISV FORUM.
- ☐ Attend an ISV Seminar.

Send more information about:

| | |
|---|---|
| ☐ CP/M® | ☐ CP/M-86™ |
| ☐ PL/I-80™ | ☐ MP/M™ |
| ☐ MP/M-86™ | ☐ CP/NET™ |

Name: ______________________________

Title: ______________________________

Company: ______________________________

Address: ______________________________

______________________________

Phone: (        ) ______________________________

Language(s) I use: ______________________________

______________________________

Main Application(s): ______________________________

______________________________

______________________________

Development Hardware: ______________________________

______________________________

DIGITAL RESEARCH®
P.O. Box 579, Pacific Grove, CA 93950

expected to be a strong shift toward networking. This is an obvious step for business users. Multiple-user stations and multitasking will more completely computerize the office and do so at a lower price than for multiple micro systems. Digital Research thinks the typical office system of the future will be a 16-Bit processor, one nice Diablo-type printer, a hard disc and four or five terminals.

As you can guess, Digital Research's recent ad and promotional efforts have been aimed at potential users of their multi-tasking system, MP/M.

And where will they be going five years from now? You can bet it will be in the direction eventually taken by the rest of the pack.

Digital Research has two regular mailings: a newsletter and an ISV letter. To get on their mailing list call Lori Forrest at 408-649-3896.

## Supersoft Associates

## Interview

Herb Schildt, President, 30, has a Master's Degree in Computer Science from the University of Illinois, and started Supersoft Associates in 1977. Herb is a tall, energetic and intense man on the move. As I talked to him it was apparent that he enjoys the business he is so thoroughly caught up in and he enjoys success. Herb has found a place that fits his temperament and talents. He enjoys people, making deals and being the boss. I think his only regret is not having the time to spend with his programs as he did in the old days. The new days make many demands on his time to organize, administer, wheel and deal his company to greater success and stronger position in the industry.

Herb: I got interested in microcomputers in 1976 and began trading programs with people. I got more and more involved and at one point began to ask for five dollars for my trouble. Money started to roll in, but there weren't enough people out there till about '79 to support what we are now doing. The real market started in 1979.

In 1976,'77 and '78 there was a real lonely sensation with your microcomputer. Whatever you did with it you were essentially alone. There was also a great sense of freedom—if you crashed the whole system, it didn't matter.

When the business started I had no clear idea of where I wanted to be in the computer business. I followed my own talents and the

*Herb Schildt and Richard Balocca of* **Supersoft**

software business grew along with me.

When I started there were only five companies selling software. The concept had barely started. When Rick and I got together we would write the programs and manuals, make the diskettes, package and ship them, all in the same room. In between we would write ads, answer the phone, run errands and take care of details.

We have grown 400% a year for the last four years. We followed the boom. Every new system increased our sales. It was a continuum. We had any other options, but the software business kept pulling us along. We were there when the time was right and we have made as much of our luck as we could.

In 1979, the area everyone had neglected was system maintenance software. The larger computers all had diagnostic programs to check the systems. One day Rick said, "How do you know the computer is working?" Here ws a need which no one had worked out

Richard Bolocca, Vice President: There was a big market gap in microcomputer maintenance software. Maybe no one had worked on this kind of software because they thought it was boring. We wanted to approach this business in a professional way; there was a gap in the market which, though not as exciting as "Tank Wars," represented a good business opportunity.

We developed a program that provided a full range of tests for the micro system. It has been tremendously successful and no one has entered the market against us.

Our test program is pretty good. The printer test makes a barber pole pattern which exercises each character in each position. If there is a character error it will show up.

Our combined diagnostics I and II package has sold thousands and thousands of units. We still don't have any competitor for it. Every major manufacturer uses it in-house.

Another break for us was when we developed our Tiny PASCAL and licensed it to Radio Shack for use in their TRS-80 line. It has been a great success for everyone involved.

We like to let Radio Shack distribute our TRS-80 compatible products for us because with so many thousands of outlets they do a great job of getting it out there.

*Diagnostics* put us on firm financial footing. It was a high quality product that had no competition and made us dominant in the whole area. If someone thinks about microsystem diagnostics, they have to think of us.

We also do spinoffs of the diagnostic program. One we have done well with is called *Disc Doctor.* This is a part of our system maintenance series.

We found a strange thing in our early advertising. We were told we should advertise no less than three months at a time and that when we reduced the size of our ads sales would drop. I also figured the lifetime of the *Diagnostics* program would be three months to a year. It didn't turn out that way at all. Sales, in fact, have gone up because new machines have come on the market that can run it. We don't see any saturation at all. Machines are coming onto the market so fast that it keeps sales quite brisk.

Herb: The crazy boom is over and has been replaced by the major boom. The crazy times were early 1979 through 1980. During those times we could do no wrong. We would buy five full pages in *Byte* at a time. I could place ads in any magazine and it would work.

The games business happened to us unexpectedly. One of our people worked out a game and asked if we would publish it. We did it mostly as a favor and it turned out to be a real performer. The author is very happy with his royalties and we smile over the unit volume. Ours was the first game to run under CP/M and so it was a great and immediate success.

Royalties on software vary between 10% and 25% depending mostly on factors of the market. A new "Tank Wars" game would probably bring the low end of the royalty scale and a wholly new and relevant program would range to the high end. Royalties are a matter of determination of estimated profit and volume potential and negotiation within that framework.

Our product line works like this: We have a System Maintenance

Series, a Language Series, Financial Planning Services (released January 1, 1982), and an Entertainment Series.

Rick: Word processing and accounting programs need a lot of user support which our more technical programs don't seem to need. We think technical support is a vital part of this business and want to provide a complete service in that regard. We have a separate "Technical Hotline" telephone number where a user can talk directly to someone who knows all about a particular program.

Our financial planning program is inbetween applications and systems. We have a Visicalc-type program called *Scratchpad.* That type of program is halfway between a computer language and a data base. It isn't one or the other.

If there are three manufacturers of an item and the fourth company gets into the market, the newcomer will get his market share just by being there. The program doesn't have to be bigger, better or stronger—you will get the market share because of the way markets work.

Herb: Just because you build a better mousetrap doesn't necessarily mean it's going to be bought. The new thing which we will see in the future is customer support.

There are some well known software firms who have neglected real hardcore customer support and this will have its effect as competition enters the industry. We are putting a strong amount of emphasis on customer support on every level, users, OEM and the lot. You have to jump when there is a problem.

Anyone can write a program, but that 1% in the program and support is real hard. A flawless program is next to impossible to produce.

Rick: The business has in the past been very mail-order oriented. You saw a lot of ads selling software that said "call between 11 and 2." That kind of company is going to fade in favor of the people who can support the product well.

We see ourselves as a package software house, which is different than a contract software house who does government contracts or a large custom software house who goes in a sets up a bank. We see ourselves as presenting a package that fits a demand. Because it is packaged its unit cost is lower, and because its cost is lower the volume is higher.

Herb: Manuals are always a problem because the manual is tangible and the program isn't. If the user has any problems he can't hate the program, but the manual is there right in front of him so he can tear it up.

Rick: There is a need for cross-referencing. You need tutorial sections, glossaries, indices, reference sections.

Look at the way hardware manuals are done. They have a lot of cross-referencing between prints, board layouts, etc. The whole point is you get the information *you* need whoever *you* are. This way the manual can address all levels of users.

Herb: Sometimes saying too much is just as bad as saying anything at all because the reader can't wade through the material. Manuals are tricky. We have a staff who works full time on the problem. Time is the biggest problem. We think you should spend as much time writing the documentation as you do the program, but it doesn't always work out that way. It's not a piece of cake to produce a good program and a good package. It's hard because creativity is involved. We attempt to completely mechanize the process of program and manual creation—that's the goal. That way we won't have a cottage industry within a big company.

We are entering the third phase of the software business. The first phase was in the late fifties and sixties—an intensive effort to produce things like FORTRAN and the first accounting programs. These were really scholarly and intense efforts. Computers were extremely expensive, very few people worked on them and it was a real clinical situation. Phase Two was during the seventies and we are just coming to the tail-end of it. I call it the Go-Go Years of software. We saw companies doing computer software on contract. Tons of government and industrial work. But the programmers were having a little bit of fun. Things weren't so clinical. When microcomputers came along things started to get haphazzard.

The third phase, now just emerging, is "let's have the business of software, not the cottage industry of software." Most software companies are a cottage industry inside a big building. Much software is still being written that way.

Rick: Software has to be sold like books and records. You have to convince the user that if he spends a lot of money on his hardware he should also make a big investment in software for the system.

Herb: That's why we have the series approach to things. Our financial series is about a thousand dollars. Our language series is about 1500 dollars. How many people buy the records of their favorite rock band all at once? They buy them one at a time. If you get someone into financial planning software series they don't have to buy the whole line, each item stands alone, but when they add the next unit they now have two complementary pieces of the package. They add the second unit when they need it. It is also a friendly way to get in. The user can take each piece at a time, learn and apply it, then go on to the next step.

Herb: Our dealer sales are 40-60% of our current revenues. The market is maturing. We used to do most of our business mail-order and we are gaining more dealer and distributor support. How exactly we should distribute our product is a subject of many meetings. Should we sell only through mail order? Should we do it all ourselves? How should we relate to distributors? There are many important questions we just don't know the answer to. The industry hasn't as yet defined a distribution system.

We look at our business this way: We are a software development and publishing company. We also do distribution. Mail order distribution was essentially a necessity of the moment. We see that phase gradually fading over a period of time. When it reaches a certain point we will find a second source and turn it over entirely. But that is somewhere down the road. We have to support it right now because it's a necessity.

There are many distribution networks in this industry. Software distributors, direct to dealers, etc.; it's all crossed up.

Rick: The essential price of software is a matter of struggle right now. Prices don't seem to follow any classic price theories. If you are selling a hard item you add your costs, add a margin and you sell it. Your competition is based on how cheaply you can add up the numbers to manufacture the item. With software you have a rather low intrinsic cost. Beyond that everything is cream. Let's say a program costs 10K to develop and your cost of reproduction, overhead and advertising is about sixty dollars. You can sell it for a hundred dollars, a thousand, or for sixty-one dollars. If you sell it for 61 dollars you make a dollar. You then sell a million of them.

A software house has to be prepared to cut its cost someday to a small percentage over direct costs. There isn't a lot of price warring now, but you have to be prepared for it. When you look at it from the bottom it seems great—spend a little time developing the product and then sell it for many times the actual cost. A great way to get rich quick. But it doesn't happen. Software was at first a get-rich-quick scheme, but all that is changing.

Herb: Phase two—the get-rich-quick thing—is just about over. Now we are going into Phase three—the time of serious competition and professionalism.

We are in the business to stay. There are new hardware developments coming along and we will develop products for them. February 1 of 1982, we will release an ADA compiler for the Z-80 system. We will be the only ones with such a program. We think this program will really take off. DOD validation is required to use their trade name for ADA. Validation costs $5000 per try and there is no guarantee of passing on the first time. It's an expensive proposition, but we believe in it.

Rick: Our development philosophy is to get a person who is enthusiastic and matched to the task. We won't attempt a project on a ho-hum basis. The programmer has to really want to do it or we won't go into the project. It also perhaps limits the things we get into, but overall this approach has worked for us.

We have seven in-house programmers. One problem we have had is we both have computer backgrounds and not management backgrounds. An old joke applies to us: "How much management experience do you have?" "What time is it?" He have brought in management types and it is helping.

Herb and Rick are the sole owners of the company and have an open attitude about the future. If the right person or investor came along they would view the situation with an open mind. They have brought great enthusiasm and expertise to a detonating market—time and the tide are on their side. It's going to be very interesting to watch them grow and prosper.

SUPERLETTER
Serving SuperBrain Owners and Users Around the World
POCKET COMPUTER
Bits & Bits
The FINANCIAL SYSTEMS REPORT
Small Business Computers
chicatrug News
DENTAL COMPUTER NEWSLETTER
THE COMPUTER CONSULTANT
THE CARL HELMERS PERSONAL COMPUTER LETTER
ISV FORUM
EMMS
ELECTRONIC MAIL & MESSAGE SYSTEMS
CCAN
CONSTRUCTION COMPUTER APPLICATIONS NEWSLETTER
NEWSLETTER Homebrew Computer Club
FEEDBACK
MICRO MOONLIGHTER
BITS & PIECES

## Chapter Eight

# PROFIT FROM YOUR OWN NEWSLETTER OR SEMINARS

## I. Promoting Seminars

Seminars are an ideal business. They can be put on with a small investment and at low risk. Seminars are low risk because you can very easily market test them.

You can market test a seminar for about $800. If it proves viable you can then go ahead with the project and the testing money will have gotten you customers in advance. If your seminar idea is a flop you can test it in a slightly altered form or in another geographic market.

Once you have proven the market viability of your seminar concept you have a very predictable business. This is because, once you have proven the idea, you know what response to expect for your promotional dollars.

Seminars are a great way to open a door to selling your other information products. Newsletters, books, tapes and other seminars are easy to sell to the people who have attended your seminars. In fact, if you're aggressive, you can hustle to the back of the room at breaks and hawk your other stuff from a table.

Seminars are flat out show business. If you need recognition or are a frustrated stage star, you will get satisfaction in excess from giving seminars. You get to be on stage and can hold the audience on your every word, particularly if you talk softly.

The seminar market is huge and expanding. There are many seminars being given and there is room for many more. The adult education market is immense. It will be an eight billion dollar market in 1982. Your few million will hardly make a dent in it.

Seminars are recession proof. During a recession, people want to improve their skills, change careers or hang on to the career they have. This initiates a need for "self-help" consulting, which you are able to provide.

To give a successful seminar, you need to determine what people need to know *and* what they are willing to pay to learn. Individuals will pay for seminars that help them become successful and for seminars that relate to their hobbies. Only employers will pay for seminars that teach skills in helping the employer. When you know who is going to pay, you can aim your market efforts appropriately.

But what about competition? Aren't all the important seminars already being offered? If you find a needed seminar that isn't being done, you'd better look at it carefully before spending any promotional money. Chances are if a seminar isn't being offered, there is not an adequately concentrated market for it.

It is possible to come up with a unique seminar and have it be a great success. Only careful market testing will tell you for sure.

Some seminar ideas are poor risks. Howard Shenson gives an example in his seminar on seminars. His example is a "How To Sell Your Own House" seminar. How often do people sell their home? They come into the market for a brief time and are gone. A person who wants to sell his own home is trying to avoid paying a commission to a real estate broker. Will this kind of person want to pay you to tell him how to do it? It's doubtful.

People will, however, pay money for personal enhancement. The EST, mind control and assertiveness seminar producers have had tremendous success in the last ten years.

People often go to seminars because they are too lazy to read a book on the subject. A large number of people see seminars as a simple and effortless way to learn a block of information.

## The Brochure

Your brochure is the most important sales tool in your seminar promotion. You should have photos, illustrations and excitement. It should emphasize and reemphasize the benefits. It is impossible to overdo the benefit aspect of a seminar. You should offer a 10% reduced price for prepaid registration. The brochure should say if you bring someone with you to the seminar you get a 20% refund on the spot. Offer a 40% discount for spouses.

THE ELEVEN BEST SEMINAR CITIES

- LOS ANGELES/ORANGE COUNTY
- WASHINGTON, D.C.
- NEW YORK CITY
- CHICAGO
- MINNEAPOLIS
- DALLAS
- DENVER
- HOUSTON
- SAN FRANCISCO
- SAN JOSE
- SEATTLE

Don't ask questions about their real marital status. Why should you care? Accept cash, checks, postage stamps and bus tokens. Make it easy for people to give you their money! If people cheat a little and bring their secretary instead of their spouse, it's OK. Don't worry about bad checks. You won't get very many and it's worth the loss when you consider the exra customers you get from this convenience.

Take MasterCharge and Visa cards. It's hard to get set up with American Express, but if you are serious about giving seminars you should try it. Shenson estimates that acceptance of credit cards increases your revenues by 11%.

Every seminar brochure should include something similar to the following:

Tax Deduction for all Educational Expenses:
Treasury regulation § 1.162-5 permits an income tax deduction for educational expenses (registration fees and cost of travel, meals and lodging) undertaken to: (1) maintain or improve skills required in one's employment or other trade or business, or (2) meet express requirements of an employer or a law imposed as a condition to retention of employment, job status or rate of compensation.

The brochure must tell the time, date and location of the seminar. It must say the price and also say whether you will accept purchase orders. Incredible as it may seem, I have read expensive brochures that didn't say where the seminar was or how much it cost. Please don't make that mistake. It would have a rather limiting effect on your responses.

The brochure should mention your other information materials. If you have books, tapes or other similar products the brochure should include it. It will help sales and it enhances your credibility.

Finally there must be a call to action. Tell them to call or write now. Make sure your address and phone number are on the brochure. Deletion of these items also has a poor effect on response. If the brochure has a coupon make sure your address and phone number appear on both the coupon, and the other part of the brochure. If your address and phone number is only on the coupon, it will be lost and forgotten when they send it in to you.

Make sure your brochure is clear, concise and specific. Don't get complicated, cute, sophisticated or in any way difficult to understand.

Include a business reply envelope with your mailings. This set up means the post office charges you for the mail that is actually sent to you. If you send an envelope that says "Place stamp here," it not only makes you look like a cheapskate, but encourages the lazier people to file it away until locating a stamp.

You might even think of offering Continuing Education Credit for attending your programs. This gives your program an ethical and scholarly image. You can find out more about how to qualify for the CEU program by writing: National Association for Public Continuing and Adult Education, Washington, D.C., 20402, (202) 833-5487.

## College Sponsored Seminars

There are 3,000 colleges and universities looking for people to run seminars for them. You have to negotiate the fee split, but it generally runs a third for you and the rest to the institution. They handle the promotion, getting the money and provide the facility. They generally do a terrible job.

Remember, these people don't live in the real world where if you do things poorly, you get hungry. The programs are usually run with the university mentality where the students don't mind standing in line and other time-wasting and maddening inefficiencies.

The worst risk of failure in promoting a seminar is from greed. Greed leads promoters to spend huge amounts of money on a seminar. Misspent dollars are gone. What if you make it up on the next seminar? You would be better off if you didn't have anything to make up!

If your seminar is good it can be repeated successfully. You must carry out your test program with care and prudence. You shouldn't test market your program in a large city. The test can be made in a much smaller city and you will be able to get the same information for 20% of the cost.

## Seven Best Test Markets

In order to test your concept, you can select certain test cities which have characteristics of different aspects and regions of our society.

Bergen County, New Jersey is the place to test your idea's relevance in big city urban America. This area replicates the responses of the Big Apple almost exactly.

Columbus, Ohio is the place to test when you want to see how your program will go in a capital city, industrial center or university town.

Madison, Wisconsin is the place to test for a sophisticated market.

Austin, Texas is a good representation of the Northeast and Midwest.

Alberquerque, New Mexico is the place to test the relevance of your ideas for the West.

Spokane, Washington is a perfect test for middle America. Spokane is probably the most tested city in the world.

Last, but not least, Santa Barbara is the place to test your ideas for relevance in Los Angeles.

## Timing

Timing can make all the difference with your seminar. You shouldn't schedule your seminar in conflict with national holidays, *any* religious holiday, major national events, elections or sports spectaculars.

## Getting There

Some seminar experts say you should ship your materials by book rate far enough ahead to be there when you are. My experience is the hotel will always lose the stuff or the one who knows where it is has the day off when you arrive.

Many airlines will allow you 80 pounds of luggage. For those who won't and for excess baggage, use a Skycap. Skycaps can put your luggage on board for free. They give a wink to the airline luggage person and it all goes for no extra charge. The only charge involved is a $30 to $40 tip to the Skycap. These luggage handlers have the whole game down to a science and make $75,000 to $100,000 a year plying their art at a busy airport. The airport luggage guy gets his too, but the Skycap takes care of it. The system works well, and though it is ignored by airline management, everyone in the system understands how it all fits together. Forty bucks is a cheap way to insure the safe and timely arrival of your materials.

## The Right Hotels

The hotel you choose for your seminar has a great influence on your success. The better hotels are usually not much more expensive than the more seamy ones and a high-class location makes you seem big-time.

When you choose a hotel you have to think of several things. Where are your attendees coming from? If you have the seminar at the O'Hare Hilton and your attendees are coming from the western and southern suburbs of Chicago, you will be asking some people to drive an hour and a half.

If you use an inner-city hotel, you may be exposing your attendees to the dangers of mugging or auto theft.

If you use a hotel that has five units scattered around the city, your attendees may wind up at the wrong one.

When you make a deal with the hotel, do it with the hotel itself. If you use the National Sales office you will always pay more for the space.

The hotel's sales department gets first rights on meeting space. They try to book the rooms in connection with renting blocks of sleeping rooms, catering services, etc. Your needs should be a great deal more simple

You will probably deal with the Catering Department, who gets to rent what the Sales office cannot fill. If you have a 200 person seminar don't tell them. Say you have a hundred. When they say you can have a certain room for a certain rate, ask them how many it will hold. If it is big enough to hold your 200, you have it made.

The hotel will usually overstate the room's capacity by 10-15%. If the catering agent says the room will hold 250 people you can figure it will really hold about 200, so you are home free.

Make sure you are renting a regular meeting room and not a converted group of guest rooms. These conversions have low ceilings, inadequate air conditioning and lots of support pillars. They are absolutely inadequate and you should be sure this is not what you have rented.

You can get an idea of how good a hotel is by its rating in the American Automobile Association's Hotel Brochure. This brochure has fairly accurate ratings of the major hotels. Use the best hotel you can find that has the facilities you need.

## Do the Numbers Make Sense?

To calculate your break-even point, first determine your fixed expenses. Here is a typical fixed expense scenario:

| | |
|---|---|
| Direct Mail Promotion: 4,000 @ .40 | $1,600 |
| Two trade ads, 800 each | 1,600 |
| Conference room rental | 350 |
| Audio/Visual equipment rental | 100 |
| Registration person | 140 |
| Your transportation | 450 |
| Hotel room, meals and gratuities | 160 |
| Total fixed expenses | $4,500 |

The Seminar Fee in this case is $195 per participant. To calculate the break-even, divide fixed expenses by the seminar fee:

$$\frac{4,500}{195} = 25$$

You have to get 25 participants to break-even.

How many people do you expect? Typical response to a well-aimed direct response mailing is 1.5%. You might expect to get 60 participants from your direct mail effort.

What about the trade ads? There are many serious studies about the subject of trade ad response but none can calculate the relevance of your program, the competition appearing in the same magazine, or your ad placement and content until the party is over.

Let's say, hypothetically, the magazine has 200,000 readers. If you got .0001% (that's really low) it would mean 20 participants from each ad. That's a total of forty from your trade ads and a grand total of 100 participants. If things go terribly wrong and only half of those people actually give you money, you still have fifty participants. Fifty times $195 is $9,750. Deduct $4,500 for expenses, throw another ten bucks per participant for support materials and your expenses would be $5,000. You clear $4,750 on the seminar. I'd take it.

There is no guarantee you can make any money at all giving seminars. But the market is there and growing. There are many people working six months a year and getting rich giving a series of fairly simple seminars.

## II. Publishing a Newsletter

Anyone involved in a fast paced technical area requires more current and specific information than they can get from books and trade magazines. A newsletter capitalizes on specific information and often represents the highest authority on a specific subject.

Since newsletters are a more expensive information source than magazines or newspapers, most people want to make profitable use of the information they find there.

An important factor motivating people to pay the price for a newsletter is it gives them a feeling of getting "inside information."

The newsletter business is one of the easiest businesses to start. All you need is a typewriter and a phone. The startup costs are for some phone calls, printing and postage. Ease of entry has advantages and liabilities. The obviously good point is it doesn't take a large investment. The downside is there are plenty of dummies writing trash that fouls-up the market for everyone.

The trick to success is to find a viable niche. There is no better way of doing this than to identify market vacuums by the gap analysis described in Chapter Three. After you pick a subject, start looking for published material relating to it.

## Writing for Fanatics

It has been said newsletters are for fanatics. They are written and read by people who are concerned about a very specialized subject. The appropriate response is to narrow the scope of your subject coverage. Aim it like a laser into the specific interest of your following. The more fanatical the interest and the more refined the subject, the higher your subscription rates can be.

How do you pick this rarified spot? Talk to people in the business. Read the market analysis chapter and act on its suggestions: Go to trade shows, travel and talk to everyone involved in the industry in any way. Identify special problems and you will uncover a special need.

Here's an example: The microcomputer industry has a big problem communicating with ordinary folk. If you don't believe it read a Vector Graphic® Microcomputer Instruction Manual, or any microprocessor or computer-related instruction manual. Is there a need for a newsletter aimed at micro-industry technical writers and the problems of this aspect of the business? There will probably be one by the time this gets published so you'll have to find another subject. There are plenty more where that came from.

## News Gathering

The trick is to find sources. Identification of the "horse's mouth" original source of general news articles written around your subject will expand your list of prime sources. Another phrase to describe this process is developing a "nose for the news."

As you locate your primary news resources you will develop a stable. You will be surprised at what these people will tell you once they discover you are trustworthy.

Attend every seminar and trade show relating to your subject and get to know the people involved. Make a card file and call certain people at least every six weeks. By doing this you will

# *VoiceNews*
## Wants To Hear From You!

VoiceNews seeks newsworthy items about all aspects of speech synthesis and speech recognition technology. Firms and individuals are encouraged to submit news items for publication. We are looking for information about:

- New speech products - Chips, boards, peripherals, systems
- New products that include speech capability - For example: data processing and office automation equipment, instruments, medical equipment, consumer products, aids for the handicapped
- Software - For speech data analysis, editing and processing, text-to-speech, system level programs, games with speech I/O
- Product price changes
- Services - Speech processing, vocabulary generation, system design, programming, chip design, board design
- Technological advances - Results of R & D programs
- New firms in the speech field - Manufacturers, system integrators, consultants, major users
- Mergers and acquisitions
- Initial public stock offerings and venture capital investments
- Organizational matters - New divisions and subsidiaries, reorganizations, new sales representatives and distributors
- Quarterly financial reports - From public corporations
- Major contract awards - For hardware or services
- People - New appointments and assignments, especially corporate officers and managers in marketing, research and development, engineering and operations
- Technology licensing offerings and agreements
- Patents - Newly issued
- Publications - Books, articles, papers and market studies
- Conferences - Calls for papers, programs
- Exhibitions - Companies attending, new products to be introduced
- Courses and seminars - Topics, dates, places, lecturers
- Implementation suggestions - Hardware and software solutions that have resulted from speech system design/implementation problems and experiences. Examples: improved support circuitry for a speech chip, novel concatenations in fixed vocabulary equipment, fix for bug in speech recognition software.
- Applications - The practical application of speech technology is one of the most important aspects of our industry and is the primary reason the industry will prosper and grow. VoiceNews desires to publicize applications in order to generate increased interest in speech I/O, to stimulate new application ideas and to highlight products, manufacturers and users. VoiceNews solicits brief, informal articles about successful applications, ranging from volume products to one-of-a-kind situations. No remuneration is offered. Guidelines for submission:

    1. Maximum length: two pages, double-spaced.

2. Suggestions for facts to be covered - Initial problem, advantages provided by speech technology solution, equipment selected (be specific), related (non-speech) equipment, special design problems, description of how system works and what it does, system cost, other applications suggested by this one, plans for the future.

3. Include author's name, address and telephone number.

Articles will be sélected on the basis of novelty, content, relevancy and space available. Articles will be edited as necessary. VoiceNews can prepare application articles for you if you submit a list of the details, product literature and any other relevant materials. Include name, address and telephone number - we'll contact you for additional details.

Publication Calendar

| Cover Date | Closing Date |
|---|---|
| January | December 10 |
| February | January 10 |
| March | February 10 |
| April | March 10 |
| May - NCC Preview | April 10 |
| June | May 10 |
| July/August | June 10 |
| September | August 10 |
| October | September 10 |
| November/December | October 10 |

Readership

VoiceNews is read by all segments of the voice industry:

• Hardware manufacturers at all levels - Chips, boards, peripherals, systems
• OEM users of speech hardware and services - Firms producing consumer, commercial, industrial and military/government products
• End users of speech systems
• System integrators and consultants
• Market research firms
• R & D organizations
• Academic institutions

Format

VoiceNews is nominally a four page newsletter. The voice industry is growing and VoiceNews expects to grow also. Depending on the volume of news, VoiceNews will expand its information content by a) reducing type size and b) adding more pages.

Other Information

Editor and contact: William W. Creitz

VoiceNews is an independent publication. It accepts no advertising.

One-year subscription: $95.00 ($120.00 outside U.S.)

VoiceNews Wants To Hear From You!

**VOICE NEWS**

**Stoneridge Technical Services**
**P.O. Box 1891, Rockville, MD 20850**
**(301) 424-0114**

develop sources of anonymous tips and hot items. When you prove your ability to maintain confidences, your sources will become increasingly informative. When you develop this inside track your newsletter will be earning its keep.

## Format

Kiplinger uses a typewritten, underlined format. A cleaner-looking, more compact letter results from a two-column typeset, right-justified, proportionally spaced format. You can also achieve an acceptable look with a word processor and daisy wheel printer. With a set-up like this you can bold face item headings by double striking. Many letters are now using this equipment, but it takes an investment of money you might need to spend elsewhere for the time being.

You should invest fifty dollars to have a good commercial layout artist set up your masthead. A distinctive and professional-looking masthead helps create a good image for your work.

The best size is 8½" x 11". This size makes it easy to store, file, handle and mail, and your printer will never run out of your paper. Do not die-cut or make you letter fancy. I know someone who published a "Frisbee Tournament" newsletter and had it die-cut in a circular form. He sold plenty of subscriptions, but always lost out when it came time to print. His die-cutting costs were his profit margin. His idea was clever but not practical.

## Writing News

The first rule of newsletter writing is *don't be afraid to take a controversial stand.* Newsletters thrive on controversy. Look at Henry Fales' HSCOOP. He has a Good-Guy/Bad-Guy Department where he "tells it like it is" regarding how some micro businesses handle their affairs. He is bound to make enemies of those cited in the Bad-Guy section, but Henry tells it as he sees it and has created a successful newsletter doing so.

Write your articles like a telegram, not a gothic novel. Use sweep lines: "Micro Manufacturers Fail Because of Poor Manuals." It gets attention and moves the reader right along. Underline, use exclamation points, asterisks and bullets!

## Predictions and Scoops

Both of these items make the reader think you know what's going on and have good inside connections. Our story might begin with a comment such as: In a confidential interview we found. . . . It shows you as an authority and authority is the lifeblood of the newsletter business.

Once you work out a format, sequence of departments, items and news coverage you should stick to it. It gives readers confidence and a feeling of security to return to the familiar.

## Production

Dealing with printers is a necessary evil in the newsletter business. You will find printers' quotes vary as much as 300%. Some of the cheap printers can't get work because they are always late or do poor work.

Some of the high bidders also do poor or late work. Price alone is no guideline to printers' services. Talking to them and looking the shop over can give you some idea of how they run their business. If three angry customers come in while you are talking, it is a bad sign.

I use the following method to select printers: Narrow the bidding down to three most likely choices. Tape their quotes on the wall, close your eyes and throw a dart. If the skewered printer does a poor or late job try another until you find the rare bird you can depend on and work with. When you unearth this gem, pay him on time so he will stay happy!

## Production Schedule

In order to get your newsletter out on time you need to set a production schedule with realistic deadlines. These times will have to be adjusted to meet requirements of local realities.

1. Writing. Allow two weeks, including rewrite and "tightening up."
2. Typesetting. Five working days or get a new service. Better yet, get a daisy wheel word processor and do-it-yourself.
3. Printing. Five working days max.
4. While your copy is being typeset and printed, work on your mailing list. Prepare labels, envelopes and attend to the housekeeping chores of your business.
5. Fold and staple work back from printer. Stay up all night

stuffing, sealing and sorting envelopes. Mail in the morning. Better yet have the printer fold and staple it.
6. Go back to step one.

## Sales

There is a lot of controversy on the best way to promote a newsletter. Space ads in trade journals are expensive and often yield few subscriptions. Classified ads are sometimes cost effective, but they should be tested. Phone campaigns are time consuming and direct mail is getting more expensive all the time. So what to do?

You should carefully test all four methods. Advertising and promotion are covered more thoroughly in chapter thirteen.

If you can get a well-qualified mailing list, direct mail is probably the best place to start. Try 1,000 names to see how the list works. Make a promotional piece, offer a premium if they subscribe (free report or booklet), include a reply envelope and a business reply envelope. Use testimonials and all the tricks of the trade as outlined in John Caples' *Tested Advertising Methods*.

The key to a promotional campaign is to sharply qualify your mail list and to continually test your promotional material. Read about testing in the ad chapter of this book.

## Renewals Are the Key to Success!

The following are the time-honored methods to get your subscribers to renew:

1. Offer an additional premium or a reduced rate for renewal.
2. Send separate renewal notices, starting five months prior to the subscription lapse date.
3. At two months before expiration send an individually typed letter asking for a renewal and offering an incentive. Include a self-addressed renewal card.
4. In the last month send a series of frantic messages on red paper, one per week, asking for renewal and reminding the subscriber of what he will miss if he fails to renew and if his subscription lapses.
5. Send two issues after expiration with an inserted red card telling the subscriber what he will be missing by failing to renew.
6. A personal phone call will sometimes bring a lapsed subscriber back into the fold.

## Costs and Subscription Price

This is the "grim reality" section of the newsletter fairy tale. Let's look at some typical numbers — you will soon see the picture.

An assumption needs to be made about percentage return from your promotion. We will assume you are promoting exclusively by direct mail. The return rate will be purely speculative until you prove your lists and test the promotional material. We will assume a 2% return.

Next estimate your production cost: probably between 30 and 50 cents delivered. We will assume the median of 40 cents. This means you have a product cost of .40 x 52 = $20.80 per annum.

How about an income for you? Can you start on $20,000 a year? It's not much but you *could* live on it.

Mail costs for promotional material might run 15 cents each. Four mailings of 100,000 would cost $60,000.

You should put in something for overhead—all those items that add up to such a large number at the end of the year. A not unreasonable figure would be $20,000/year for a small operation.

| | |
|---|---|
| Cost of filling 2,000 subscriptions: | $40,600 |
| Your income | 20,000 |
| Promotion costs: | 60,000 |
| Overhead: | 20,000 |
| Total: | 20,000 |
| | $140,000 |

Divide total subscriptions (2,000) into this and you get your break-even subscription cost: $70/year. This should be the minimum price of your subscriptions if your numbers match those above.

Will this market be elastic? That is, will it increase as the price drops? You can only tell by testing. There is a certain minimum price below which people think the product is "cheap" in the inferior sense. A good way to test price is to send out mailers with different prices offered and chart the result.

## Add-On Sales

There are many ways you can earn supplemental income with your newsletter. Advertising is an obvious method but may reduce your authority and independent image.

You can periodically offer special reports or a booklet to

subscribers at a "reduced rate." The more faith your subscribers have in you, the more you can charge for these extras.

You might provide a research service to your subscribers and charge them an hourly rate for it. The research will most likely turn up items for inclusion in later newsletters.

Back issues often become valuable. Some publishers have had to reprint back issues to keep up with increasing demand. Often new subscribers will want to purchase a year's worth of back issues to catch up on the subject.

Seminars are probably the best way to make extra cash and also increase your subscription base. People are anxious to pay you for saying the same things you have been writing.

You can make money by renting your mailing list to one-time users. Prices go from $40 to $200 per thousand for single use rights, with you supplying the labels.

Syndicated offers or "per inquiry" deals can be a good source of extra newsletter income. You simply add the promo material as an insert in your regular subscription fulfillment mailings and forward the orders to the promoters. These deals generally pay 40-50% of the item price. Sweet!

Finders fees have retired many newsletter editors. They are in a position to know what is going on in the industry. The editor knows who wants to buy, sell or merge. *Fees for making these connections typically go from 3-10% of the gross amount of the transaction!* A single fee could give you more than five years of subscriptions.

## A Different Approach

A newsletter idea was taken by Jeff Love and Steve Pizzo and tured into *The Community Computerists' Directory,* a quarterly listing of people and businesses•involved with computers.

They originally started a company called Data Access, a data base for local computerists. They found a list of personal computer owners and offered them a free directory of other owners if they would fill out a questionnaire. This launched what is now a 72 page, quarterly publication with growing circulation. Jeff and Steve are sitting on a tiger and enjoying almost every minute of it!

Whether you want to see how they approach the informaton access business or just want to get the directory for personal use, you should subscribe. Write them at PO Box 405, Forrestville, CA

95436. It costs ten bucks a year, complete with quarterly updates. You shouldn't be without one.

## Henry Fale and HSCOOP

HSCOOP, a newsletter aimed at Heath computer users, was started in April 1980. Henry Fale promoted his newsletter in free news releases in the computer journals and with a small mailing list of H8 owners. Subscriptions were slow at first. He got only 200 to start and was mighty worried. Henry started offering other H89 compatible products and his sales volume steadily increased.

Circulation was up to 1,400 fourteen months later. Henry says he gets four or five new subscriptions a day from ad and news release residuals and by word-of-mouth.

Henry claims the most important aspect of starting a newsletter is to *know your subject* and to use good judgment on what you write.

Henry feels it is best to have your newsletter offset printed and that copy methods are really not good enough. Regarding printing, he says you should print more than you need because you will be sending out many back issues and it's a bummer when they are gone.

His choice format is to use a word processor with a daisy wheel printer, reduced 15% for offset printing. Proportional spacing combined with pica type gives the maximum characters per line. He uses an 80 line per page two-column layout to get 50-70 characters per line. This way you can get a maximum amount of information in a minimum space.

I have included an example of Henry's newsletter so you can see how he does it. It is, incidentally, an invaluable source of information if you are an H8 or H89 owner.

HENRY E. FALE
2918 S. 7TH. ST.
SHEBOYGAN, WI 53081
(414) 452-4172

# H8SCOOP

OCTOBER 1981
ISS#1902090981


## BITS & PIECES

### SUBSCRIPTION RENEWALS

Just a reminder on how your subscription works. When you receive this newsletter your mailing label contains a number opposite your name. This is the number of your last subscription. The current subscription number is found in the banner such as ISS#1902101081. The first two digits are the current issue, this is issue #19. When you are getting close, send in your $15 for another year, when you are at your last subscription, the word LAST appears in place of the last issue # on your mailing label. This means that no more issues are mailed out until payment is received. Try not to let this happen, as it could delay your subscription by a month.

I wanted to give fair notice that H8SCOOP will be raising its subscription price soon. Those who want to renew yet at $15 can do so. If your number on your mailing label is getting close (4 or 5 numbers) to the current issue #, it may be a good idea to renew at the current rate.

### ON MX-80 GRAPHICS

A note from Bob Moss from MNET on MX-80 problems with graphics. "It sounds like people are getting their parity bits stripped off... I would suggest that people adapt the H14 method of handshaking for the MX80 only because it permits a greater uniformity amoungst users with Heath equipment and allows use of existing drivers and patches (i.e. ctrl P) without significant modification. If you want to use both, this is possible by cabling both and taking one straight off and one off the NOR. Then you can plug into a machine that uses the DSR high=disable without recabling.

For using graphics which uses the 8th bit, you'll have to modify the ASM source code for the driver and reassemble. Modify so the ANI 377 is not stripping the 8th bit.

### A TERRIBLE OMISSION

Last month I was forced to cut my editorial short because of lack of space. I wanted to give the subscription information and addresses of BUSS, and REMark for those who do not have this information.

BUSS/ 325 Pennsylvania Ave, SE/ Washington, DC 20003. Pricing is one year which is about 18 issues for $25. REMark (I hope you all know this one) is $18/year initial ($15 renewal) for 10 issues. Address to Heath Users' Group/ Hilltop Road/ St. Joseph, MI 49085. Besides these, there are many fine local HUG newsletters that allow the public to subscribe to. I hope to publish a list of some of them in a future issue.

### HEATH RUMORS

I have heard rumors (true or false?) that Heath is going to introduce a package called SUPERCAL for about $200. This is about equivalent to the program helping sell thousands of Radio Shack computers, VISICALC. It's something I have been long waiting for. Also, as reported earlier an 8" 10 Mbyte hard disc with tape capability backup for about $6000, priced right out of range of most hobbiests. There is expected to be about 25 new software products coming out, many to run under the newly persued (by Heath) CP/M, which is supposed to be slowly overtaking HDOS. The H8 is to be supported through the middle of 1983 when the new super computer is expected out. There are expected to be more improvements and cards coming for the H8.

Around October, there should be, as reported earlier, the H89 double density card for about $395, with the H8 card to follow in December. CP/M 2.37 is to be released shortly. I hope it supports those Tandon 400K drives. The H14's price is to drop even more as they try to clear their 2000 inventory to make room for the H25, which is supposed to be a $1000 kit high quality, high speed dot matrix graphics (same set as H19!) printer. The price is expected to drop to $395! You may want to pick one up as Epson is struggling to deliver the MX-80 due to its popularity. They can't keep up with demand anymore! There is to be a new serial card for the H89 with 2 serial ports and 1 parallel port to support the MX-80. Look for a 12" green monitor for under $150, but don't ask me what that is to be used for. The new HDOS 3.0 expected to be released in November of this year, is said to be 0-org as previously reported, and have an MX-80 device driver on it. I guess we'll have to wait and see how much of this comes true-- and on schedule. Oh yes, I also heard DG is supposed to come out with a hard disk drive for the H8, probably under $2,000.

### NPS COBOL?

Captain Steven Tinius sent me an add showing The Software Review, Selling the NPS COBOL for $69.95. This he can't understand as it is in public domain, unless the $70 is for the 3-ring binder that comes with it. As reported in a previous H8SCOOP, this is the same COBOL he gives away!

### 3 DRIVE H17 MOD--HORIZONTAL

Several individuals have written in to me that they are running the H17 3 drive mod putting feet on it and turning it on its side. This way the drives are in the horizontal position instead of vertical which most individuals seem to prefer (and is better for the discs and drives!).

### ON SPELLBINDER

I have decided to sell SPELLBINDER at the price of $295 as mentioned last month. It is the word processor (sold as office management package) that I prepare H8SCOOP on. In my opinion, it beats ANY other word processor out there, costs less, and is MUCH easier to use since it makes use of the special function keys of the H19/H89 (although not necessarily logically). As a dear friend of mine, D. C. Shoemaker puts it "You're completely correct about Spell Binder. Compared to WordStar, this is a truly professional word processor. I'm constantly amused at the folks who go overboard about WordStar (Amen--ed); clearly their experience with the available processors is limited." D. C., by the way, is the one who turned me on to SPELLBINDER--I owe you one Major! He has also been evaluating word processors for the Army.

Anyone wanting to order a package, or receive more information, feel free to contact me.

### NEW SOURCE FOR LABELS & DISKS

Bob Sloat writes in that he has had good luck dealing with Disks, Etc./ POB 327/ Center Valley, PA. They have a good price on 5.25" discs and a real good price on labels with tractor feed holes. $10 and change for a box of 5000 mailing labels.

### ON 1.6 and 2.0 INCOMPATIBILITY--H8

D. C. also writes in (See also Request column) "By the way, you might mention that there is an easier way to solve the incompatibilities between HDOS 1.6 and the org-0 modification board. I understand that the patches to the 1.6 discs don't always work, but the following method is infallible and applies to both HDOS 1.6 and CP/M 1.42 and 1.43 disks. The procedure is as follows:

a) Do a cold-start by pressing RST and 0.
b) Press MEM.
c) Set the address to 000.362.
d) Press OUT.

You're now ready to press GO and boot up the system."

I did! See page 2, May 1981 H8SCOOP! Remember my slogan H8SCOOP--Contact with the future!

### NEW HUG CLUB

A HUG is forming in Philadelphia and will be meeting at the Heathkit Electronic Center (Roosevelt Blvd) on the second Wednesday of every month at 7PM. That was sent in by Henry Beechhold.

### REPORT ON LINDLEY SYSTEMS MX-80 DRIVER

Brian Hanson wants to pass this information on to you about the Lindley System MX-80 device driver.

For those who want the info, Lindley Systems, 21 Hancock St, Bedford, MA 01730/ Phone (617) 275-6821, price $20 postpaid. "I was very impressed with the original version 2.1, that I had purchased in early June. Lindley systems has now updated the driver and they gave me the oportunity to update, at a very nominal charge, to their version MXV34.DVD.

"I would like to tell you some of the features which have impressed me. All printer controls are programable with normal text characters. The text can control Double Strike, Condensed and Emphasized print modes. Form length and automatic line skip at page break can be used if desired. Spaces can be added to the left margin if desired. The driver can set the high bit so that programs (like B.H. Basic) that output seven bits to print files, can access the graphic mode in the printer. Either DSR or CTS, RS232 protocol can be used. The driver can access 5 device names (LP0:, LP1:, LP2:, LP3:, and LP4:) through a single I/O port and each has a 16 character initalization sequence that is preprogrammed but can (also) be reprogrammed to any desired sequence, such as 40 characters per line normal print, 66 characters per line normal print or any other configuration desired."

**ON MAGNOLIA CP/M**

I'm asked about CP/M so often, who has what, and what will handle the Tandon drives I want to add this section. It deals with the Magnolia CP/M, since this is what I mostly get questions about.

The Magnolia Microsystems (of whom I am a dealer) CP/M with their double density card for the H89 has a CP/M that will run only with their board, and only with the H89 to give the standard drive about 180K CP/M and the Tandon about 750K. This card is only for double density H89, and since all their CP/M BIOS use Z80 code, it is not transferable to the H8.

They have a single density package, again using Z80 codes (but A converted H8 CPU could handle this) and using the standard Heath drives. Although they specify the H89, I see no reason why it would not run on a Z80 H8. It will support the Single Density Tandon drives giving about 350K for CP/M.

There are still those out there working on the CP/M BIOS for the Heath CP/M, but I haven't heard any word on the progress of these. One thing to keep in mind, anyone working on this project should know what Magnolia is doing, since they have set the "standard" in non-standard Heath drives. I'd sure hate to see a half dozen different modified CP/M's going around that were not compatible. We have enough compatibility problems, let's leave it at that.

I also hear the Magnolia CP/M will support only 128 directory entries, while Heath's will support 256 (for their new version).

**GOOD PRICES ON PRODUCTS**

Lum-Buckles, a Zenith factory-authorized distributor, is holding an inventory reduction sale. All prices include shipping to a street address. Orders may be prepaid or COD (COD with 20% deposid, add 3% for COD). The items offered are

Z-89-FA (disk, 48K, serial I/O) for $2100*
Z-89-GA (48K, serial I/O) for $1900*
Z-87 dual drive for $850*
Z-47 dual 8" drive with controller for $2500
Diablo/Xerox 630 printer for $2000*
Z-19 terminal for $706
CP/M, HDOS, or AutoScribe for $125 each
Scotch or BASF 5" 10 sector discs 10 for $26, next 10 for $23
Diablo Hytype II film MS ribbons 12 for $45, next 12 for $40
Diablo Titan 10 metal print wheels for $35

Starred items--order 2 or more, get free dust covers. Quantities limited to stock on hand. Order from Lum-Buckles/ 7 Gateview Ct/ San Francisco, CA 94116. Phone (415) 731-7793.

**ONLINE CLEARINGHOUSE FOR MICRO INFO**

A new source of information and advice on micros is now online. Called "The Micro Advisor", it is accessible through the CompuServe Information Network (Micronet) to anyone with a terminal or personal computer. It contains features of interest to anyone using or thinking about using microcomputers, including individuals, professionals; executives, small business people, etc.

To find out more about it, play around with it. You can access it by typing "TMA" while in CIS mode. Others interested should contact Battery Lane Information Services/ POB 30214/ Bethesda, MD 20814.

**DATA TERMINALS CORRECTION**

Data Terminals & Communications/ 590 Division St/ Campbell, CA 95008/ (408) 378-1112 wrote to inform me that the information published in last month's **H8SCOOP** (page 3) on **Re-Conditioned Keyboard Diablo Printers** was incorrect. The refurbished 300's sell for $1295 plus tax and shipping, and the DTC 382's sell for $2,000 plus tax and shipping. The 300 uses a Diablo HyType I print mechanism while the 382 the HyType II print mechanism.

**NEW PRICES ON 400/800K TANDON'S**

Because of my increased quantities of ordering the Tandon drives, I am now able to reduce my price to you. Single quantity of drive alone is $460, the second for $450. Quantity orders can be discounted greater than before, write or call for complete information.

I'm still waiting for the modified CP/M BIOS for these drives. Magnolia has several configurations if you want to buy the whole CP/M over again, but so far nothing for the H8. What happened to all you guys that said you'd have the Heath BIOS modified? I haven't heard a word on it as of yet, and there are lot of individuals waiting.

**UPDATE FROM MI-8**

MI-8/ 822 E. County Rd. 30/ Ft. Collins, CO. 80525/ (303) 669-4116 has a price reduction on the V-8 Model II speech synthesizer for the H8. It is currently being sold for $324.95 and includes full software (3 disks). In November, there may be another H8SCOOP exclusive on the PC-12 parallel board with a special 3 port price when purchased with the V8.

A question has come up which deserves some space. I have been asked, and so has Ted of MI-8, so I'll let Ted tell it. "With the introduction of various voice systems available for most computers as well as the Heath, one most frequently asked question is "Which one is best for the Heath computers?". I would like to say the V-8 Model II is without a doubt. However, the answer depends on the users' application and requirements of his voice system.

"For a low cost limited application, the Digitalker can fulfill a good number of requirements. The Digitalker consists of two ROM's containing 143 words and phrases along with a speech processor. The voiced output is very high quality. The vocabulary is broad enough to meet a great number of applications. A talking clock, volt meter, voice prompted terminal, and a good number of talking educational programs, such as math quizzes and spelling. The Digitalker also requires very little programming.

"For the person requiring more versatility and unlimited vocabulary in English or any language, the V-8 Model II would have to be the logical choice. I am often asked how the V-8 compares to the Type-N-Talk. My response would have to be that there is little comparison. While Type-N-Talk can speak with virtually no programming, it lacks the intelligibility of the V-8. Both use the SC-01 speech synthesizer chip, but in a different way. The Type-N-Talk produces its English speech with the use of a ROM English algarythm. The algarythm is about 90% accurate, which is quite good when dealing with the many rules of the English language. The speech it produces is, however, a direct result of that algarhythm and may not be the speech the user would like to hear. On the other hand, the V-8 uses a look-up dictionary of words and speeks them exactly the way the user wants to hear them. Any word can be changed and any number of words can be added. Changing or adding a word in the dictionary is quite simple with the utility "SPEAK" program. SPEAK allows the user to configure a new word to sound the way you like before adding it to the dictionary. An example of this would be the word "coffee" which can be pronounced in any number of ways depending on where you live. Anywhere from upstate New England or Southern California and anywhere in between. The user can also add inflection to his words and sentences to give them the clearest sounding speech available today."

"MI-8 has gone to great lengths to provide software to support the V-8. There is virtually no software provided with the Type-N-Talk. (There is a device driver disk available with demo programs and sounds from the Keyboard Studio, by Tom Jorgenson--ed). Our programs include a 1,000 word dictionary, which is user expandable, and several utilities to support the V-8. There is also the device driver "VB.DVD" which allows the user to add speech to any BASIC program or other language that recognizes device drivers. There are also several BASIC programs for the V-8 user. A talking clock and talking game puzzle. There is more coming in from V-8 owners everyday. To further encourage this, MI-8 is offering a full disk of programs to anyone submitting a program of their own along with written permission to redistribute it.

"I can honestly say there is no other voice system available for the Heath computer that offers the versatility and support of the V-8 Model II. After all, we are entering our second year of voice for the Heath computers. But don't take our word for it, ask around, or better yet, compare yourself. For versatility, support, and voice experience with Heath computers, there is no comparison.

"The V-8 Model II sells for $249.95 kit or $349.95 assembled and tested. The Digitalker sells for $119.95 kit or $149 assembled and tested." To order, contact MI-8.

# NEW STUFF

### MORE FROM HOYLE & HOYLE

BAUDOT to DISK receiving and correcting programs for $15 are available from Hoyle & Hoyle Software/ 716 S. Elam Av/ Greensboro, NC 27403 (NC residents add 4% sales tax). This program runs on the H8, H17 and H19 combo requiring HDOS 2.0 and 16K memory (I guess the H89 will also work?--ed).

Using the Baudot to Disk Receiver, your H8, a Ham rig and the standard interface between the Ham rig and the H8, you will be able to receive and decode 60 or 100 wpm baudot/murray code. The program is also set up to receive 110 and 300 baud ASCII code. The info is stored in a buffer which can be saved on your disc.

Features include the following: Prints on the screen what you are saving, clears the screen instantly by pushing one key, single key changes receive speed at any time, 10 automatically named files, protection for already named files, stores incoming data when buffer is full, easy buffer clear to store new data at any time, clear, constant display of free space in disk and buffer.

A simple, small screen editor is included to correct pictures, with the special ability to strike over characters on the same line by giving the user the option of eliminating the LF on any lines desired. It allows you to read in 20 lines at a time, make corrections on the screen and store the corrected version.

This program package is ideal for receiving and editing pictures or copy (Including Military transmissions and press bulletins) received on Ham operating equipment. A small collection of pictures received and edited using these programs is also included on the disk.

### DISK DUMP UTILITY FOR CP/M 2.2

New from Elektrokonsult/ Konnerudgaten 3/ N-3000 Drammen/ NORWAY for $29.95 including disk and documentation (not source code) is DDUMP, a sector oriented disk dump utility which makes it possible to examine and modify any byte(s) on any sector, addressed by track and sector number, OR addressed by allocation block (or 'group') number. Sector contents are printed and/or displayed - and may be patched - in both HEX and ASCII formats. DDUMP allows you to dump and patch data not otherwise accessible by CP/M, and it may, for example, be used to examine text files for control characters, tabs, etc., to study how CP/M allocates disk storage, examine and repair a damaged disk and recover deleted files and lost data.

DDUMP works with most types of drives and disks used with CP/M, including 5" and 8", hard and soft sectored, single and double density, single and dual sided disks. The program automatcially adapts to the actual number of tracks and sectors per track for most types of diskettes without manual intervention.

To order, include $4 postage and handling. Check or VISA accepted.

### H8 BUSS PC BOARD HEAT SINK EXTENSIONS

From MI-8/ 822 E. County Rd. 30/ Ft. Collins, CO 80525/ (303) 669-4116 comes a "HOT" item for the H8, Heat sink extensions for the PC board. It's a well known fact that a fully loaded H8 generates a considerable amount of heat. On some boards the 7805 5 volt regulators operate close to their thermal shut-down limit, and the convection cooling of the H8 can be quite insufficient. Heat is one thing that can damage expensive computer IC's, which was the reason for many H8ers installing fans in their H8.

MI-8 has developed a simpler and quieter solution, the addition of HEAT-SINK EXTENSIONS. They connect to the PC board mounting brackets and can be installed in just a few minutes, without any modification to the H8 enclosure. Tests have shown up to a 65% of heat reduction on some boards. These extensions are made of fast heat dissipating aluminum and come complete with mounting hardware. Price is $3.25 for 1 to 3, $2.99 for 4 to 6, and $2.49 for 7 or more. Include $2.50 handling and shipping per order.

### INEXPENSIVE 8" CONTROLLER

Here's more info on the 8" controller I mentioned last month. This is available from Livingston Logic Labs/ 2386-323 E. Del Mar Blvd/ Pasadena, CA 91107. The 8" disk controller is very simple, made up of only 14 IC's, the controller chip being the Western Digital WD1771. Total cost of parts should be under $100 from most suppliers.

In operation, the controller is virtually identical to the H-47, except that it does not support double density. The total disk capacities for the two formats supported by this controller are 8" single side--250K, double side is 500K. There is a version for the H89 and the H8, but since it uses Z80 non maskable interrupt capability, the H8 must have a Z80 board or a Z80 mod to the CPU. In addition to this, you must have at least 32K RAM, 0-org mod, and 1-4 Shugart compatible 8" drives. Presently, CP/M is required and supported, and proof of ownership MUST be supplied before the software can be shipped to operate this system. This is necessary because much of the software, including the BIOS is derived from standard CP/M, and Ray Livingston doesn't cherish the thought of spending time in jail for copyright violations. This may change in the future as software "patches" are being developed to work with CP/M. Hopefully the next few months will produce the HDOS drivers to operate this under HDOS as well.

Your present 5" controller can be used as normally for your 5" drives. When you purchase the controller you receive the controller board (the same size of standard H8 boards for the H8, and slightly shorter than the H89 boards for the H89), complete documentation including schematic, parts list, source code, a replacement monitor ROM which is identical to Heath's except the H-47 boot routines have been deleted and replaced by the routines necessary to boot from any drive connected to this disk controller. The new monitor ROM operates exactly the same way your standard ROM (boot from any device, etc.). In order to keep costs low, you are requested to send your old ROM in after receiving the new one so it can be reused (there is a deposit). A complete set of software is also supplied, which includes: Bootstrap loader, Bios loader, Bios, MOVCPM, CONFIGUR, FORMAT--all come with complete source code except MOVCPM which comes with source code for the modified part.

Pricing as follows. No personal checks only cashiers or money order. For the H89 systems, the basic price is $75, $200 assembled, and $15 ROM deposit. The H8 basic price is $85, $215 assembled, and $25 ROM deposit. This ROM deposit is refunded when you send back the ROM (if you elect to do this). The IC's needed to build the kit are commonly available small scale TTL logic type IC's. Specify the disc you want your software on, 5" or 8". If you want 5" add $15 as it requires several of them to hold all the software. Projected dates are September 15 for H89 controller, and October 1 for H8 controller. If you are interested and would like to be placed on the waiting list for the order, contact Ray Livingstone of the above mentioned address. Do not send any money until you hear from Ray, as he will inform you when things are ready.

Other products in the works are new serial/parallel I/O board for the H89 which will contain 2 serial ports and 3 parallel ports using the 8255). A high resulution color graphics interface for the H89 is planned for under $200.

### ALSO EPROM BURNING SERVICE

If you need an EPROM programmed, Ray can do it for $5. Just send him the EPROM, or he'll supply one at a reasonable price. Also send the software in one of the following formats: HODS .ASM or .ABS, CP/M .ASM, .MAC, .HEX, .PRE, .REL, or .COM, or an already programmed ROM or EPROM. If either .PRE or .REL format is supplied, specify the origin address you desire. If disk is supplied, use either Heath 5" or 8" Single density (single or double sided). Any questions on any of the above, Ray can be reached by phone at (213) 792-4763.

### SOFTWARE FROM REICHERT DIGITAL SYSTEMS

Henry Beechhold told me he purchased two programs from Reichert Digital Systems (29 Blazier Road, Warren, NJ 07060), both of which are winners. LOGIC, is a digital-logic simulation program designed to produce a truth table showing the state relationships of all outputs of a digital circuit for all possible input conditions. The program has numerous features, including an editor, and runs under HDOS MBASIC. The cost is $29.95.

The other is really two programs, XYPLOT and BARPLOT, both of which are sophisticated plotting programs. This package sells for $29.95. These can be used whenever data is needed to be plotted on screen or printer.

### SOFTWARE TOOLWORKS T-SHIRTS

For $6.50 you can have the Software Toolworks T-shirt featuring a picture of Leonard, their H89 dreaming of a floppy disk and their moto, "Without software, it's just a paperweight". It's silk screened in black on gold color, 100% cotton. They may be ordered in mens size S, M, L, or XL. These are top quality shirts so they run slightly larger than most. These are available only from Tri-Arts/ 7854 Lankershim Blvd./ North Hollywood, CA 91605, and will be shipped only in the 48 contiguous states. California residents add tax. Price includes shipping--allow 3 to 4 weeks for delivery.

### CP/M BUSINESS SOFTWARE FROM VANDATA

For those looking for business software on the H89 format, contact Vandata/ 17544 Midvale Ave. North/ Suite 205/ Seattle, WA 98133/ (206) 542-7611. They have available the complete Osborne business package consisting of General Ledger with Cash Journal ($295), Accounts Receivable ($295), Accounts Payable ($295), and Payroll with Cost Accounting ($295). Buy all four for $995. These require CBASIC2 2.05 or higher which is available for $110, and CP/M 1.4 or higher.

These require an 8080 or Z80 system with minimum 48K RAM, double density 8" or two smaller capacity disk drives. Three diskette drives are the optimum configuration. The format supplied and supported is the 5 1/4" single-density format. A 132 column printer is required for printout, and the H19 or H89 or a similar type terminal with addressable cursor.

This is a much modified, enhanced and debugged version of the original Osborne package. Comes complete with very adequate documentation and user manuals.

They also have available for $700 dBASE II a relational database, and PEARL III for $650, a program generator. VISA, MC, and COD orders accepted.

### 8" DISK SYSTEM FOR H88'S AND H89

Floppy Disk Services/ C.N. 5212/ Princeton, NJ 08540/ (609) 771-0374 has available for H88 and H89 owners a disk drive system using the CDR controller card. It is capable of single and double density at the same time. This is presently for CP/M (I think--ed). They can supply the BIOS to drive the thing if you have CP/M. The complete package including 2 single sided double density drives, cabinet, hardware, manuals--everything needed is $1600. Complete with single drive in double cabinet is $1300. Assembled and tested controller only is $600.

### H19/H89 AUTO REPEAT AVAILABLE

From R Peterson/ POB 122/ Livermore CA 94550, for $60 comes Auto-Rep-89. This allows the H19 or H89 terminal to automatically repeat any key by holding down the key, thus eliminating the need for holding down the key and the repeat key simultaneously.

Any key will repeat at a specific rate, after a 300ms delay to avoid double strikes. No modifications are made to your terminal. It's simply a small module that plugs into the existing connector on the keyboard, and the other end to the cable that used to go to the keyboard (in series). No external power is required, and its use in no way affects the normal operation of the terminal.

### APPOINTMENT CALANDER BY SUNFLOWER

Sunflower Software/ 6304 W 76th St/ Prairie Village, KS 66204 has for 39.95 an executive appointment calander package eliminating the need for an appointment book. This package is comparable for some selling as high as $295. It's called EASY for Executive Appointment SecretarY. It is written in ABS so execution is fast. There are three modes of operation, Calander Mode, Full Screen Mode, and Sectioned Mode.

In the Calandar mode, the screen displays a full representation of the current month with the prompt at todays's date. There are a multitude of options available, with the numeric key pad allowing you to move forward or backward a day at a time. An "H" is displayed on dates for holidays, and a "V" may be placed in days for vacation.

At this point, the blue key takes you to the Full Screen Mode, from which you may enter appointments of messages and edit them with the numeric key pad. Any information on the screen in this mode can be printed. Pressing the "shifted 7" key will cause the times of the day to be superimposed on the screen in 15 minute intervals starting with 8AM. This is the "Sectioned Screen Display Mode", making the appointments more meaningful.

The times displayed are protected fields and may not be deleted. When you delete a line from this mode, only the appointments themselves are affected. This looks like an excellent package for the businessman or busy hobbiest, for a very affordable price.

### CROSS REFERENCE FOR REMark

REMREF is available for $12 at most Heathkit stores or from Keyboard Studio. What is REMREF? It is a data disk for use with Keyboard Studio's Keyword Index Program, KEY-IT. REMREF is a data file containing author, title, keyword information for all articles appearing in REMark issues 1 through 20. With REMREF together with KEY-IT, you can quickly obtain all references in REMark to a specific subject, author, or other keyword. It is designed so that the reference keys not only tell you which REMark to look in, but the starting page number of the article! Also, since REMREF is an ASCII text file, it can be edited to include future issues of REMark. It is available in both CP/M (REMREF-C) or HDOS (REMREF-H). For more information, contact Keyboard Studio/ 125 Aspen/ Birmingham, MI 48009 (313) 645-5365, or the author, Dave Powers/ Box 1154/ Troy, MI 48099 (313) 879-1115. Bob Ellerton of REMark tells me in a near future REMark, the entire REMark index will be printed, FYI.

### NEW STATUS PROGRAM

In the beginning, there was the STAT command of ver 1.6 of HDOS. Some useful information, but not much! Then came version 2.0--some new useful information but what happened to all the old information? NEWSTAT is a program that gives the user more complete details of their system status, which includes all the information of 1.6 and 2.0 (except DVD status), in both split octal and decimal. Also, the types of disk errors are broken down for hard and soft errors. It is interesting to note that all errors are not reported by the system as errors in the STAT command--this program reports ALL detected errors! Also included is the last volume number mounted and track accessed for each drive. This program will, if errors are encountered, ask the user for permission to clear all errors. As an assembly option, the user can elect to have all errors cleared after displaying them or to eliminate entirely the error clearing routines. If the user has any routine that puts the time (in ASCII) in the 'S.TIME' cell, this program will print it in its header. The source code is included. Runs on ver 1.6 or 2.0 H8/H89. For a copy send $15 or $12 and a disc to Gregory Marsh/ 5279 Miles Ct/ Woodbridge, VA 22193.

### NEW ROOTS BY COMMSOFT

COMMSOFT/ 665 Maybell Av/ Palo Alto, CA 94306/ (415) 493-2184, is releasing ROOTS/M. It is almost identical to ROOTS89 which is currently offered by Heath and COMMSOFT for HDOS, but will run on CP/M or MP/M and is available on 8" or 5.25" disks. The program supports a number of CRT terminals including the H19 and H89.

ROOTS/M allows you to store, retrieve and display thousands of facts about your family. It uses standard genealogical conventions to print pedigree charts (family trees) and family group sheets. With the program you can prepare a print out of your family trees back to 1AD! Another of the seven modules in the program allows you to compute the relationship between individuals. With the aid of ROOTS/M you can settle the argument about whether an individual is your grand aunt or second cousin once removed.

ROOTS/M comes with an illustrated typset manual which provides an extensive course in how to trace your family tree. The price for ROOTS/M or ROOTS89 is $124.95. For more info, contact Howard Nurse of COMMSOFT.

### NORTHSTAR BASIC CP/M ON H89?

BaZic is a BASIC interpreter that will allow any H89 eqivilent computer to run any NorthStar BASIC program under CP/M, and run it faster and more efficiently. Since it uses Z80 code for optimization, if you want to run it on an H8 you would have to have the Z80 CPU. It is available for $150 from Micro Mikes Inc/ 3015 Plains Blvd/ Amarillo, TX 79102.

Micro Mike's claims that baZic is 28 to 60% faster than North Star BASIC. It provides several terminal control facilities within the language such as statements to clear the CRT screen and position the cursor at a specified location. The greatest improvement over NorthStar BASIC is the executable APPEND statement, which enables you to write a software package containing many different programs and APPEND subroutines common to more than one module while the program is running. The advantage of this is each common subroutine need appear on the program disk only once, which results in disk space gained, and program maintenance is much easier. INFOWORLD, April 27, 1981 rated Usefullenss as excellent, Documentation as good, ease of use as good, and error handling as excellent.

### MONEY MAESTRO HOME BANKING SYSTEM

InnoSys Inc, a leading supplier of software to the banking industry since 1973 is pleased to announce its entry into the personal computer market with its **MONEY MAESTRO** home banking system. This new package written in FORTH under CP/M is designed to provide financial recordkeeping, tax reporting and budgeting for professionals, clubs, families and very small businesses. Those who recognize the benefits of accurate records but don't require full-blown double-entry accounting systems will find MONEY MAESTRO to be the fast, simple and complete money management package they seek.

Based around the user's checkbook, the system will record all deposits, payments, and charges by category (or group of categories) and payee while simultaneously keeping and accurate check register. These records are supplemented by entries of all financial transactions which don't affect the account ballance (charge cards, cash payments, etc.) so that MONEY MAESTRO can give complete reports on budget status, payment histories, and all income or expenses by category. Its powerful stockpiling feature will allow the preview of bills before payment and will hold partial payments or regularly occuring payments for later payment.

For more information, or to order, contact InnoSys. Price of user's manual alone is $20, price of complete package is $200. Specify 8" or 5.25" CP/M disk. The address is 2150 Shattuck Av/ Berkley, CA 94704, phone (415) 843-8122.

### BIBLIOGRAPHY UPDATE

September 1981 Microcomputing had an article written by Kathleen and D. C. Shoemaker (he's got the wife in the act now) titled "Relief for the Hassled Clerk". In the article they describe a timekeeping program whereby you enter timekeeping information by clock and job number. It is written in MBASIC under HDOS. This starts on page 162.

Another on page 92 by James Ingram "Tame That Blackboard Jungle" is a program written under MBASIC and HDOS for an H8/H17/H9, although he states H19 modification is straightforward. The program contained performs three main functions, entry of activities, insertion and deletion of activities, and display of current information. It was written mainly for a teachers use in a class, where a disk record is kept of every day and date of every actual class throughout the school year.

## OFFERS

I make all software available an an as-is basis, in other words, no money back policy if not satisfied, mainly because it's too easy to copy discs. You take your chances. At my prices, you really can't go wrong. I try to get software out as fast as possible so you canget the newest stuff fast, and as thus, don't get a chance to carefully screen and test everything. To do so, would delay all software at least 3 to 4 months. I do the best I can and sell without assuming responsibility on the accuracy or runability of a program or disc. I don't think I've let anyone down in the past, and will continue to do my best not to.

The following are past offers made by H8SCOOP, which are and will continue to be made available to those interested readers. Note I have dropped a few items from the list, and as time goes on, more will be dropped so my inventory doesn't go crazy around here.

| | |
|---|---|
| Tandon Drives W/Software | $485 |
| Tandon Drive only | $460 |
| 2ND. Drive | $450 |
| Single Cabinets W/PS | $100 |
| H89 DD Magnolia board W/CP/M | $510 |
| H89 CP/M For 400K Tandon +16K add on | $250 |
| SPELLBINDER Office Management Pkg. | $295 |

PROJECT ARTICLES FOR PARALLEL PORT--WRITE FOR CATALOG

| | |
|---|---|
| 9/80 File Dumps & Utilities. | $10 |
| 11/80 Pictures, Lables, Word Processor. | $15 |
| 12/80 Pictures & Utilities. | $10 |
| 1/81 H19 Graphics program disc. | $10 |
| 2/81 Plant, Swarms, Starwars, Utilities. | $10 |
| 3/81 Potpourri Set(2). | $15 |
| 3/81 Adventure Set(2) Pirates, Lost Dutcm. | $15 |
| 4/81 THINGS--H19 Graphics, Biorythm, Utility | $10 |
| 5/81 HDOS 2.0 PATCHES | $10 |
| 7/81 MISC I--OREGON TRAIL, ATOM20 | $10 |
| 7/81 ODDS & ENDS--Sort, Calculator, Finance | $10 |
| 8/81 HVC; Bigfont (excellent), cake, chair | $10 |

If the bootlegging of these software offers does not cease, this column will be discontinued. Once that happens, it will not be re-instated! When only 20 discs sell to my entire readership, I know something is wrong. This makes it not worth my effort, or my contributers effort.

This months OFFER 9/81 is MIXED BAG OF SOFTWARE for $10. It contains a modified verson of my Selectric device driver to work with 2 or 4MHz computers, settable baud rates, ports, and echo or no echo to console, and uses the H8-4 4 port serial card. The driver was written long ago as one of my project articles, back in the days when I had time to do assembly programming, even though I did not even know what an assembler was months before that. It has come a long way since then. It also contains some programs of interest to those using the 400K drives. EDUMP is a very quick one line change to fix HUG's DUMP which allows dumping of all 160 tracks. PNDUP.ABS is a relatively major modification to HUG'S DUP program which allows copying between any two drives and will copy more than the normal 40 tracks. Both drives must be the same type. It also preforms a byte by byte comparison on verification and will display track, sector an byte of any difference. PNDUP19 is the same, but for the H19 terminal. DATE.ACM is an assembly language program which will code and decode an ASCII date into the HDOS two-byte format.

## TECHNICAL FORUM

### CUSTOMIZED BOOTABLE HDOS DISKS

This item is printed by permission from **CHUG**, Capital Heath Users' Group, Inc., POB 341/ Fairfax VA 22030. CHUG is an independent local HUG with USA and Canada addresses membership rates of $12 and all others (foreign) $25/year. It is an excellent newsletter to have. This article is taken from August 1981 page 4.

Although most users of the HDOS Operating System are now familiar with the use of PROLOGUE.SYS files, there is a little known method for creating "customized" bootable HDOS disks which uses a similar technique. When HDOS boots up, it checks to see if a file named PROLOGUE.SYS exists on drive SY0:. If the file is found, it is automatically executed when the booting process is completed, thus providing the user with a pseudo turnkey capability. This technique can be carried one step further, however:

1) INITialize and SYSGEN an HDOS disk in the usual manner.
2) Mount the SYSGENed disk on a drive other than SY0:
3) Remove the Lock flag from the file SYSCMD.SYS using the HDOS DUMP program to modify the DIRECT.SYS file (or use an equivalent method).
4) DELETE the file SYSCMD.SYS!
5) COPY an ordinary HDOS.ABS file to the SYSGENed disk.
6) RENAME the .ABS file to SYSCMD.SYS.
7) Install the modified disk in drive SY0: and boot HDOS.

At this point you will have created a SUPER PROLOGUE.SYS! When the disk is booted, the program names SYSCMD.SYS will automatically be executed at the end of the boot process. The big difference, however, is that when the program terminates, it is automatically reexecuted again! This is precisely the way that the normal HEATH supplied SYSCMD.SYS receives control when a user program finishes executing.

It is impossible to perform any operation other than execute the program named SYSCMD.SYS with this configuration. Typing a double Control/Z sequence merely starts the program at the begining again!

Two obvious uses for this technique are:

1) Create a limited operating enviornment for an unsophisticated user who only needs to know how to operate a single program.
2) The replacement SYSCMD.SYS can be written as a MENU driven selection program which is used to specify which program from a set of programs on the disk is to receive control via a LINK SCALL. When the selected program terminates, control will be returned to the MENU "SYSCMD.SYS" and the next program (or function) can be specified. Two programs which illustrate the use of this technique are ZENITH Electronic Typing (AutoScribe) and the newer HUG Dungeons and Dragons game.

It should be noted that all unnecessary files can be deleted from the bootable disk since they cannot be executed from

HDOS command level. The only files really required are the new "SYSCMD.SYS", HDOS.SYS, HDOSOVL0.SYS, HDOSOVL1.SYS, SY.DVD (for V2.0) and possibly ERRORMSG.SYS.

## GOOD GUYS and BAD GUYS

**GOOD GUYS**--ALL HEATH OWNERS & USERS ACROSS THE WORLD. This nomination came in from Janet Hoyle of HOYLE & HOYLE SOFTWARE. Janet writes "Back in May when we started a software business our personal banker told us to expect 10% "bad" checks and strongly advised us not to ship to anyone until the check cleared. Well, we ignored that advice and shipped to everyone who ordered, the same day. As we expected, in over 500 orders, we have had no checks returned for insufficent funds or any other reasons. More than just good financial relations, our customers have been good to meet (via mail & phone) and pleasant to deal with. We enjoy the 2 to 3 phone calls a week asking for help or hints. The letters from people with questions or frustrations are still friendly and complimentary, even if they complain that we mispelled scabbard or left out an ending quotation mark, etc...(Yes we always have to have the spelling critics--gives them something to do--ed).

"In our new, soon to be released A Galactic Experience any word mispelled is deliberate because that's the way it's 'posed to be in the far reaches of outer space... Please express our thanks to all the fine folks who use Heath." I must say I agree with Janet, I have had the same experience. The majority of my subscriptions, offers, and drives are shipped by check, before they ever clear, and I have not yet to be burnt. It makes me feel good that in this crazy mixed up world we live in, the Heath group are indeed "GOOD GUYS"--a rare breed of human beings that play it straight (mostly--see editorial) and are excellent people to talk to, meet, and work with. My getting into this field has been the most rewarding experience of my life, a move I have never regretted. Hats off to all you Heath owners and users.

**BAD GUYS**--BEAL AGENCY/ 4141 Fairmont Ave/ San Diego, CA 92105. Georges Troupin ordered a disk doubler kit for $10 to convert his discs to double sidded discs and hasn't heard a word from them. They were mentioned in May 1981 H8SCOOP under NEW STUFF. This is the first offense against them, so we'll kind of play it cool and see what happens.

**BAD GUYS**--ADVANCED COMPUTER PRODUCTS. This outfit has been written up twice already, July 1981 and April 1981 H8SCOOP. It appears this column may be neglected, and if that is the case I will discontinue it. Send in your feedback, either you want this column or you don't. I'm not writing this for my health, I have plenty of other things to do, and a lot more to fill H8SCOOP with besides this column. When I started out I choose this column to try to help guide my subscribers to who is worthy of our support, and lot of feedback tells me this column is being neglected. If that's the case, I'll stop printing it. Let me know your views.

Anyway, Gordon Richards ordered some Verbatim discs from them, and has problems. The price was good and he received them in good time, but after using some he discovered some would not mount because they were 16 sector rather than 10. Even the label said 10 sector (wait till you hear my story --ed). After contacting ACP, he was told since the order was over 30 days old, they could not exchange or help in any way, he should have checked them ALL right away! Now what kind of bull is this? I buy discs in the hundreds, and I check them as I use them. If a company has this reputation, plan to spend lot of time checking an order after receiving it--in this case impractical! Anyway, suffice it to say they offered no satisfaction.

His next call was to Verbatim, who said this should be handled by the store selling them, but in this case they would exchange them (They are the GOOD GUYS) in this case. There has been much BAD stuff written in about ACP, for your own good, stay away from them. You may have had some good luck, but don't count on it continuing!

Now for my experience. The same thing happened to me using Memorex. My 10 sector hard discs had a 10% error giving me 1 sector soft, even though labeled 10 sector hard. I got these from PACIFIC EXCHANGE (see next GOOD GUYS) and they promptly shipped me my replacements. I also wrote a letter to Memorex and they never even had the decency to respond or acknowledge my letter! If they didn't have such reliable and good discs, I would not be buying from them. Especially after they claim every disc is checked bfore it leaves the plant--hogwash!

**GOOD GUYS**--PACIFIC EXCHANGE/ 100 Foothill Blvd/ San Luis Obispo, CA 93401, (1-800-235-4137) or (805)-543-1037 in California. I mention them because this is the only place I now buy discs from, and have not only been totally satisfied, but have not had one complaint against them. They handle various types of disks in all kinds of configurations--your one stop headquarters. They ship COD UPS, after your first order Cashier check, they will chip Company check OK. You call in an order, and it usually arrives within 5 working days. Very impressive. They advertise lowest prices available (which they are) and stock the items (which a lot don't).

There was one time they were out of stock. What did they do? They shipped me double side 10 sector hard sectoring for the same price as standard single side. Now that's what I call a GOOD GUY. They go out of their way to help you. I recommend all disc users to go through them as they won't let you down. Small or large quantities, you get the best prices and the fastest service.

**GOOD GUYS**--Hoyle & Hoyle Software/ 716 S. Elam Ave/ Greensboro, NC 27403. Tom Kyle writes in to tell me how they go out of their way to help him, and I have heard this from several others. For $1 to cover postage and handling plus the original disc they provide an updated version of their "A Remarkable Experience" adventure game. The updated version corrects some bugs that existed at the end of the game.

Tom has also purchased their second offering "Steer Kleer", which is a real time absolute, variable speed, graphic, manual dexterity skill game, requiring the player to navigate a ball through an obstacle course. For $10 one receives a 5" disc containing 2 assembled games, 2 unassembled games, plus the documented source code. They have been more than helpful. Judging by their new offers, they are on the way to the top, and that comes by being a GOOD GUY. You can have all the software and hardware you want, but your sales and life are based on whether you are a good guy or a bad guy. This is what seperates the men from the boys.

**GOOD GUYS**--William Campbell, MD/ 855 Smithbridge Rd/ Glen Mills, PA 19343. Doc Campbell sells an assembly language primer for the beginner that covers some of the basics for HDOS assemebly programming. Cost is $15. He also provides a 3 page addenda to clarify some points in the main papper. I have to agree. Reading some of his articles in REMark, and just my dealings with him nominate him for the GOOD GUYS colmn.

Tom adds--I have yet to be disappointed with any outside (Heath) product I nave purchased for the H8. The budget doesn't allow me to buy many of them (the story of our lives), but when I do part with some of my rare extra bucks for a product, it is gratifying to find a supplier that provides the extra support for the product and purchaser.

## CLASSIFIEDS

**FOR SALE**--H11A with 32K RAM, 2 Serial I/O and 2 adapt cables. Original cost over $2000, will sell entire setup for $1500 or best offer. Also H8 with 3 16K RAM boards for a total of 48K. Selll boards for $230 each, or best offer. Write for more information. John Hong/ Box 85/ Nome, AK 99762.

**FOR SALE**--Godbout 12K Static memory board for $60. Heath H8-5 Serial/Cassette interface with manual and cassette software for only $50. Heath Assembly Language Programming Course for $25. Will sell all for $110. Thomas Bessire/ 7600 Pacific Place, #2015 Bld. Ft. Worth, TX 76112. Phone (817) 451-3912.

**FOR SALE**--DG 32D RAM Board less memory chips, $150. Heath 8K Ram board $50. Omnitec Modem- Acoustic, 300 Baud $60. Michael Couch/ 1218 18th St/ W. DesMoines, IA 50265. Phone (515) 223-0549.

**FOR SALE**--Z89 FA factory built H89, brand new, for $2200. Also 100K Seimens disk drive, steps at about 12ms for $150. Frank Rinkleff/ 2036 E. Ridgeway Rd/ Waterloo, IA 50702. Phone (319) 234-6566.

**FOR SALE**--12K Godbout RAM for $100, 8K Heath Ram for $60. 2-Heath 8K RAM boards without memory chips or sockets for $25 each. H8-7 breadboard without breadboard sockets for $40. Gordon Richards/ POB 7211A/ Orlando, FL 32854. Phone (305) 298-8729.

**FOR SALE**--Complete Heathkit H8 based 48K system. Includes H19 and H9 terminals, H17 dual disk, H8-5 serial I/O, 16K extra RAM, H8-4 multiport serial I/O, H8-2 parallel I/O, H8-7 breadboard, HTB-0 Mullen extender board, 25 disks with programs, 16 new disks, interface cables, Zenith Word Processing, Much software including Microsoft and Extended BH BASIC, HDOS 2.0, many cassettes, new Diablo 1640 with extra type/fonts and 21 carbon ribbons. All manuals. All in excellent condition. Best offer over $2000 on H8 system, and best offer over $2000 on Diablo. Robert Ackerman/ 5870 Country Ln/ Aberdeen, SD 57401. Phone (605) 255-7057.

**FOR SALE**--1 DG Electronics DG-32D 32K Ram board for H8 fully populated, factory wired $250. 2 Heath WH8-16 16K Ram boards for H8 factory wired $155 each or both for $290. Allan Moser/ Route 1, Box 16/ Samuels, ID 83862. Phone (208) 263-3726.

**FOR SALE**--Two WH-8-16 16K memory boards, $200 each. Jack Van Zandt/ 350 Sharon Park Dr., Apt Q-4/ Menlo Park, CA 94025. Phone (415) 859-4718 during day.

**WANTED**--Z89 compùters (used-below $1500) at a reasonable cost. Contact Allen Bernson/ POB 68/ Boston, MA 02167.

**FOR SALE**--H8 up to 40K memory, with or without H8-5, H8-2 and PC-12 interface boards. Make offer. Ted Benglen/ 822 E. County Rd. 30/ Ft. Collins, CO 80525. Phone (303) 669-4116.

**FOR SALE**--NOGDS HA8-2 music synthesizer board for H8, complete with on board 1 watt stereo amplifier, sufficient for two 8" speakers with an output level greater than one would likely use at home. 3 discs of software, schematics, and full documentation also included. $85 or best offer. D. C. Shoemaker/ 2000A Foxridge/ Blacksburg, VA 24060. Phone (703) 552-5764.

*********************************************************************************************

"HEATH" and "HEATHKIT" are registered trademarks of Heath Co.

NOVEMBER issue deadline--October 16

Subscription Rates--$15/Year ($21 overseas Airmail)--current issues

Back issues #'s 1, 2, 3, 7, 8, 9, 10, 11 no longer available. Remainder through March 1981 (issue 12) still available at $1 each while supply lasts. Volume 2 back issues available at $1.25 each to current issue.

PHONE HOURS: 9AM to 9PM as I am available, except sunset Friday to sunset Saturday. NO COLLECT CALLS.

Reprinted by permission of John Fale, publisher, H Scoop.

# References

*How to Start Publishing Newsletters,* Stevenson Publishing Co. Distributed by Towers Club Book Sales Division, P.O. Box 2038, Vancouver, WA 98661.

*Editing Your Newsletter,* Mark Beach, Coast-To-Coast Books, 2934 N.E. 16th Avenue, Portland, OR 97212.

*Newsletter On Newsletters,* Howard Hudson, 44 West Market Street, Rhinebeck, NY 12572, (914) 876-2081.

*How to Make $25,000 a Year Publishing Newsletters,* Brian Sheehan, Parker Publishing, West Nyack, NY 12572.

*Newsletter Publishing Guide,* The International Entrepreneurs Association, 631 Wilshire Blvd., Santa Monica, CA 90401.

You might consider joining the *Newsletter Association of America,* 900 Seventeenth Street, N.W., Washington, DC 20006, (202) 785-0550. They sponsor conferences and an annual meeting.

The following list of Newsletters reponded to our request for a sample copy:

Arcadian, Games Newsletter, 3626 Morrie Drive, San Jose, CA 95127

BUSS, for Heath computer users, 325 Pennsylvania Avenue, S.E., Washington, DC 20003, (202) 544-0484. $18/year.

CHICATRUG NEWS, Chicago TRS-80 Users Group Newsletter. I couldn't find an address or phone number in my copy (Oct. 81). There was a coupon with the subscription price of $12/year, but it orthe newsletter had no address. Incredible!

Computers in Psychiatry/Psychology, 26 Trumbull Street, New Haven, CT 06511, (203) 562-9873. $25/year.

Constrction Computer Applications Newsletter, 1105 F. Spring Street, Silver Springs, MD 20910. $48/year.

Dental Computer Newsletter, 1000 North Avenue, Waukegan, IL 60085, (312) 233-5077.

Dits and Bits, Amateur Radio Microcomputer Newsletter, P.O. Box 10101, Dallas, TX 72507, (214) 690-1063. $15/year.

Electronic Mail and Message Systems, Technology, user, product and legislative trends in graphic and record communications. 30 High Street, Norwalk, CT 06851, (203) 866-6914. $170/year.

Feedback From Fujutsu, News of the Japanese computer, telecommunications and electronics industries. Ruder and Finn, Inc., 110 E. 59th Street, New York, NY 10022.

HUG, For Heathkit users.

HSCOOP, An excellent newsletter for Heathkit H8 and H9 users. Henry E. Fale, 2918 S. 77th Street, Sheboygan, WI 53081, (414) 452-4172. $15/year.

ISV Forum, For independent software vendors. Digital Research, P.O. Box 579, Pacific Grove, CA 93950, (408) 649-3896.

Micro Moonlighter, For people starting and growing their own microcomputer businesses. 2115 Bernard Avenue, Nashville, TN 37121. $25/year.

Newsletter Homebrew Computer Club, P.O. Box 626, Mountain View, CA 94042. $6/year or Donation.

Pocket Computer Newsletter, P.O. Box 232, Seymour, CT 06483. $30/year.

Small Business Computers Newsletter, 39 E. Hanover Avenue, Morris Plains, NJ 07950, (800) 631-8112. $12/year.

Superletter, For Superbrain owners and users. P.O. Box 3121, Beverly Hills, CA 90212, (213) 277-3410. $17/year.

The Carl Helmer's Personal Computer Newsletter, A great, highly technical general subject newsletter for the computer professional. North American Technology, Inc., Strand Building, 174 Concord Street, Peterborough, NH 03458, (603) 924-7136. $200/year.

The Computer Consultant, An information resource for consultants, authors, systems houses. Battery Lane Information Services, P.O. Box 30214, Bethesda, MD 20814. $48/year. If you fit the description above, don't missthis one.

TRANSNET, Newsletter of "Appropriate Technology." P.O. Box 567, Rengeley, ME 04970, (207) 864-2252. Donation.

## Chapter Nine

# How To Become A HIGHLY PAID INDEPENDENT CONSULTANT

A consultant is an outside person who gets paid for his analysis, advice and implementation. You don't necessarily have to be an expert to consult. All you need is to know enough to be of real help to your clients.

Clients have many reasons to use a computer consultant. Occasionally they have no EDP staff, their present staff can't handle the load or don't have the experience required to solve certain problems.

Clients use computer consultants because it leaves them and their employees free to do what they do best—make money in their regular business. Sometimes a consultant is called in because a client needs an objective viewpoint he or his employees can't have.

Some clients need an expert opinion and look to someone they can trust to give it. If someone knows little about computers and yet needs to computerize his business or improve his present system, who can he trust for advice? A systems house will push their own hardware lines and the client knows it. As an outside independent party, the client trusts a consultant to help him make this kind of tough decision.

Clients know that systems analysis, feasibility and cost-effectiveness studies are best done by an unbiased expert and often rely on consultants to do this kind of work.

As a consultant you may be called on to design and develop an entire system for your client. To do this you must be familiar with the equipment and software market and be able to match these things to your client's unique needs.

Many consultants specialize in research and development, market research, or evaluation of new products. But no matter what approach you take, the computer consulting business is booming. Whether you decide to sharply focus your area of expertise and limit your practice to one kind of client, or whether you decide to offer a broad general service, if you do a good job you will soon be busy as a beekeeper in the spring.

## Consulting Opportunity Areas

Most microcomputer stores aim their wares at the small businessman. An obvious but often overlooked way to get in on this business is to specialize in straightening things out after the system installers have left.

System installers *always* leave problems when they depart. Micro stores and OEMers make money from selling and installing equipment and software. It's not economically feasible for them to hang around for a long time after the sale. In fact, many encourage the customer to solve his own problems.

Imagine the situation in a small business after the equipment and software installers have left. A few people in the firm have a vague idea of how things work; the systems are partly or wholly operational. Things seem to work OK when the installers are there, but what happens when there is a glitch?

The distraught businessperson screams for help. "My god, the business has stopped!" The computer store owner wants to sell another system, not nurse a past sale. Enter the hero.

I know a consultant who started this way. He originally worked as a system installer for IBM. He couldn't help noticing when they left there were a few loose ends.—actually more than a few, and they got worse the longer the business was on its own.

This guy quit his job with IBM and started working with the businesses left holding the bag by the system installation people. I met him at a Harvard Business School seminar for presidents of small companies. He was clearly the most successful company president in the group of more than four hundred!

He was puzzled because there were so few companies doing what he does. He told us his group was so busy helping the Fortune-500 companies there was no time to get to the really vast market for his service among medium-to-small companies.

Many of the presidents at the seminar had horror stories to tell of "What Happened When The Computer Installers Left," and wanted to know if there was anyone at all they could call for help. Barry's answer was, "I've hired everyone I know who has the appropriate knowledge, we're booked for the next 24 months and I need more help!" The problem is bigger now than it was then.

## Mail Order Consulting?

Mail Order Consulting is a growing field. This kind of consulting is done by placing a small ad in the computer and business consumer magazines. Advertise that you specialize in helping first-timers select the right items for their microsystems. For fifty dollars you can guide them into a system appropriate to their needs. Advertise "free information" and send a two page description of your service on response to inquiries. When they remit, send a questionnaire, analyze it, phone them *once* and print out a recommendation report with two alternatives for each component system. Summarize the recommendation on a computer printed form.

Never underestimate the magic of that computer printout. We have all been conditioned since the first grade to believe in the printed word. People can read a lie and believe it while disbelieving the spoken truth. Add to this the reverence people have for computers and computer-generated products and you have a powerful propaganda tool.

I know a physicist who works for a military research think tank. They have found computer printouts of their research summaries have considerably more credibility and impact than conventionally typed or even printed reports. These reports are submitted to folks who should know better.

Have I made the point? Submit your survey summaries on computer printout forms, printed on your dot-matrix printer if you have one. It may not be as easy to read but will do a better job of conviction. If your work is good and the recommendations appropriate, so much the better.

If you are hardware oriented you might specialize in helping people modify or install new features and peripherals on their systems. Many people are intimidated by the hardware aspect of computers and would rather pay someone to deal with the problems hardware presents. This kind of work is endless because no computer system is ever fully evolved.

This method opens the door to selling parts, software and hardware. It also makes you the repair and maintenance resource if you want that kind of work. When the computer starts smoking the first call will be to you.

## Technical Writing

Technical writing consulting is a lucrative and important resource, and is often an overlooked area of the computer business. Hardware manufacturers and software publishers do a great job developing, packaging and promoting their products and do a terrible job of writing their manuals.

I interviewed many computer business owners and every one of them was in some way concerned about poor manualization.

Manual writers are confused about who is going to use the product and don't know which level to address. Often manualization is considered an ugly stepchild and the job is given to the low person in the company pecking order.

The real culprit responsible for poor manuals is orientation. Hardware and software designers become business owners who sell hardware and software. They love to deal with design and product problems. They excel in designing circuits and assembling machine instruction sequences. They are, as a group,

scientific, technical and linear left brainers who view the world as though everyone had a technical background and computer mania.

The best manuals are written assuming a high degree of computer acquaintanceship and scientific savvy. The worst of them are sloppily assembled, ungrammatical and omit large blocks of syllogistic logic while assuming the reader will make intuitive leaps along with the system designer. All of this makes the concept of "user friendliness" increasingly relevant.

This creates a great opportunity for technical writing consultants. The growing number of computer entrepreneurs who realize poor manualization is hurting their business are eagerly looking for someone who can translate their product into plain English.

## Custom Software

People who do this kind of consulting unanimously feel their biggest problem is to establish clear boundaries for the job. An open-ended customizing job could disrupt your life by upsetting the customer with large bills or enraging your spouse or other partners because you aren't billing all your time.

Most customers have no idea of their exact needs and the tendency is to bite off too much. At first, carefully select small jobs you can clearly define and can see the end of.

Here's why. What happens if you bid on a job, only to find it is much bigger than you expected or that the customer expected much more? If you raise your bid halfway through the job you will probably not do much more work for that customer or his friends. If it takes much longer than your estimate, not only will you loose money, but the customer will be unhappy—a no-win situation.

Start small and carefully work your way into complex jobs—it will make your life more enjoyable and help you sleep better when it's over.

## Getting Started

Hubert Bermont in his book, *How To Become A Successful Consultant In Your Own Field,* discusses how he started. When he started his consulting business and no one volunteered their services as client, he took a page from Mark Twain's adventures as a cub reporter. He phoned the president of one of the most prestigious firms in his industry and offered his services free! He was, of course, immediately taken on as an unpaid consultant. He worked hard for this new client. Within a few weeks the president invited him to lunch and and asked him what kind of retainer he wanted. Bermont mentally added up his monthly expenses and said that number. Done! He had his expenses covered and also had a prestigious client to mention when prospective clients asked the inevitable question, "Who have you consulted for previously?" Now his fishing expeditions began to produce results.

If you are making the transition from working for someone to being an independent consultant there are a few adjustments you will have to make. When you're an employee, no matter how high on the scale, there is always someone taking charge of what you can do. Even if it is only acknowledging a good job done or hammering you for a perceived shortcoming, there is someone to herd you back into line, adjust your compensation and generally make the rules governing your life. Over all this is the power to end your income.

When you go on your own all this changes. But there are difficulties hidden in this new freedom. One of the biggest problems penal institutions have is called recividism. This is the tendency of inmates to return to the scheduled certainty of prison life. Most recividistic prisoners would vehemently deny this trait. But prisons see long-term inmates returning after a short time of freedom for minor or unlikely crimes. They create a situation which will return them to the hated but comfortable routine of prison life.

Recividism affects anyone who sees their cage door open. Whether you one day decide the rat race is bad even for the rats and tell your boss to shove it, whether you are fired for doing too much too well, or whether you leave in a planned sequence of careful strategic moves you will many times and in many ways wish you still had the security of the employee collar.

If you recognize the situation and realize fear and insecurity will eventually be replaced by a feeling of security in your own ability to survive, your first days on the street will be easier.

## Office Equipment and Setup

The first rule for a one-person office is to get the best answering service you can buy. It gives a "doctor is not in" professional image and enhances your professional status. Every call could be vitally important to your new business and people often hang up or give incomplete messages to a machine.

Visit the service office and meet the supervisor and operator who will be answering your calls. The better they know you, the more they will come across as your private secretary. Make regular visits because there is often a high turnover in these companies.

When you call in for your messages be polite and even sometimes funny. Lead the operator to feel you are a nice, but very competent professional and she will answer your calls with the same attitude.

If there is a mistake, report it to the supervisor immediately—let the operators know you expect accurate and courteous professional service.

Hubert Bermont says getting a client to sign a contract cuts your potential work in half. Clients are typically intimidated by a legal document because of past experiences. A formal contract is like a marriage and the honeymoon is often over when the clients' daydreams of what you could accomplish are brought to reality. If the client is disappointed for any reason, the contract complicates the problem of getting rid of you. The worst situation is when the client is unhappy but paying you to stick around. Who needs it? It's disagreeable to work that way and it also hurts your reputation.

On the other side of this argument, what if the job eats more of your time than you estimated? What if you find the client is into unethical or illegal dealings? With a contract you may be stuck with an unpleasant, unprofitable, or dangerous situation.

Bermont asks his clients for a letter of intent stating the kind of work required and the fees to be paid. Included in the letter is a thirty-day bilateral severance clause. Asking for a letter like this instead of a contract makes it easier for the client and it can be as legally binding as a full-on contract.

## How Much To Charge

There is not an unlimited amount of working hours to be spent on consulting. Reasonably you must expect time off for vacations, holidays, and the flu. A viable working year might appear as:

365 days minus weekends = 261
261 minus approximately 40 days
(holidays, illness, vacation) = 220 days

Multiplying 220 days by eight hours totals 1,760—the number of hours you can reasonably expect to be available to consult.

Even when your business is fully developed you won't be able to bill out every working minute. Administrative problems, errands, collections, prospecting and a host of other trifles will reduce your net billable time to 50 or 60% of your available working hours. Even 60% gives you only 1,056 billed hours a year and this assumes great efficiency and lined up clients.

You will have overhead expenses. It isn't unreasonable to assume at least $800 a month expense for a small office, telephone, answering service, lights, supplies and gasoline. This totals $9,600 a year.

How much do you need? $30,000 a year minimum? Add this to your yearly overheads. This equals $39,600, for the sake of our example. Divided by the maximum reasonable billable hours, 1,056, you get $37.50 an hour. If you know what you are doing or can learn quickly you should have no trouble getting twice that.

I guess everyone has heard the story of the giant mainframe computer that broke down and seemed unrepairable. The distraught owners finally called in a maintenance consultant who was said to be the best in the business. The consultant looked the machine over for a few seconds and gave it a kick in the I/O port.

The machine hummed to life and worked perfectly.

The consultant presented a bill for $5,000. "What!" the owners exclaimed simulataneously, "Five grand for five seconds of work?" "Nope," said the consultant, "the work was only five cents. The other $4,999.95 was for knowing where to do the work."

Hubert Bermont says your fee will never be questioned if you have come to the client recommended by another of your clients. If, however, you talk to a client without the benefit of a third party introduction, your fee will inevitably be suspect. Typically a client like this wants you to "Show me how you work." You may spend a number of hours for free.

The prime rule of fees is to set a reasonable fee and *never lower it for even a trial period.* When a prospective client questions your fee he is really questioning your ability. If you lower your fee you are admitting to your client and yourself that your quoted fees and reputed ability are bogus.

By questioning your fees the client is really only asking to be assured you can help him. Don't tell a potential client your fee over the phone. Wait until the first exploratory visit, and feel out whether you think you will be able to work together. If you think a productive working relationship is possible then bring up the subject of fees before the end of the meeting.

Avoid contingency arrangements and deals where the client pays you only if he is happy with the result of your work. A typical deal is made where the consultant says, "I can improve your profitability 100% and if I do I want 10% of the improvement." Clients love deals like this. The problem is there are too many short-term ways to increase sales and profitability that will eventually bring the business to ruin. Cut the R&D budget, fire the QA department, and promise anything for a sale. This list of quick cures is long and usually suicidal. Can you think of quick ways to increase productivity of the EDP function that carry a hidden bomb? I can think of ten right off the cuff and you are probably thinking of ten different ones.

The contingency arrangement often works to the client's disadvantage and so will eventually hurt you too.

Collecting money is another matter. If you feel embarrassed about collecting your fee from an overdue client you should get over the feeling. If you have the slightest hesitation about getting the money owed to you, you won't collect much of it. Many clients are psychic when it comes to whom they have to pay and whom they don't. It's a part of the RLC factor which is thoroughly discussed in Volume II.

Send your bill right after performing your service. If you expect your bills to be paid immediately, after 30 days, or on the first of the month following billing, you should call if the money is late. Be polite but firm. Don't be belligerent or insulting. Follow the advice given in assertiveness training books: Be firm but unrelenting. If you don't get a promised check within 3-4 days, call back. Be firm and polite every time you call no matter how many times promises are broken. Repeated requests without threats or nastiness will get money out of the hardest stone.

The following are descriptions of some different kinds of successful consulting businesses:

## COMMUNICATIONS TECHNOLOGY

Joan Strassman, 29, owns COMMUNICATIONS TECHNOLOGY, a Denver based consulting firm specializing in marketing and communications. She started her business five years ago.

"It was the right time for me to start my business. I had no children, few responsibilities and some money I saved from my last job. I was working for a small agency and we parted on good terms. I didn't pirate any accounts so there were no burnt bridges.

A business like mine is fortunate in that it has a small overhead. My major investment was an electric typewriter which IBM financed for me. I put down a deposit for a phone, bought a good file cabinet and rented a corner of an office.

When I opened I sent brochures to *everyone* I knew. I think people remember you even though they may not call right away. I sent a newsletter to people I thought might be prospective clients.

It was slow at first, but the pace has picked up steadily this last year. The first six months I was worried, but after the first year I knew things were going to work out all right.

Any business is 99.99% selling no matter what field you are in. If you can't sell, you won't stay in business—it's as simple as that."

## STRATEGIC INCORPORATED

STRATEGIC INCORPORATED, located at 4320 Stevens Creek Road, Suite 215, San Jose, CA 95129, 408-243-8121, is a company whose produce is research. They work on a customer basis or through a series of reports based on research done for some of their clients. Their clients include an impressive array of companies such as ATLANTIC RICHFIELD, HEWLETT PACKARD, IBM, RCA CABLE, SPERRY UNIVAC, SONY, TI, and WANG LABS.

Here is an example of the research SI does. The announcement in April, 1981 of AT&T's videotex standard and the May, 1981 ruling permitting direct satellite-to-home transmission created a hugh new market for information services.

SI has published a series of studies sorting out the opportunities existing in this newly created market. The papers are entitled *Local Area Network Markets and Opportunities, Electronic Publishing, Home Fax and Other Peripherals for the Mass Information Market.*

The prices for these reports run between $1,200-$1,500. But they offer a volume deal: 12 reports for the bargain price of only $9,500! If you want to order a few reports or just find out more about what they do, sent for their catalog or send a check.

## INTERNATIONAL RESOURCE AND DEVELOPMENT

INTERNATIONAL RESOURCE AND DEVELOPMENT, 30 High Street, Norwalk, CT 06851, 203-866-6914, also specializes in high-priced, high-quality market studies. They offer studies of portable terminals, computer peripherals and consumer electronics all priced in the thousand dollar range.

They do something which is extremely clever. They publish "Directional Intelligence Reports" on the strategic directions of major companies in the computer/electronics business. These reports cover 45 of the aggressive corporate trendsetters in the computer and electronics industry. They are priced fairly low: $145.00 each. Why is this wise?

If you are investing a lot of time or money in a high technology startup, one of the biggest fears is that you will invent the wheel in parallel with a big corporation and they will introduce it to the world a month before you are ready to present yours. A classic example of this is what happened with the daisy wheel printer business. The R&D effort to develop a daisy wheel printer is long and expensive. One small company worked on it for four years and introduced it a month after a huge company had amazed the world with theirs.

How do you minimize the risk? Do a detailed investigation on the strategic and tactical directions of the major electronic technology companies. Which would be cheaper: thoroughly researching each of 45 companies or spending five grand for summaries of this same investigation? How much are you willing to spend for insurance on your electronics technology startup? Write for IRD's literature. You will find it inspiring.

### FROST AND SULLIVAN

FROST AND SULLIVAN, 106 Fulton Street, New York, NY 10038, 212-233-1080, is an international market research company. It has been around for over twenty years providing market research reports, seminars, conferences and Wall Street research that analyze and forecast the market for industry segments in the United States, Europe, the Mid-East and Latin America.

The following newsletter, *The Computer Consultant,* is so relevant and filled with practical ideas I decided to include it in its entirety. If you are thinking seriously about being a consultant, this newsletter will be a source of advice and communication with others who follow the same line of work.

THE **COMPUTER CONSULTANT**

*Vol 2 No 8*

*An information resource for: consultants • contractors • software authors • systems houses.*
*Published by Battery Lane Information Services. ISSN 0196-4445. Editor: Eric Balkan.*

*THIS MONTH:*



## FROM THE EDITOR

"Software Wanted: How and Where to Sell Your Program" is a collection of material appearing in past issues of CC: a survey of 75 software marketers plus relevant articles. It's available to CC subscribers for $15.

The consultant directory is still on the way; expect it next month. Copies to subscribers are $5. We're now taking listings ($23) for the next issue, due out in April (?).

While the new subscription price for CC is $48, we're holding the line on renewals: $29 if you extend your subscription now.

Output magazine, which recently folded, was directed towards managers who use DP output. Are these people who hire consultants or contract programmers? We initiated a survey to find out. Based on the first few returns (note: this is not statistically significant), we can report that almost none had hired a consultant or contractor but would be interested in doing so. The reasons most often given for wanting to hire a consultant were to get specialized expertise and objective opinions. For hiring a contractor, the motive given was to avoid long-term commitments.

Do you offer services of interest to CC subscribers? CC is starting a new classified section: 25¢ a word. Software Wanted and Consultant Wanted listings will remain free.

CC is still looking for contributions from readers. We'll extend your subscription a year for any article published. We can also use short items, tips, news, etc. of interest to readers.

## CONSULTANT PROFILES

by Phillip Good

II George W Gebhardt

"I plan on spending a day and a half on the phone each week making sales calls, that is if I want to work the other three and a half days," says George Gebhardt, head of Management Consultants, P.A., Columbia MD (301/465-5039).

George has been the head of his own operation for over ten years. He didn't plan on being a consultant exactly, things sort of worked out that way. "I was going through a messy divorce and one day I found myself unemployed for the good of the firm. I bounced around from bed to bed for awhile, till my current girlfriend asked me what I wanted to be. "A consultant," I told her wanting to get into something else. "O.K." she replied, "No more sex until you become a consultant."

"The next day, I got on the telephone and got a client, and my girlfriend. I've never stopped since and I've no intention of working full time for anyone else again. But being a consultant means I've got to be a salesman 50% of my time.

"You can't play at being a consultant. You've got to sell yourself all the time. Whenever I've got a spare moment, I go through my leads and make a telephone call. I do that even when I'm on the road. And I ask to speak to the president of the firm, not some techie.

"Even if someone calls me, I find out if he's the boss. You've got to speak with the decision maker. They sign the checks, and they understand that hiring a consultant whatever his price, will save their firm money.

"I end the telephone conversation by making an appointment to go to the decision maker's office. There I show him samples of my work and my client list, and then talk to him about what I can do for his firm. I'd say that 3 out of every 20 calls I make result in work for me."

George's leads come from widely available books and government publications. He has profited from lists supplied by the county and state governments for manufacturers and high-tech firms.

George uses direct mail as well as the telephone. When he does, he goes first class. His résumé and client list are typeset and printed on his letterhead. And he writes to the president of each firm.

He stays in contact with the management advisory services in his area. "They may refer smaller clients to me, or they may take advantage of my expertise in training and documentation. It pays to stay in touch."

Naturally, George has been offered a number of permanent jobs along the way. Has this been a temptation?

"The big advantage of being a consultant is that once they've hired you they listen. When I go back to a client, I can see the results of my previous efforts. This is something I never could have accomplished as an employee."

## CONSULTANTS' CONVENTION

American Society of Professional Consultants meets Nov 8-11 in Houston Texas to bring "basic 'how-to' pointers to the many consultants around the country who are struggling to build a successful practice." Speakers will include: Howard Shenson, Hubert Bermont, Viola Finefrock. For more information, contact Mary Bass, ASPC, 713 D St SE, Washington DC 20003.

## NEWSLETTER/DIRECTORY

Newsletter for design firms: Design Compudata Exchange. Will be including: list of computer consultants who work in design firms, list of design software available, software swap section, hardware and software reviews, case studies. Practice Management Associates Ltd, 45 Van Brunt Ave, Dedham, MA 02026; 617/326-4103.

## SOFTWARE WANTED

Packages for the IBM System 3 Model 10 needed: Payroll, A/R, A/P, GL, Inventory Control. Also interested in any other software for the S/3. Anand P Agarwal, A & A Management Inc, 129 Juneberry Ct, San Jose, CA 95136; 408/629-1862.

## FARM COMPUTING

by Alan Radding

The speed at which small farmers are turning to microcomputers is creating a great opportunity for computer consultants who can develop appropriate software for commercial sale. A computer programmer who understands farming (or can learn about it) will find an eager and substantial market waiting for his software products.

Where farmers currently need the help most is with bookeeping and accounting programs. Richard Uhrenholdt, a Nebraska farmer, uses a TRS-80 Model II, but he has had to adopt commercially available software which doesn't really fit his needs. So too, Bibb Inc., a Tunica, Louisiana farm has also reluctantly conformed to Radio Shack accounting software.

The problem is that most standard accounting software does not fit the way farmers operate. Many small farmers use single entry bookeeping while most commercially available programs are for double entry record keeping. Accounting programs designed specifically for farmers would be welcomed, says Uhrenholdt, who called around to most commercial software suppliers seeking out a program he could use.

Terminology is another problem with the general accounting programs. Farmers tend to think in terms of bushels and acres, crops and seasons and heads of cattle, rather than in terms of liabilities and assets, credit and debits and inventory. Certainly farmers can adopt commercial bookeeping programs and terminology, but given their choice, they will spend their money to buy programs written specifically with farming in mind. The problems for which farmers will use a computer may be no different, essentially, from the problems of any other business, but "they perceive of themselves as different," says Robert Jolly, an extension economist at the University of Iowa. In truth, farmers do follow rather unique accounting procedures and have highly varied operations.

Even small farms are complex businesses. In fact, the problem with some commercial software is that it isn't complex enough, notes Wesley Bailey Jr., another Tunica LA farmer who uses on Ohio Scientific microcomputer which he programs himself. Each field is a small production facility, each crop is a different product line with its own production schedule, and every farm must account for a wide variety of equipment and supplies. On a dairy farm, for instance, the farmer would want to keep detailed computer records that could track production on a day to day basis by cow, by herd, or by any number of classifications and deviations.

Only slowly are farmers beginning to put the computers to work on their actual farm operations. Much of the slowness can be attrubuted to the lack of available software. Bailey has written his own programs to chart crop rotation, direct his spray rigs, and to keep field records. Other farmers are using their computers to calculate the best feed mixture to give their livestock at the best price or to calculate the proper fertilizer or irrigation schedules. Commodity pricing, market projections, budgeting, financial planning, and more should be available on programs for farmers, but for the most part the software is generally unavailable except to the farmer who will write his own programs.

Financial modeling programs, cash flow programs, and financial analysis programs designed specifically for farmers are what is needed most, say staffers at the Mississippi State University farm extension service. After that, they believe that there will be a need for sophisticated financial management programs and capital investment programs, again geared specifically to the world of agri-business.

The large university agricultural extension services are attempting to fill this software gap. The University of Nebraska has organized AGNET, an agricultural computer network with 150 farmers participating in seven states. AGNET allows farmers to input their own data and run a variety of operational programs to help determine feed, irrigation, budgeting, commodity forecasting and other such operations and marketing tasks.

"When I started there weren't any programs available at all," says Gerald Schmidt, a Jansen, Neb. farmer who participates in AGNET and writes some of his own programs for his Radio Shack computer. Because he could't find an appropriate general ledger program, Schmidt wrote his own which records physical transactions as well as financial transactions -- "sort of combining inventory control and accounting," he explains. He probably would have bought one if it had been available.

Besides the university extension services, a variety of agri-businesses are beginning to supply farmers with programs that correspond with the products that they sell. Fertilizer firms are giving farmers programs to help calculate the proper fertilizer mix, for instance. So are feed and seed suppliers. Many of these programs are designed to run on programmable calculators, but as more and more farmers add micro-computers, programs must be correspondingly upgraded.

Computer consultants who think they can write programs for farmers will find a large and untapped market waiting and growing. To begin:

Contact the local or county extension office and see what is happening. "What we are seeing is a grass roots cry for help," says John Nevins, a leading researcher in computer applications for agriculture. Farmers purchased microcomputers and then found that they didn't have the programs to use with them. As a result, they have turned first to the local extension services.

Check out the university agricultural departments and see what they are offering. A number of universities are attempting to build a library of agricultural programs, such as Mississippi State, University of Nebraska, Iowa State.

Touch base with the farmer organizations in your areas. For instance, the New England and New York apple growers association has only recently become aware of the increasing number of members who are buying small computers. The associations may have to begin to provide some level of computer support.

Keep in touch with the computer stores in farming areas. The farmers interviewed by Computer Consultant all purchased their machines through retail stores and turned to the stores again when they started looking for software.

Be aware of the increasing number of farming conferences, meetings, and conventions focused on computers. The agricultural trade press and the university extension services can probably keep you up to date on the meetings.

For the computer consultant with a green thumb who can write small and medium size farmer oriented agricultural programs for personal computers, there is an opportunity to reap a harvest of software sales.

## COST OF A SALE

Ever figure out what it actually costs you to make a sale? McGraw-Hill's Laboratory of Advertising Performance (LAP) surveyed different industries last March and came up with (for someone selling business services): $143 per sales call and 5 calls for each completed sale, giving $800 average cost to close a sale. Obviously, if you can get a new client without preparing lengthy proposals or making repeated trips to the client's site, your cost will be much less. But the consultant who has qualified his prospects before visiting them starts out way ahead of the game. Ditto for those who have packaged their expertise into a seminar, book, software product, etc. -- something that doesn't need to be done over constantly.

## MANAGEMENT INFORMATION

Small business computer and office automation product reports are a specialty of Management Information Corporation, 140 Barclay Center, Cherry Hill, NJ 08034; 609/428-1020. A free catalog describes their line of periodicals, reports and special services.

## COMPUTER PUBLICATIONS REVIEWED

Computer Books Review is a new publication covering computer publications (including periodicals) world-wide. Numerous pithy reviews. "Highcroft", Gunhouse Lane, Bowbridge, Stroud, Glos. GL5 2DB, Great Britain. $44/yr.

## HOW THE NEW TAX LAWS AFFECT COMPUTER OWNERS

*(Courtesy of Financial Systems Report)*

by Vernon K. Jacobs

Should you buy your first (or next) computer this year or next? Should you lease or buy? Are there any other areas of the new tax law that might affect those who own or are thinking of owning a computer? There are at least 109 specific provisions in the "Economic Recovery Tax Act of 1981", and it will be months (perhaps years) before the impact of all the provisions is evaluated. It's almost certain that we will have another tax bill early next year to correct the inevitable errors and flaws in this hastily drafted and complex set of tax law changes. Nonetheless, here is a brief summary of some of the provisions of the new tax law that should be of specific concern to computer owners and lessees.

### Full Write Off For Small Computers

One of the provisions of the new tax law will permit businesses to deduct the first $5,000 of business equipment acquired in 1982 and 1983, the first $7000 of purchases in 1984 and 1985 and the first $10,000 of purchases after 1985. This means that many small desktop computers could be fully expensed in the year acquired. No investment credit would be allowed on such purchases but the immediate write off would usually be better. If the cost of the computer exceeds the deductible amount, the excess would be eligible for the new depreciation method. This full write off provision is not available for investors. It's only available if the equipment is to be used in a trade or business.

### New Depreciation Rules

If you purchased a computer in 1981, the 100% write off won't be available, but the new method of depreciation (called the "Asset Cost Recovery System") does apply to 1981 equipment purchased. Under the new method, computers will be depreciated over a five year period using specified rates for each of the five years. (If computers can be classed as research and development equipment they can be depreciated over a three year period.) For five year class equipment purchased in 1981 through 1984, the first year's depreciation will be 15% of the cost. The second year's depreciation will be 22% of the cost and the rate will be 21% in each of the next three years. The entire cost will be deducted over the five year period.

By contrast, the prior law permitted a computer owner to write off up to 40% of the cost in the first year if the equipment was placed in service before July first. An additional 24% of the cost would be written off in the second year, 14.4% in the third year and 10.8% in the fourth and fifth years. This assumes a five year life, which has been typical for computer owners. Consequently, owners of larger and more expensive computers won't fare as well under the new law as under the old, but owners of desktop size computers will be better off -- assuming no other equipment purchases in the year.

If the tax deductions won't be available because of other tax deductions or business losses, computer owners will be able to elect to write the equipment off over a 12 year or a 25 year period using a straight line method of depreciation. However, the election to use the slower method is mandatory for each years purchases -- meaning you can't change your mind after a year or two. The main reason to use a slow method of depreciation is to avoid the possible loss of deductions during a prolonged start up period due to the existing time limit on offsetting losses of one year against profits of future years. The new law provides substantial relief in this area -- which may make the slower depreciation method unnecessary. Previously, business losses could be carried forward for seven years, but the new law extends this to 15 years -- retroactive to 1976.

### Changes in Rules for Investment Tax Credit

Computer buyers will realize a small increase in the amount of available investment tax credit for purchasing a computer. Under current law, equipment with a five year useful life is eligible for 2/3 of the full 10% tax credit. Equipment with a five year life will now be qualified to claim the full 10% tax credit for equipment that is depreciated over a period of five or more years. If the equipment will have a three year useful life (autos, trucks and certain R & D equipment), the tax credit will be 6% of the cost of the property rather than 10%. These new tax credit rules take effect in 1981 -- including property that was acquired before the law was passed. (It was signed on 8/13/81.)

There was no specific change relative to claiming the tax credit on the full cost of a system that included both hardware and software. However, if the tax credit is claimed on the software because the price is combined with the hardware, then the buyer must depreciate the software with the hardware. If the software is purchased separately, and is licensed rather than purchased, then the full software cost can be deducted in the year of acquisition.

New Rules for Defining Leases

Taxpayers and the IRS have been arguing for years about whether a lease is really a lease or just a method of financing an equipment purchase. The new tax law attempts to simplify some of the complex rules that have cropped up in this area of controversy. Basically, the parties must clearly agree that the transaction is a lease and the lessee must not acquire ownership of the property at any time during the lease. The lessor must be a corporation and must have an investment of at least 10% that is "at risk" in the investment. Generally, the property must be new property.

Vernon K. Jacobs is a CPA who practices as a tax consultant in the Kansas City area. He is the author of Tax Angles, a nationally circulated tax planning newsletter, and he is the author/publisher of the Financial Systems Report -- a monthly report about computer systems for financial specialists. In his spare time he develops tax oriented computer programs for desktop computers. A copy of either of his newsletters can be ordered from Research Press, Inc., PO Box 8137-P, Prairie Village, KS 66208. Send $3 for each sample to cover postage and handling costs.

## STATISTICS & FINANCIAL PROGRAMS

Need a quickie program to make a statistical or financial calculation? Simple BASIC Programs for Business Applications is the title of a new book that very well might have the program you need. Over 50 short programs are included: probability, continuous distributions, regression, analysis of time series, loan repayment amortization schedules, sinking fund payments, etc. Each listing is accompanied by the mathematical formula, input requirements, actual program output with explanation, references, and sample program. Available from Prentice-Hall, Englewood Cliffs, NJ 07632. $15.95 (hardbound), $8.95 (paper).

## BUSINESS ADVICE

The Business Owner is a monthly journal offering advice primarily on the financial aspects of running a business. A recent issue (June) discussed estate planning, insurance, bad debt write-offs and other such topics. $48/yr from 383 S Broadway, Hicksvill NY 11801. 12-month full refund guarantee.

## PERFORMANCE AND PRODUCTIVITY

How to Measure Programmer Productivity is the title of a new book by CC subscriber Garish Parikh, a leading authority on software productivity techniques. Topics include: measuring productivity, how it's affected by goals, future directions, etc. Available from Shetal Enterprises, Dept CC, 1787 B West Touhy, Chicago, IL 60626.

The EDP Performance Review, published since 1973, is a monthly report covering new tools, techniques, literature abstracts, etc. on the subject of performance improvements in DP. Publisher is Applied Computer Research, PO Box 9280, Phoenix, AZ 85068. ACR also puts out a monthly newsletter previously reviewed in CC: System Development, which discusses programmer productivity issues. Editor of both publications is Phillip C. Howard.

## PROGRAMMER'S TOOL BAG

by Phillip I Good

V - DBMS: Micro B+, dBASE II

A good language or report generator can reduce program development costs. Ron Parker, an independent consultant in Portland, OR, told us bluntly: "Without the availability of dBase II, I would not have bid on the job."

Not all software is as good as dBase II, in fact, some does not even meet advertised specifications. In other instances, the costs of installation and training far exceed any benefits.

Make your own evaluation

A favorable review is just the first step in your evaluation. A review can guide you to your best choices. The rest is up to you. Take your own look at the manual(s). Are they comprehensive and easy to follow? Are demonstration files included?

In evaluating data base management systems, I look for:

record and file limitations -- number of records, number of characters per record,

number of fields, number of fields per record, number of files accessible simultaneously
. RAM, disk and processor limitations
. RAM requirements at execution
. flexibility of search criteria, number of keys
. speed of execution of searches, sorts, and merges
. language interfaces, number, ease of use, quality of documentation
. data entry -- full screen is a definite plus
. command structure -- command files or subroutine calls?
. report generator -- is it flexible?

There may not be a "best" solution. Trade-offs in flexibility, space, speed and cost are inevitable.

As the final steps in your evaluation, call the vendor "hot-line"... is help readily available? Ask the vendor for the names and telephone numbers of existing users. Call them and ask for their reactions.

For speed of execution

Micro B+, $260 from FairCom, 2606 Johnson Drive, Columbia, MO, 65201 is a true DBMS, consisting of a set of integrated subroutines designed to be accessed from your applications programs. It comes in two versions -- CBasic or MBasic. CP/M and 64K of RAM are also required for its use. It has few limitations on records and files other than those imposed by the CP/M file structure.

RAM requirements at execution include a low 7K or less for Micro B+ itself. You also will need room for the Basic interpreter and for file buffers. The number and size of buffers is optional, allowing you to "fine-tune" the system.

There are two main approaches to locating records in a database according to key values: hash coding and index tree search. Hash coding is very, very fast. However, it doesn't support sequential processing, nor does it support multiple keys. Micro B+ supports sequential processing -- thus minimizing the need to perform time consuming sorts -- and up to ten simultaneous search criteria. Time trials run by Tab Products put Micro B+ head and shoulders above the far more expensive MDBS in speed of execution.

Data-entry and report generation are strictly up to you in your choice of CBasic, MBasic or Fortran-80. The assembly language routines needed to interface any or all of the three are supplied with the system. The subroutine calls are straightforward. The documentation is excellent.

Bill Fairman, Micro B+'s designer, runs a strictly one-man operation. He may not be there when you telephone; but he will get back to you. Users rate vendor support at 95%.

A word of warning

Regardless of which data base management system you use, inserting 100 or so records in a 10,000 item file can be an all-night run on a CP/M based system--even when a hard-disk drive is employed!!

The problem lies with CP/M's approach to blocking and file allocation. CP/M was designed in 1976 for use with floppy disks. Digital Research never got around to developing a "hard-disk" version. Good news, bad news: I have been contacted by four manufacturers, each making extravagant claims for his new, improved CP/M compatible operating system. There was no supporting data.

Strong support from the vendor

dBase II is $700 from Ashton-Tate, 3600 Wilshire Blvd., Suite 1510, Los Angeles, CA 90010; 213/666-4409. Though dBase II is sold as a relational data base management package it's actually a complete program development system. Unlike the program development systems we've reviewed in past columns, this one comes highly recommended. Ron Parker claims he put together a file conversion system in two hours. Three other reviewers have assigned it excellent ratings.

Changes to files are trivial -- programmers can add, enlarge or compress fields and restructure files with minimal effort. Programs can be run interactively during debugging, but files of commands may be used also.

Provision of a special command language has its pros and cons. On the one hand, it is just one more language you'll have to master. On the other, it is block structured. If. . . Else. . . ENDif and DO WHILE. . . ENDdo structures lend themselves to documentation. The language you'll use in constructing the data base is the same language the end user will use for making ad hoc queries. (This seems to be an attribute of all "true" relational DBMS's.)

dBase II is written in assembler, and uses B+ tree indexing. Limitations on file size are identical with those of Micro B+, namely those of CP/M itself. Accessing a record in the maximum size file (65,000 records) will take only two seconds. (Again, adding a record to that size file can take all night.)

There are drawbacks. Construction of reports can be time-consuming. Computations are best done using CBasic. Direct interface with other application programs is impossible, though you can exchange information through files.

The documentation consists of three parts: a verbose and confusing end-user guide allegedly written by a naive end-user; a comprehensive reference manual for fine-tuning; and, the Rosetta Stone, Appendix A which takes you step-by-step through an example supplied on disk.

Ron Parker says he only thought of bidding on a job after he came across the dBase manual. "I'd have said two men, six months, otherwise."

All reviewers agree that the use of dBase can speed up program development 5 to 10 fold. Here is the way I score it:

Documentation
    Completeness 95
    Ease of use 85
Price/Performance 90
Vendor Support 100
Error Recovery 95

If you are interested, but still lack faith, Ashton-Tate has a unique money-back offer. Two disks are provided. One is unwrapped; it is a demonstration disk which permits only 15 records in a file. You can play with the demonstration disk for 30 days, then return the package for a full refund if the seal is unbroken on the other disk.

What next?
This is the last of the originally planned articles in the series on programmers' tools. If you would like to see this feature continued, let us know. If you would like to see a particular software package reviewed, let us know about that too.

## TECHNOLOGY ASSESSMENT

The Mini-Micro Computer Intelligence Report is a new $288/yr newsletter dealing with technology assessment and market analysis. 221 Columbus Ave, Boston, MA 02116.

## CANTON ON CONSULTING

by Alan Canton

Q: When interviewing for a contract I know what to wear. But how should one dress during the course of the assignment -- over-dress or under-dress?

A: I have been asked this question many times and, while I am not an authority on style or color, I think I have found the right approach in dressing.

You really have two choices. You can go the "power outfit" (the pin stripe three piece suit) -- or you can take the casual approach by wearing an open shirt and jeans. My feeling is that you should be comfortable. You cannot create good software or give good advice if you are not at ease in what you wear.

Many consultants want to project a super successful image and thus they wear their best suits to work, even though they hate 3-piecers. Others don't give a damn and wear jeans and a t-shirt. It is my feeling that most of the employed staff will resent a new contract programmer coming on board. They know we make good bucks. By wearing a "power" suit, we are just rubbing this in their faces. We are saying, "Look at me... I'm really successful and you are just a working stiff".

On the other hand, if it is a casual shop and you really wear the old grub outfit you are saying, "Look, I'm so successful in business I can get jobs and look like a slob at the same time." So what should you wear? My answer is (you're gonna hate this) the prep-look. It really is a functional uniform. It is dressy without being snobbish and it is casual without being grubby. I hate to wear neckties. I don't like to wear vests. I have found over the years that by wearing a nice pair of cords, a button down shirt and a blue blazer (sans tie) I can be comfortable and not project a snob or grub image. I keep a tie in my briefcase so that if a user-meeting comes up, I can look the part. But for sitting around and coding in the customer's shop, I have found the prep-look to be right for me. Most of my clients are big outfits and they have staff that run the gamut from $500 suits to the jean and t-shirt guru. I have found that both groups seem comfortable in working with me when I simply wear my cords, button-down, and blazer.

Q: Some of my consultant friends have incorporated their business. Should I do the same?

A: Don't listen to me or anyone else about this subject. Talk to your lawyer and/or your accountant. I could go for pages on this topic but it has been covered very well by an excellent book called Inc. Yourself by Judith H. McQuown, Macmillan Publishing, ISBN 0-02-583720-6. This book gives all the pro and con arguments for incorporating your business, and it is must reading for anyone thinking about going this route. I incorporated my business about six months ago, but I was forced to since one of my really big clients refused to do business with me until I was eligible for workmans compensation insurance. As an employee of my own corporation, I can now get that insurance. However, in California, a self-employed person can not get coverage. Stupid, I know, but that's the law. Anyway, I am working on an article for CC about the pains of incorporation so look for it in a later issue.

Q: Do I need fancy forms to bill my clients?

A: I always ask my consultant friends how they bill and what type of forms they use. Some have really nice pre-printed invoice forms and some just send a letter. Those who have spent the money to have the forms printed up swear that they get better results from the more professional form. I have tried both and I have not seen much of a difference in the response rate. I simply use a letter-head bill these days.

****** Readers: If I offend you or if you disagree with one of my answers, let the editor know. I am not perfect and I do sometimes screw up. My motto is "Often wrong, but never in doubt!" Let me hear from you. Dear Abby I'm not, but I'll try to answer you or respond to your gripes.

## SOFTWARE PUBLISHERS/MARKETERS DIRECTORY

This continues the series started last December. It consists of information about organizations that will buy software from independent programmers and market it through their own distribution network. CC will attempt to list only reputable firms, but readers should do their own checking before signing any contracts. Caveat venditor.

This section will be continued in upcoming issues. Periodically, the information will be gathered together in a special supplement available to subscribers.

ASCII (Attn: Lawrence Teich; PO Box 516, Valley Stream, NY 11582; 516/791-4890)
- in business 1 year
- average monthly gross $700.
- sell programs both retail and wholesale
- outright purchase from programmer only
- no contract required
- requires 2 weeks for evaluation, on average
- company retains copyright
- documentation required can vary
- provides programming assistance
- Looking for: utility, game or practical application for the TRS-80 Model I/III 16K (Level II).

A-T ENTERPRISES (Attn: Bob Maxwell, 221 N. Lois, La Habra, CA 90631; 213/947-2762)
- in business 5 years
- average monthly gross is $20K-$25K
- sells programs both retail and wholesale
- purchases program copies individually
- no contract required
- company requires copyright
- cash on delivery
- partial documentation O.K.
- will provide programming assistance
- looking for: real estate and property management related, including investment analysis
- "We market real estate, investment analysis and property management software packages on a national basis"

BRILEY SOFTWARE (Evaluation Section, PO Box 2913, Livermore, CA 94550; 415/455-9139)
- time in business: 2 1/2 yrs
- not currently profitable
- programs sold both retail and wholesale
- royalty: 25-30% of gross, depending on length of contract
- contract signed after initial evaluation
- evaluation time, on average, 6 wks
- company holds copyright
- pays annually, sometimes more frequently. Pays interest on royalties account
- complete documentation required. Author must also provide back-up consultation services.
- programming assistance can be provided, but will affect royalty rate
- looking for: professional and special purpose business applications. Machines: Pet/CBM (must run on all ROMs), TRS-80 Mod I Lev II, Atari 800. Must be able to use more than one of these printers: Anadex, CBM, Epson, Centronics (i.e., no special graphics symbols, auto-formatting, or "tricks")
- SASE must accompany sumittal if materials are desired to be returned. Recommend sending written abstract first.

COMPAL, INC. (Attn: Mitchel Kadish, 6300 Variel Ave, Woodland Hills, CA 91367; 213/992-4425)
- in business 6 yrs
- sells programs retail only
- financial arrangement is negotiable
- requires signed contract after acceptance
- takes 30 days for evaluation, on average
- copyright arrangement negotiable
- requires complete documentation
- looking for: business applications, engineering, statistical, word processing.
- "Compal is interested only in serious business and scientific applications of microcomputers. Programs must be full function for the application."

ALLEN GELDER SOFTWARE ( Box 11721, Main Post Office, San Francisco, CA 94101)
- in business 3 yrs
- sells programs both retail and wholesale
- royalty basis - varies
- requires signed contract after acceptance
- takes 30 days for evaluation, on average
- copyright retained by programmer
- requires complete package from programmer, except for source code
- looking for (1)cross-assemblers running on TRS-80 Mod I/III; (2)BASIC/machine language program development aids for TRS-80 I/III.

Reprinted by permission of Eric Balkan, publisher, The Computer Consultant.

## Directories of Consultants

Association of Consulting Management Engineers, Inc.
230 Park Avenue
New York,NY 10017
212/697-9693

Independent Computer Consultant's Association
P.O. Box 27412
St. Louis, MO 63141
314/567-9708

Institute of Management Consultants
19 West 44th Street
New York, NY 10036
212/921-2885

Association of Management Consultants
331 Madison Avenue
New York, NY 10017
212/490-3113

Directory of Management Consultants
Templeton Road
Fitzwilliam, NH 03447
603/585-2200

## Consultant's Publications

*Managing Your Accounting and Consulting Profession.* 2 inch handbook on administrative, nuts & bolts aspects from time-keeping and bookkeeping to partnership agreements and conpensation, fee setting, billing, filing systems, liability, insurance, etc. (Matthew Bender) 640 pp. Consultants News, Templeton Road, Fitzwilliam, NH 03447. $50.00.

*How to Become a Successful Consultant in Your Own Field.* A great book on consulting by Hubert Bermont. Bermont Books, 815 15th Street, N.W., Washington, DC 20005.

*The Professional Services Enterprise: Theory and Practice.* Categorizes professional employees, describes client buying psychology. Los Angeles Publishing Company. 211 pp. (out of print—supply may be gone) $10.50.

*Management Consulting—A Guide to the Profession.* First and only basic text on the business. (International Labor Office) $22.50.

*Management Consultants in Action.* Case histories of 3 dozen of author's consulting assignments. (Hawthorne) $8.95.

*Consultant's News.* The confidential newsletter of the consulting profession. Monthly. $56.00/Yr.

*The Computer Consultant Newsletter.* Battery Lane Information Services, Box 30214, Bethesda, MD 20814.

## Other Publications

*Consulting—Establishing & Maintaining an Independent Practice.* Stemms Information Systems & Indexes, P.O. Box 42576, Los Angeles, CA 90050.

*Directory of Management Consultants.* Consultants News, Templeton Road, Fitzwilliam, NH 03447.

*The Marketing of Professional Services.* McGraw Hill Book Company, New York, NY.

*How to Start, Operate and Promote a Consulting Business.* Dollar Power Financial Publications, 750 North Salina Street, Syracuse, NY 13208.

*The Howard L. Shenson Report.* Up-to-date strategic info on the business side of consulting. Also many other consultant's aids available. Howard L. Shenson Inc., 20121 Ventura Blvd., Suite 245, Woodland Hills, CA 91364, 213/703-1415.

*How to Become a Successful Consultant in Your Own Field.* Hubert Bermont Books, 815 15th Street, N.W., Washington, DC 20005.

## Chapter 10

# 21 STEPS TO SET UP YOUR BUSINESS

The following action steps fall into three categories. The first are commitment decisions you must make before starting out. The next sequence involves satisfying the legal requirements various government agencies have for your new business. The last group of items involves getting a place to work and setting up lines of communication. It may seem like a long list, but do them systematically and you'll be surprised at how quickly you have launched your new business!

1. Make your personal commitment decisions. This involves deciding whether to work full or part-time, whether to take in a partner, how much time you expect to spend with the business and when you expect to spend it.

How much of your savings or income are you willing to commit to the startup?

The most important question of all is whether your family will support you and your effort. Starting a new business can sometimes be a greater strain on your family than on you. If they understand and support your efforts, the project will have a much greater chance of success and your life will be easier. When you have a clear personal answer to these questions you are ready to start working.

2. Decide what your product or service will be and write a description of it. This step might seem silly at first, but if you sit down and write a single page of *exactly* what kind of product you plan to offer, your focus will become distinct. A written description of your intentions makes you think clearly about it and will also give your product its first definite form.

A technique used by some of the best mail-order entrepreneurs is to write an advertisement for the product before you develop it. This forces you to think about your product's market relevance.

3. Write your business plan. Refer to Chaper Eleven and follow the outlined steps closely. This business plan allows you to think clearly about the entire business function, not just about your product. Your product description is a part of the general business plan but necessarily takes the entire operation of your business into account.

4. Make a cash requirement projection and a budget. The form for this is given in Chapter Two. Projecting cash requirements forces you to project sales and enables you to see the cash requirements of the business in the startup phase. A budget is a natural corrolary to your cash needs projection. If you determine your needs for cash and decide when that cash will be spent you have automatically created a budget.

How many entrepreneurs have determined how much money they need to start their business, found the money and then blown it all in the first two months of operation?

A reasonable, well-thought-out budget serves as a pacesetter for portioning out your available funds. Don't leave home without one.

5. Decide on a name for your business. This name should sound professional, dignified and not too presumptuous. Most of all it should be vague enough to allow you to expand into different areas.

If you call your business BIG JIM'S DISC MAINTENANCE SERVICE it will be difficult to convince people they should pay you for software consulting. If you call your company DELTA TECHNICAL SERVICES or DELTA TECHNICAL LABORATORIES it may make your receptionist weary saying all those long words, but the name is scientific (Delta sounds scholarly), obviously oriented to high technology, and the word laboratory calls up the image of someone in a white lab coat who is a tireless, devoted scientist. All these images work in your favor.

Some names are restricted. You can't call yourself a foundation unless you have "Not-For-Profit" tax status. You will hopefully be a "For-Profit" outfit, so calling yourself a foundation is out of the question.

A short name is useful if you come up with one which covers your activities and meets the image requirements cited above. If you have a long name which can be shortened to an appropriate acronym, all the better. If the acronym sounds legitimate, scientific and believable then you have a winner. I have always thought INTEL is a fantastic name for a high technology company. It sounds like an abbreviation of the word "intelligence" so it meets and exceeds all the image criteria I have mentioned.

I recently started a profit center called OMEGA TECHNICAL LABORATORIES. To those who are familiar with the Greek alphabet this name means the ultimate or final technology. Also the shortened form, OMEGATECH, sounds like an institution for advanced learning. The name is non-specific so can be used as an umbrella for a great number of different activities. What does OMEGATECH do? It's a fancy machine shop.

There was a time during the seventies when crazy names were the fashion. It was considered very hip to let everyone know you were just playing a game in the world of business, and whimsical names were a sign of this disaffection.

But the eighties are more sober and serious. If you call your company INTERGALACTIC MEGALITHIC INDUSTRIES you will eventually wish it had a more neutral, dignified and mature sounding name. Eccentric names soon wear thin and need to be changed, so why not start out right?

Do not call your company your name followed by the word "Enterprises." This sounds like a company run by an egomaniac who promotes rock concerts and maybe sells contraband on the side.

You will notice my publishing company is called WILDFIRE PUBLISHING. This contradicts all the advice I am giving here. It would be better named TECHNICAL BOOK COMPANY, DELTA BOOKS or something more digified and neutral. I did it in a moment of egomania and would probably change it if it could be done over. The industry knows us by that name, books have that imprint and I have a lot of stationery. We all have an albatross of one kind or another to carry. When you name your company do what I say, not what I did.

6. Decide the legal form of your business. The following is a comparison of the three main forms of business organizations done by the Small Business Administration.

# WHAT FORM OF BUSINESS ORGANIZATION?

## SINGLE PROPRIETORSHIP

ADVANTAGES

1. Low start up costs
2. Greatest freedom from regulation
3. Owner in direct control
4. Minimal working capital requirements
5. Tax advantage to small owner
6. All profits to owner

DISADVANTAGES

1. Unlimited liability
2. Lack of continuity
3. Difficult to raise capital

## PARTNERSHIP

ADVANTAGES

1. Ease of formation
2. Low start up costs
3. Additional sources of venture capital
4. Broader management base
5. Possible tax advantage
6. Limited outside regulation

DISADVANTAGES

1. Unlimited liability
2. Lack of continuity
3. Divided authority
4. Difficulty in raising additional capital
5. Hard to find suitable partners

## CORPORATION

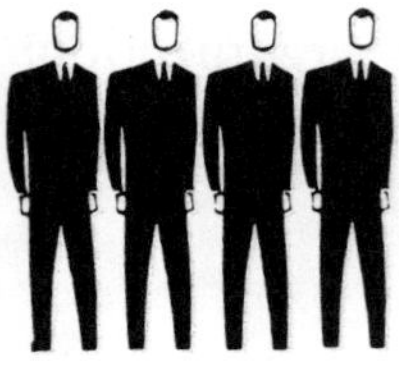

ADVANTAGES

1. Limited liability
2. Specialized management
3. Ownership is transferrable
4. Continuous existence
5. Legal entity
6. Possible tax advantages
7. Easier to raise capital

DISADVANTAGES

1. Closely regulated
2. Most expensive form to organize
3. Charter restrictions
4. Extensive record keeping necessary
5. Double taxation

What should you decide? If possible do it yourself and be the sole proprietor. If you take a partner, you must of course use the partnership structure.

Only when you start to make significant money is it time to think about forming a corporation. Forming a corporation when you start out is probably a poor choice. It costs about a thousand dollars unless you do it yourself. Do-it-yourself corporations are about as effective as chastity belts.

There are two main reasons to elect a corporate business form. The first is for tax purposes; the second is to limit your personal liability. The corporation is a legal person, created by you to hold assets which you create by loaning the corporation money, by outright purchase or shares in the enterprises, or by making and retaining profits.

The corporate entity is theoretically liable for its own debts and if it is unable to pay, the creditors have no personal legal handle on you. There are a few slight hitches in this plan. If you haven't followed proper form, such as taking notes at regularly scheduled Board of Directors' meetings, maintaining a minute book, etc., a creditor might call the corporation into default and "pierce the veil" of protection given to you by the corporation.

I don't know why such suggestive terminology is used to describe the inadequacy of corporation protection. In any case, this veil piercing is why do-it-yourself corporations are about as effective as chastity belts in protecting your interests.

The next point that makes corporate veils ineffectual is everyone who loans the corporation money will surely ask you to guarantee it personally.

The third item about the fallibility of corporate veils is they give no protection from being sued for personal negligence or malfeasance as an employee of the entity.

7. Choose an attorney. Word-of-mouth reference is the best possible way to select both your attorney and accountant. Talk to friends who are in business or people in your industry for a recommendation. Look for someone you trust to give you a reference.

You shouldn't necessarily go to the biggest firm in town or a super-specialist. You may not be able to afford the best attorney unless you need one who knows your business and he happens to be expensive.

The fee spread between the worst and best is between $70 and $300 an hour. Fees are set by the size of the firm and the nature of the clients. It's obvious that sophisticated clients who are paying

COMPARING LEGAL FORMS FOR A BUSINESS

| | HUMAN RESOURCES | | | INITIAL FUNDING | | |
|---|---|---|---|---|---|---|
| | Management Control | Personnel and Expertise | Continuity, Transferability | Organizational Requirements and Costs | Ability to Raise Capital | Liability for Losses/Debts |
| SOLE PROPRIETOR-SHIP | One owner in total control | Depends mainly on owner's skills; hard to obtain quality employees | Ends on death of owner; free to sell or transfer | Costs lowest; (filing fee if under name other than owner's) | Limited: all equity (funding) must come from proprieter; loans based on strengths of individual | Owner liable for all debts |
| PARTNERSHIP general or (limited) | Divided among two or more partners; decisions by majority or by pre-established agreement; (limited partner can not manage) | Depends mainly on partners' skills; hard to find suitable partners or employees | Ends on death of partner (unless agreement provides otherwise); transfer conditions vary with agreement | Costs low; General: agreement optional but recommended; (Limited: agreement stating liabilities and responsibilities of each partner required | Limited to resources of partners; loans based on strengths of partners | Partners liable for all debts (Limited partner has restricted liability and involvement, as per agreement) |
| CORPORATION | Corporation acts as one person, but board of directors (influenced by votes of share-holders) hold legal, formal control; working control by those who manage day-to-day | Broad-based; allows for flexible management; easier to secure quality personnel with broad expertise | Continues with overlapping management; most flexible in transfer of "interest" (e.g., ownership) from one shareholder to another | Costs highest; legal forms, documents, and fees required | Greatest equity potential: can sell new stock; loans based on corporate financial strength and expertise, thus larger borrowing base | Corporation liable for debts (i.e., shareholders are liable only for amount invested, but if personal guarantees were given they are personally liable for more) |

## COMPARING LEGAL FORMS FOR A BUSINESS — PAGE 2

| | GOVERNMENT REGULATION | REVENUE | | | OTHER* CONSIDERATIONS | FOR MY BUSINESS | |
|---|---|---|---|---|---|---|---|
| | | Taxes | Profits | Growth Potential | | Key Advantages | Key Disadvantages |
| SOLE PROPRIETORSHIP | Little; few records needed with minimum formal regulation (possibly a license, license fee and state tax) | Taxed as individual (through personal income tax) | All go to owner | Limited options: reinvest profits, obtain loan on credit of owner | | | |
| PARTNERSHIP | Limited; few records needed with minimum formal regulation; should have "articles of partnership" drawn up | Partners pay taxes as if in business as individuals (through personal income tax) | Divided among partners | Limited options: reinvest profits, obtain loans on credit of owners | | | |
| CORPORATION | Greatest; extensive record-keeping required; differs from state to state, but includes "articles of incorporation," by laws, initial tax and filing fees, and shareholders' meetings. | Corpo-ration as entity pays taxes, and share-holders pay taxes on dividends as income (couble taxation) | Retained in corpo-ration and share-holders receive dividends | More options: reinvest profits (at discretion of board of directors); sell additional shares; obtain loans on corporate credit | | | |

This area is often the most complex and important. It focuses on the concept of taxable entity. Discuss it with your lawyer.

*These might include optimal starting size, managerial expertise required, etc.

$300 an hour for attorney services would not continue to pay that large sum if they didn't think it was worth it.

You shouldn't spend money on an attorney until there is a legal problem or there is a patent issue. Don't talk to a lawyer unless it's in connection with forming a corporation or selling investment interest in the deal.

Many attorneys have finances themselves or have clients who might be interested in taking part of your deal.

There is, in fact, a reason to stay away from attorneys when you are just starting an unproven business concept. The attorney may not understand your business but may proffer a business judgment on its likelihood for success. If the attorney happens to say your widget will never sell you might believe him and there goes your business. Being an attorney doesn't necessarily give you the qualifications to judge products and markets.

Most attorneys are willing to render services to a small startup business for a reduced rate. This is based on the theory that someday the firm will expand and they will then have a substantial client. You should discuss this situation openly with your prospective attorney.

Most lawyers, particularly business lawyers, will be willing to make some accommodations depending on your financial condition and their prediction of how well they think you are going to do. If they don't think you are going to succeed it's unlikely they will make an arrangement.

On the other hand, the fact they don't think you will be successful should not sway you.

If your business is merely a gleam in your eye, other than basic understanding of how well the patent laws work, there is absolutely no reason to go to an attorney.

You should, however, go to a patent attorney if you have a patentable product. With patent attorneys especially you should select someone who knows your particular technology. There are lawyers who know about computers and others who know about chemical compounds, etc.

If you have something patentable, it is your birthright. In that case you should go to a very well-known and prestigious patent firm. The reason is twofold. First, they didn't become well-known and prestigious without being efficient. Second, since they are writing your birthright their firm name means a lot in further negotiations with other companies or potential licensees of the technology. If they know you have an outstanding law firm they will give more credibility to your patent and they are less likely to challenge it. It's similar to receiving more respectful treatment in junior high school if you had a tough big brother.

Some patent attorneys will do your patent work on a reduced rate basis if they think your idea has merit. It depends on what they think of the technology. If Thomas Edison walked in with the light bulb he probably could have gotten a deal. You must also keep in mind that a patent attorney is no better judge of what is going to fly than anyone else.

Just remember everything is certainly negotiable. Whether or not they choose to negotiate shouldn't indicate to you whether your invention is good or bad. It just means that attorney's assessment or financial policy caused him to make a certain decision.

8. Choose an accountant. Approach this situation the same as you did acquiring an attorney. Reference from someone in your business or a similar business is the best way to find an accountant who will be competent and in tune with your business needs.

Ask the accountant, "What do I need to set up minimal books at the lowest possible cost?" Tell him that if you succeed you will want to set up a sophisticated cost and budget system and you will be using him to help prepare financial forecasts for second round investors, etc.

You don't need a Cadillac accounting system when starting out. You want a good accountant, but you want him to do a cost-effective job, not what he would do for General Motors.

Most of the large accounting firms have a small business department. The theory many of the large firms go on is if these small businesses grow it will eventually mean a substantial client for the firm.

A starting entrepreneur usually has extreme loyalty for his original accountant or lawyer, as long as they continue to provide adequate services.

9. Register with the County Government. The County Clerk's Office is the place to go. Tell him you want to register your new proprietorship. They will ask you to look through a listing of already registered names to see if yours conflicts. They will ask you to fill out a simple form asking for information similar to a credit application. You then pay a fee, usually less than $20.00, and they will give you two copies of a registration certificate. At this point ask the clerk if you have to register with the city. Avoid registering with the city if you can.

10. Register with the city. This will be like the county proce-

dure. Cities often charge on the basis of your projected business volume, so tell them you don't plan to be very successful.

City governments can be a real pain. They will ask detailed questions about the kind of work you are doing and where you expect to do it. If you are building a few widgets in your kitchen they might see this as a violation of some zoning ordinance. Be careful what you say on your application. Characterize your business in bland, understated terms. Tell them you are doing library research. Say you are doing consulting by mail. Just don't tell them something that will call the dogs on you.

This is a fairly free country, but one of the places where it is the least democratic is in regard to city or county government harassment of home start-up businesses. Remember, they work strictly by classifications, not by judgment. If you make one widget in your house they may say you are manufacturing and need to do it in an M-1 zone.

Use good sense when you tell the government agencies what your intended business will be — it can save you the cost of moving your operation before you are ready.

11. Register with the State Sales Tax Board. You must be careful with these people also, but for a different reason. They are in existence to collect sales tax from as many transactions as the law allows. If you are making non-exempt sales you must collect taxes for these people, turn in the money and a report of your activities on a regular basis. Not only do they want to get money for every transaction they can, but they expect you to collect if for them.

The laws vary from state to state, but usually only the end-user is taxed. Thus, if you are in the retail business you will have to collect tax on every sale. If you sell an item to another company which they do not resell but utilize themselves it is also taxable. You are expected to keep track of the exempt or non-exempt status of all this, collect taxes and send them in with a report. It is really not so bad and they will give you a booklet that explains their dirty work.

What is bad is they don't trust you. They ask you to estimate your yearly sales and to tell them whether they will be of exempt or non-exempt status. If you will be making non-exempt sales you will be accumulating money for them. They are afraid you will take the money and run off, so they will want a deposit equalling some proportion of your yearly collections; it can run into thousands of dollars.

I'm sure you have better things to do with your capital so it is a good idea to be very conservative when estimating your sales. If your sales are very low and are all exempt from sales tax you won't have any taxes to collect and won't have to make a deposit. Get it? If your sales turn out to be larger than you project and they happen to be in some cases taxable, then you report it on your periodic report and turn in the money. They will then probably ask for some deposit. If you only report every year then you will be able to operate for more than a year before having to put up the deposit money. I'm not advocating fraud but only prudent judgment.

12. Advertise your fictitious business name in the "business announcements" section of the newspaper. Go to the newspaper office classified ad window, tell them you want to run a fictitious business name ad and show them the receipts from the County and City Clerks, and the Sales Tax Board. They will ask you for about $25 and give you a special receipt. The fee covers running the ad the appropriate number of times. The newspaper must verify your registration with the appropriate agencies before accepting the ad.

13. Open a commercial bank account. You don't have to wait until the newspaper ads have appeared. The receipts from the government agencies and the newspaper are your tickets to opening a commercial account. There are many choices of checkbook style, type of check charges, etc. You be the judge of this. Get two bankbooks: one with big impressive checks with no logo and another portable one you can carry easily in your briefcase. You are now a business!

14. Get a place to work. The rule here is to keep overhead as low as possible. Though there are drawbacks, working at home is the best way to start because you have a phone, lights, heat, etc., all set up. If you decide to get an outside workshop or office just the incidental move-in costs can be overwhelming. To work at home all you need is to make some room, get a desk, file box and maybe some bench space. You should write this motto on a piece of paper and paste it on your forehead so you can see it every morning in the mirror: NO OVERHEADS.

15. Order your stationery. The best, cheapest and most reliable source for stationery is NEW ENGLAND BUSINESS SERVICE. You can call them toll free at 800-225-6380, or if you live in Massachusetts 800-252-9226. Ask for a catalog. They also sell a line of computer forms which appear in a separate catalog. You have to ask for both catalogs because if you don't specify they will send only the standard one. NEBS will send your custom printed

stationery usually within a week and they will bill you. It is a good way to build up your credit history.

I generally order the following items:

Invoices: You need four copies — customer gets the top one, you need a sales copy, office copy and a packing slip. For part forms with billing and shipping address space separate; Product #105. 8½ x 7", 250 sets. $33.75.

Window Envelopes: #771, $9.75/150.

Return Envelopes with your company name printed in the address position: #710-1, 500 or $16.00. Very important!

Letterhead: Use product #810-1, 500 for $25.95.

Envelopes: #745-1, 500 for $26.50.

Mailing Labels: #72-1, 250 for $12.95.

If you are shipping discs or printed material use "Jiffy Bags"; they are the best protection for the least money and they are light. If you use them, be sure to cover the address label with clear tape because label stickum doesn't work very well on them.

16. Let the world know you are in business. Refer to Chapter Thirteen and send news releases to every magazine on the list. Plan your ad campaign and follow the Chapter Thirteen checklist.

17. Get an answering service. Get the best service in town and get to know the operators so you can run around town and do errands, meet people, etc., and not worry about missing that big order. A machine just doesn't have the same effect that a real live operator who knows you and comes off as your secretary can have.

18. Get your office furniture and whatever shop fixtures you need. There are many good deals in the classified section of the newspaper. Get a strong secretary's chair for yourself. These chairs are easy to move around and are available cheap. Don't get a big executive chair—it's a waste of time and is too comfortable. Your business will keep you lean; your chair should keep you mean. When it comes to getting a typewriter I suggest a very good IBM Selectric. Remember the first phases of your business are strictly promotional, and the more professional your correspondence looks the more effective it will be. Branch new Selectric III's aren't that expensive and IBM will finance them for 10% down.

19. Set up your bookkeeping system. Get an accountant to suggest the proper set up; get the supplies and organize the system. If you have actually operated the system yourself, then it will be easier to teach it to someone and you will have a better understanding of how it all works.

The weakest point of most entrepreneurs is their avoidance of account books and accounting. If you make this a part of your business discipline you will be ahead of the game from the start.

**WORKSHEET FOR MEETING TAX OBLIGATIONS**

**This worksheet is designed to help the owner-manager to manage his firm's tax obligations. You may want your accountant or bookkeeper to prepare the worksheet so you can use it as a reminder in preparing for and paying the various taxes.**

| Kind of Tax | Due Date | Amount Due | Pay to | Date For Writing The Check |
|---|---|---|---|---|
| **FEDERAL TAXES** | | | | |
| **Employee Income Tax and Social Security Tax** | | | | |
| **Excise Tax** | | | | |
| Owner-Manager's and/or corporation's income tax | | | | |
| **Unemployment Tax** | | | | |
| **STATE TAXES** | | | | |
| **Unemployment Taxes** | | | | |
| Income Taxes | | | | |
| Sales Taxes | | | | |
| Franchise Tax | | | | |
| Other | | | | |
| **LOCAL TAXES** | | | | |
| Sales Tax | | | | |
| Real Estate Tax | | | | |
| Personal Property Tax | | | | |
| Licenses (retail, vending machine, etc.) | | | | |
| Other | | | | |

Source: *Small Marketers Aids* No. 142, "Steps in Meeting Your Tax Obligation," Small Business Administration.

20. Set up a regular and definite work schedule. If you approach working for yourself as you would approach a regular job it will help keep you tracking straight.

Too often entrepreneurs try to work every minute of every day. In the long run it just doesn't work. You may be there every minute, but the human system can't take massive loads of work with no breaks or diversion.

If you overload your personal capacity your efficiency drops; you sense it, feel guilty and try to work harder. Working harder makes you space-out even more, you feel more guilty and try to work harder. It's a bad cycle.

The way to avoid this problem is to set up reasonable and regular hours when you will do your work. The remaining hours should be spent with your family, exercising and relaxing. The word recreation means to create anew. Recreation regenerates your energy sources and clears your mental decks for further action. Approach rest and recreation as a necessary part of the work/success cycle.

21. Keep your head on straight. Remember no matter how hard you work and how smart you are, you exist in a matrix of time and circumstance which will have more effect on your success than any of your efforts. Events regulate themselves, and forces of history and the market are vastly more powerful than you.

The best you can hope for in your business is to be working with this wind of change and not against it. The best buggy whips in the world rotted on the shelves when the automobile came out.

If luck goes with you and you make some good decisions backed up by smart work you will be a great success. If the pattern doesn't fall in your favor you will not succeed. So relax, make your best decisions and work as intelligently as you can. Your life is going to be damned interesting.

N

## Chapter Eleven

# DEVELOPING YOUR BUSINESS PLAN

Everyone knows you can't raise money for your business without showing the lender a neatly typed business plan. Most entrepreneurs think of a business plan as a tool to get financing and they make up the first one the night before going to see the friendly banker.

Believe it or not there is another reason to plan your business with written formality. A careful plan can prevent business failure and can lead on to real success. Careful advance planning helps you avoid pitfalls and problems way ahead of their occurrence.

A business plan provides a drummer which you and your employees can keep time with and provides a framework to build on.

Harvard Business School has a program designed for entrepreneurs called *The Smaller Company Management Program.* This program is run on the case method where you are given 20 to 40 page case studies of particular companies and are asked to comment on the cases the next day. As you go to each class you are asked to analyze a company's situation from the viewpoint of each discipline.

When I attended, the first class on the schedule was marketing. The class had been asked to read a case about a company that had a group of problems involving exclusive territories, unhappy sales reps, pricing problems and loss of market share.

The next day various members of the class were asked to give their opinion. Naturally everyone in this group of entrepreneurs had a strong opinion on what to do with salesmen, how to handle big customers who want exclusive territories, how to cope with shifting pricing and market conditions, etc., etc., etc.

Everyone wanted the floor. Everyone had a slightly different idea of how to handle things. The session degenerated into anarchy, with private arguments among groups of students. Some were shouting to be heard and no one agreed on any single issue. There was pandemonium for thirty minutes, the arguments getting serious by this time. Everyone had a way to fix the situation and an opinion as to the source of the problems.

Professor Martin let the situation build to a frenzy and then quietly asked the class if they wanted to know what was wrong. Of course everyone wanted to hear that their ideas were what Professor Martin would champion.

"WHERE ARE YOU GOING?"

| POLICY | STRATEGY | STRATEGIES | |
|---|---|---|---|
| WHAT TO DO | HOW TO START | HOW TO DO IT | EXACTLY WHAT TO DO |
| • Purpose<br>• Mission<br>• Goals | • Action Steps<br>• Resource Allocation | • Functional<br>• Supports Strategy<br>• Basis for Tactics | • Tactics<br>• Programs<br>• Projects |

"The problem," said Professor Martin, "is not that they handled their salespeople too softly, or that they are too locked into their distributors, or that the R&D people are dogging it. The problem is this company has no *plan*. There is no strategic framework to guide daily decision making." You could have heard a pin drop.

Professor Martin had purposefully let the class get out of control and descend into a chaotic shouting session to dramatize what goes on in a company without a plan.

## What is a Business Plan?

It is a set of strategic ideas that determine your business attitude and guide your business to a clear set of goals. A plan isn't some long range forecast of what you would like the company to be. A plan does, however, make decisions about your best estimates of the future.

Your business plan is not a cast iron mold to lock up your ability to gain from windfall or change. A good plan is a process, an ongoing adaptable framework which you can cast your business in.

A good plan is the way you match your capacities with opportunity. To start you first need to see your choices:

THE THREE PHASES OF YOUR GRAND PLAN

- Ask questions and make best-guess assumptions on the nature of your business, its environment and its expected sales and earnings.
- Develop a cash planning and control system—a budget—to insure application of available assets consistent with the assumptions made during Phase One.
- Develop a cash flow prediction and management system so your cash assets will be in place in time and in the amount required by Phase Two of your Grand Plan.

## Idea Flow in the Planning Process

This chapter has been put in the last section of the book for a reason. Assembling a workable, realistic and effective plan for your business is an evolutionary process. It doesn't happen during a single meeting, or while sitting in front of a roaring fire for a whole evening. It happens as an evolutionary outworking of the reality you deal with. Your business plan is a working document and is a blueprint for everyone, including yourself, to follow. After you have evaluated your needs and dreams, the market and competition, and your particular edge you will have the raw materials for "The Master Plan."

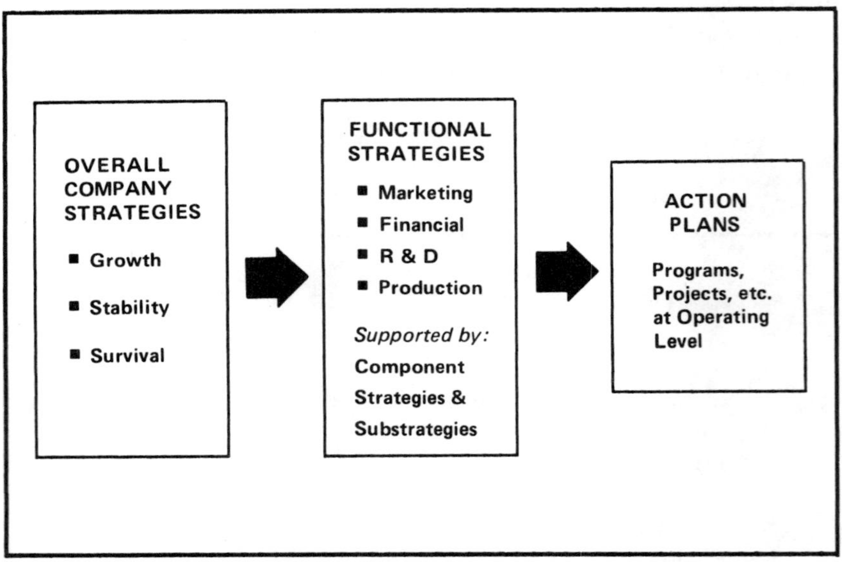


## Please Put It In Writing

As you change your plan to meet the evolving realities of your business, put those changes in writing. The document you create will be a record of where you have been and how you got where you are.

Write your business plan yourself. Do not hire a consultant or anyone else to write your plan. Volume II tells you to definitely hire a consultant to write up the business plan, but that is for a different reason. Volume II assumes you have grown, have become in some degree profitable and want to continue growing, and that you need to negotiate for outside money. Investors and lenders like to see a slick business plan and they respond like

Pavlov's dogs to certain buzz words and buzz concepts. A good financial consultant knows where these reactions live and knows how to orchestrate them for max effect.

Your first business plan is for you and your employees. Write it yourself. You'll be glad you did.

## After the Horses Have Gone

Most business people looking for financing eventually come to the point of writing a formal business plan. In a way this is terribly sad because it means the business has come along on technical muscle, marketing luck, and good horse-sense.

I know a man who was a contender for the World Professional Archery Championship, quite a feat in itself! But he was always second best. One particular guy kept edging him out of the top spot.

My friend went to a Zen Archery Master (what else?) and said, "Why can't I beat this dude?" The Master asked him if he could win if his opponent were blindfolded. "Of course!" was the natural answer. The Master then said, "How do you expect to win if you have no target? You have no plan, no series of small goals leading to an ultimate goal? With a plan every arrow has a purpose and *must* go along the path leading to your goal. With a plan your arrows and your goal will converge on the same target." Eventually my friend gave up archery and bought a computer.

## The Planning Process

Planning combines prediction, calculation, goal setting and identifying courses of action. There are five steps in setting up your plan:

1. Analyze the business environment, determine what is really going on out in the real world.
2. Realistically appraise the present situation.
3. Set goals. What do you want for yourself and your business in the next year? Two years? Five years?
4. Strategic guideposts. What are your present choices? How can you make your plan work? What is holding you back?
5. Step-by-step strategic plan. Exactly what are you going to do, when are you going to do it and how are you going to measure the success of the operation?

> **"Beware that you do not lose the substance by grasping at the shadow."**
>
> —AESOP, circa 550 B.C.

The plan gets down to three questions: how are you going to grow, prosper and survive? The organisms that have survived the test of time have been the ones who meet reality with adaptive honesty.

## Growth

Has there ever been a business that projects a decline? It is the way of entrepreneurs and the Western World to live and breathe growth. I am going to assume you want your company to grow. The problem then is to determine a rate of growth consistent with your resources and needs.

Planned growth is the area where most successful enterprises get into trouble. Growing faster than your available cash or human resources can lead to loss of profits or tragedy.

It is sometimes smart to grow a little more slowly than the maximum possible rate. This conservative growth approach can yield a consistently good cash position and stability. Moreover it holds a reserve so you can take advantage of windfall opportunities that often bestow themselves on a business in a rapidly evolving technical market.

## Survival Strategy

It is sometimes hard for entrepreneurs to imagine their business turning sour. But it can happen and when it does, it does so with astonishing swiftness. Thus it is prudent to have a survival contingency plan.

Even a powerful market can hiccough. A new discovery or market trend could put your product and company on the dusty end of the trail herd. If hard times hit, the effect will be amplified if you have stretched things thin by running out in front of your available cash. A business plan that provides stability and a *predetermined risk exposure* is your best insurance for survival when things go wrong.

Planned contraction, consolidation and recovery should be a part of your contingency planning. A good book on the subject is Joseph Eisenberg's *Turnaround Management: A Manual for Profit Improvement and Growth,* published by McGraw Hill. Survival planning doesn't forecast doom—it merely prepares you with a contingency action list in case bad weather hits.

Below is a block diagram of the flow of concepts that need to be explored. Each area should be examined and policy decided. Each of the overall strategic areas is then conceptually divided into divisional, functional, and strategic plans. Each of the divisional plans is implemented with an action plan—some contingent and some which will be operational every day.

This might look like the planning scenario for General Motors. And it is. It is also appropriate to a single-person operation. If you are the only person in the company you still serve each of these functions. If you are able to clearly recogize this division of tasks within yourself you can organize your time and and energy more efficiently.

By creating a clear divisional strategic plan you can expand your activities and effectiveness and can build other people into the system as you add to your organization. But your business is an organization even if you are the only employee. This sort of planning creates a framework of concept strategy and action which are really the unifying concepts of your business.

A sound, thorough and reasonable plan can expand and contract to suit the ebb and flow of your fortunes. With it you will make your life much more bearable.

## Market Strategy

What products are you going to sell? How are you going to let people know about your product? How much of your time and money will you spend on this activity?

How will you approach the market? Mail order? Direct selling? Wholeselling? Retailing? Service? By word-of-mouth? If you make these decisions clearly and write them down, your life will be much quieter and simpler.

Here is an example. My company specializes in technical books sold through ads in National magazines. These points are the result of policy decisions.

1. To be in a technical "how to" market. This policy is

changing, or more accurately, has been recently improving its aim. We are localizing the market to computer-related, technical, how-to books.

2. We sell the product in a defined way. A new policy may soon emerge. We are testing direct mail as a possible way to increase sales. Should tests prove this method appropriate to our product, the policy will be modified to include it.

By analyzing the available choices and setting out a clearly defined plan we avoid arguments and wasted time. For example, if someone offers us a book on Modern Drama it would be politely turned down. Everyone in the organization knows the policy. Modern Drama doesn't fit our planned business direction.

Should we sell to a bookstore who just sent an inquiry? No, not nust now. We sell through the mail for advance cash. Everyone knows the policy so there is no trouble making the decision.

We may someday decide to sell our books through the established book distribution channels. Right now it is our policy to not do so because of the problems of slow pay (up to six months) and returns.

## Periodic Re-Evaluation and Review

You will need to re-evaluate your policies as time and the tide change. We do not at present plan to sell to conventional bookshops. Something may change in the future which tips the scale to the other side. If that happens the new developments will be evaluated and our policy will be adjusted (I hope) appropriately.

Big companies often have problems because people making policy are quite removed from the scene of action. The bigger the organization the harder it is to change and implement policy. Your great advantage as a small business person is your ability to quickly and effectively adapt to changes in the times.

## Financial Strategy

This is the subject almost universally ignored by entrepreneurs. It seems so far removed from the everyday realities of the business. "If my product is good, sells well and makes a profit, why worry about financial strategy?"

Because a sound financial strategy coupled with good and timely soundings will tell you about trouble before it arrives and can guide you to high ground. It begins with understanding ratio analysis.

## Ratio Analysis

Accountants and financial types place great faith on a technique called "Ratio Analysis." This faith is partially dead wrong and partially right.

Financial statement ratios control nothing, nor do they provide explanations of what has happened. If you rely on these numbers as absolute arbiters of your business policy you should probably have taken up accounting. Accountants feel comfortable when they can give advice by the numbers. But ratios can lead you to incorrect conclusions and inappropriate performance measurement.

Ratio analysis is, however, not all bad. If used wisely, ratios can help you spot situations which are out of tune. They can be a signal for you to further investigate an area you have been ignoring.

Here is a brief and incomplete summary of how it works. Please do not be offended if you already know these first simple concepts.

The financial statement is composed of two parts: a balance sheet and an income statement. A balance sheet is only a list of assets (things your company has that are worth money) and a list of claims on those assets (liabilities). Your total assets minus total liabilties is how much your company is worth (net worth). Simple?

The second part is your income statement, sometimes called Statement of Financial Condition. It shows what happened in your company during a certain period of time. It shows how much you sold and spent during that period (usually three months or a year). The difference between what you sold and what you spent is roughly how much money you earned during that period.

Ratio Analysis is a technique of relating various categories of assets, liabilities, profits or losses to each other creating a thumbnail sketch of your business health. It is sometimes done the same way paramedics monitor vital signs of a traffic accident victim.

There are many ratios and each interested person has his favorites. Bankers are interested in how well you can pay your bills, how much money is coming in right away and what you could get by a quick liquidation of your assets. (Can this be my friendly banker?)

Investors are interested in long-term earning power and operating efficiency. You are interested, more or less, in all of it.

There are four types of ratios:

1. Current Ratio = $\dfrac{\text{Cash + Receivables − Inventory}}{\text{Trade dept. + Note payments + Taxes Owed + Wages Owed}}$

2. Quick Ratio (Acid Test) = Same as current ratio but doesn't include inventories.

The quick ratio measures your ability to pay your bills without reducing inventories (sometimes not so easy to do). You can see when the quick ratio equals less than one, you hurt.

Leverage Ratios measure how much debt financing you have. The debt to equity ratio shows how much you have invested in comparison to how much you have borrowed. This ratio is of great interest to creditors for obvious reasons. If you don't have much invested you might someday send them a key to the place instead of a check.

3. Activity ratios measure how effectively you are using your resources. These ratios are in some ways a measure of your managerial effectiveness.

A. Inventory Turnover = $\dfrac{\text{Sales}}{\text{Inventory}}$

It shows how quickly stuff moves in and out of your place. If everyone else in your business turns their inventory four times a year and you turn yours eighteen times it probably means you don't have inventory and are shipping items as soon as you can wring it out of your suppliers. If your inventory turns once per year you either brought the wrong stuff or you are a farmer.

B. Average collection period is calculated in two steps:

a. Sales per day = $\dfrac{\text{Total Yearly Sales}}{360}$

Average collection period = $\dfrac{\text{Total Receivables}}{\text{Sales Per Day}}$

This shows how well you collect from your customers, what deadbeats your customers are, or both.

4. Profitability Ratios show the bottom line; the net result of your business effort.

A. Profit On Sales = $\dfrac{\text{After Tax Profit}}{\text{Sales}}$ = a percentage

B. Return on Assets = $\frac{\text{After Tax Profit}}{\text{Total Assets}}$ = a percentage
(Return On Investment)

This is the one your investors will want to see. The ROI is a measure of how effectively your assets function to produce a profit.

There are many other ratios and other ways of looking at them. Ratios can give a capsulized view of a company's strengths and weaknesses though they explain little of the reasons behind the condition.

## Trend Analysis

Ratios are exactly like your balance sheet. They are a stop-action view of your company's activities at a particular moment in time. To see evolution or decay you need to add the element of time.

The graph shows trend analysis of a hypothetical company's sales, current ratio, debt ratio, fixed asset turnover and return on net worth.

What happened in mid 1980? This company followed industry trends until that time and then something went wrong. As you can see in this example, trend analysis can lead you to ask the right questions.

Ratios and trend analysis are not only for outsiders to use when they want to evaluate your company. Profit planning is an integral part of your business plan. You can accurately estimate profits by looking at your historical ratios.

Financial forecasting is an important part of your business plan. You can use ratios to help budget your cash. The amount and timing of your cash needs can be determined by looking at asset requirements and flow of funds from profits.

Here there are three issues to keep in mind:

1. Technical Forecasts. Where should your money be spent? What R&D directions will be the most fruitful? For most technical people this one isn't a biggie. Planning how much energy and money to spend on R&D is not the toughest part. Sticking to your plan is.

2. How much of the R&D investment of money and effort is going to be spent immediately and how much is going to be spent over the long term? A sound policy here will be a big help to track straight.

3. How much of your time will you spend working with new

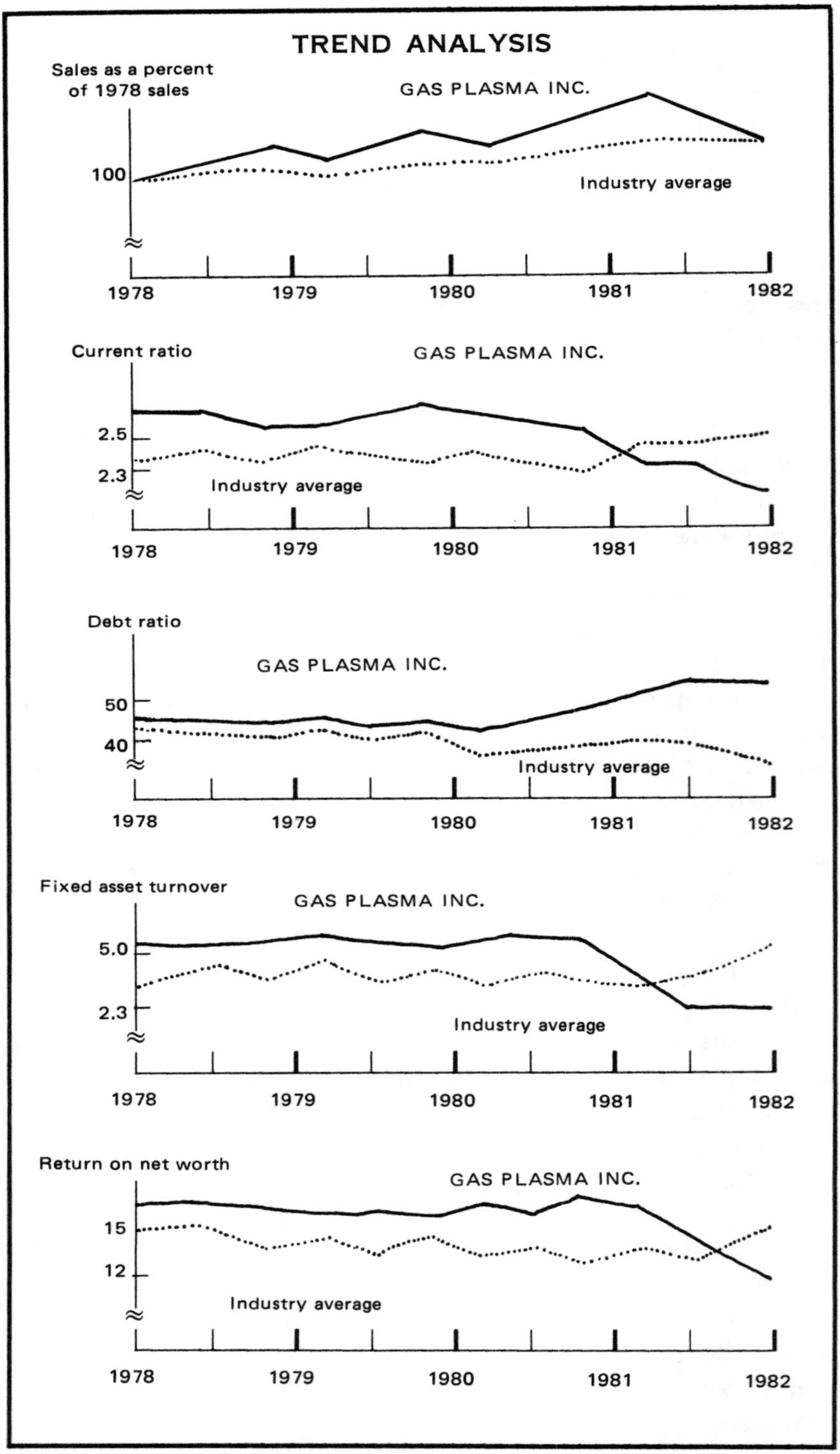
TREND ANALYSIS
Sales as a percent of 1978 sales
GAS PLASMA INC.
100
Industry average
1978
1979
1980
1981
1982
Current ratio
GAS PLASMA INC.
2.5
2.3
Industry average
1978
1979
1980
1981
1982
Debt ratio
GAS PLASMA INC.
50
40
Industry average
1978
1979
1980
1981
1982
Fixed asset turnover
GAS PLASMA INC.
5.0
2.3
Industry average
1978
1979
1980
1981
1982
Return on net worth
GAS PLASMA INC.
15
12
Industry average
1978
1979
1980
1981
1982

projects? Managing yourself and your time is just as important as managing the time of a large staff of employees. If you run a one-man-band you are the whole staff. Each segment of your time needs to be apportioned and managed just as though it were a separate group of people doing the job.

## Worksheet

EVALUATION OF YOUR BUSINESS STRATEGY

Question #1. Can you list the opportunities and potential threats to your business? Explain: ______________________________

______________________________________________

______________________________________________

Question #2. Can you realistically reach your sales and profit targets in the next 6 months, or 12 months and how? Explain: ___

______________________________________________

______________________________________________

Question #3. Do you have adequate cash and earnings to finance your business? ____________ How much is required? ____ and what are the sources? ______________________________
Explain: ______________________________________

______________________________________________

Question #4. What about your sales, production, and other supervisors and workers? Do they know your targets and can they achieve them? ______________________If not, why not?
Explain: ______________________________________

______________________________________________

______________________________________________

Question #5. How about yourself and your management style? Do you have the time to concentrate on managing the operations and making and directing strategies? ____________ Do you feel adequate to manage a bigger firm when business expands?
Explain: ______________________________________

______________________________________________

______________________________________________

Question #6. What is your firm's problem now? Low profit, suffering losses, doing great, ready to expand? Or __________
Explain: ______________________________________

______________________________________________

______________________________________________

Question #7. Do you have a strategy for now? ______________ And is it effective? ______________ A strategy for the next six months to a year? ______________ A vague idea where you want to be in 2 or 3 years? ______________________________
______________________________________________

Above is a list of questions to ask yourself when you begin to formulate your business plan. Each one of these questions is designed to provide you with a framework for your entire plan.

The first question addresses the problems of market analysis and future trends. Question two asks how you plan to sell your company's product. Three is your financial picture. Four addresses the issues of production and personnel management. Five is a checklist for you. How are you holding up to it all? Are you hitting some personal limitations? How do you plan to work around your own weaknesses? This question is critical if you want to become a real pro at what you do. Question six is about your ability to see the big picture and how you view the five functional areas in relationship to that picture. The last question is about how your prior planning has worked and asks you to commit yourself to commit yourself to a long-term blueprint.

These questions aren't simple to answer. But if you do answer them well, the answers will turn into promises you have made to yourself. And those promises will come true.

## References


*Entrepreneurship: Playing to Win.* Gordon Batty. Reston, Virginia. Reston Publishing Company, 1974.

*Breaking the Barriers to Small Business Planning.* Management Aid No. 179. Washington, D.C. SBA, August 1973.

*Up Your Own Organization.* Donald M. Dibble. Santa Clara, CA. Entrepreneur Press, 1971.

*Fun and Guts: The Entrepreneur's Philosophy.* Joseph Mancusco. Reading, Mass. Addison-Wesley Publishing Company, 1973.

*The First Two Years: Small Firm Growth and Survival Problems.* Kurt Mayer. Small Business Research Series No. 2. Washington, D.C. SBA, 1961.

*Starting and Managing a Small Business of Your Own.* Wendell Metcalf. The Starting and Managing Series, Volume I (3rd edition). Washington, D.C. SBA, 1973.

## Chapter Twelve

# MARKETING AND PRODUCT DEVELOPMENT

I read a book called *The Marketing Mystique.* It discussed the great dark mysteries of the marketing process. But this chapter is about a different kind of marketing. It shows the practical side of how to find products and get people to buy them. How can anything so straightforward be mysterious?

Marketing is an ancient and simple idea. It is determining what you want to sell, who might buy it, why they would buy it, and it makes a best guess on the way to get them to give you their money.

Marketing is not selling things. "Writing Paper," as my Uncle Henry used to say, "is the result of good marketing." Marketing gets you ready to sell your products and is the job of sales to write the orders.

Marketing is understanding who your intended customer is and what he wants and needs. The study of the way your customer lives and breathes is called Demographics. Demographics gives you a place to start.

## Filling Needs

Marketing is discovering your customer's unfilled needs and desires. In a rapidly expanding industry it is impossible to provide a product for every opportunity. The horizon of expansion in the microcomputer industry produces many large and profitable vacuums.

In a technology-dependent industry it takes time to develop need-filling products. In a strong market everyone is busy trying to fill orders. Everyone wants to have a fast-moving, new product effort. Not only is it impossible to cover all the developing trends, but also it is a mistake to spread yourself too thin. No one company has time to cover every base and so there are many opportunities with virtually no competition.

## Analysis

Marketing is analzying your competition or potential competition. In this part of the marketing function you ask: How big is the market? How much of the market do I want? How much can I handle? Will other companies get in on this market? How soon? Is someone already working on this product? When will it break? Will they do it right? Should I wait to pick up the pieces if they make a mistake? Will their success create other markets? Good marketing research answers these questions and guides you to realistic decisions.

Marketing is selecting products that give you maximum competitive edge, maximum profit margins, the least R&D expense and the greatest product longevity.

Marketing selects a price for your product giving you the best tradeoff between competitiveness, profit and market size.

Marketing determines the best way to promote and present your product to the customer. It analyzes media for relevance to the intended customer and determines the best way to tickle money out of them.

It is impossible here to give a complete marketing course. There is a list of recommended reading at the back of the chapter. You might also consider coming to one of our marketing seminars. To get on the list send me a line at the address in the front of this book.

## The Microcomputer Consumer

Just who are the micromarket consumers? We know a few things about them and most importantly we know where they are headed.

They don't all own equipment, but of those who do 49% use their machines for games, mostly because they just don't know what else to do with them. I know a bright mechanic who owns an Atari. He uses it to keep a record of who he has loaned tools to, a job more easily done on paper (he doesn't loan out that many tools). He also uses it to play "Tank Wars"—but that is the limit of his imagination right now. He is a prime customer for someone who can stimulate his interest.

Micro buyers read! Almost half of the *Popular Electronics* readers also read *Byte.* 4% of *PE* readers who own computers read *Byte!* Does this tell you that when a person invests in equipment his interest peaks?

Micro prospects and owners are smart and educated! 75% of them went to college and 43% graduated. 37% *of those who read PE* also read *Scientific American.*

They are business minded! A large proportion of them regularly read a business magazine like *Business Week.*

They are mostly male, estimated at 95.1% in 1982, though this trend may be changing. They are about 32 years old. They average about 27.5K income (1982 figure). Quite a group!

Looking at these people a little more strategically we find they are the leading edge of the War Baby Boom. It is this same group who made the Diaper Service industry boom in the late 40's and early 50's.

They are the same war babies who caused suburban spread and the vivification of the college and university systems across the nation.

Their parents are the product of the Great Depression and WWII. Their parents wanted them to have the "best of everything" and raised them with a baby in one arm and Dr. Spock's book in their free hand. These people are used to being indulged, are well-off, educated and can get the material things they want. And they do want.

This group *makes* markets. In their college days they wanted leather belts, sandals and marijuana. These products became national industries in the 60's and 70's.

When they graduated or left college their back-to-nature zeal turned more civilized (they were growing up) so jogging, hiking and bicycling became the next phenomenon.

Now the war babies are in their thirties. They are slowing down physically but speeding up mentally. *They are becoming more cerebral.* Their growing interest in books and computers is creating the biggest boom these industries have ever seen. And it is just now starting.

The war babies who are fueling the microcomputer market are the leading edgers. The pack is close on their heels. The war babies bespeak individualism but have incredibly strong herd instinct—possibly because of the competition created in such a dense group.

As this group passes to middle age (40 and up) they will consume educational materials and other forms of cerebral stimulation in impressive and accelerating qualities.

This group passes through its developmental stages like a marauding army, creating and destroying whole industries as it passes. It is now creating the microcomputer industry, of which we have only seen the beginning.

Tuning in to the war babies is tuning in to the electronics markets of now and the ever larger future.

## Richard White's Market Gap Analysis

The concept of market gap analysis, as described by Rich White in *The Entrepreneur's Manual,* is a matrix method of determining large numbers of grand opportunities, fast buck opportunities and mirages.

Gap analysis works like a wheat harvester, separating a market into increasingly divided categories. Rich White says in an evening's session you can easily uncover 40 long-term, viable gaps in the market, 20 short-term targets-of-opportunity and as many as 100 mirages.

Many entrepreneurs start their businesses by going for short-term opportunity targets that give them a quick flow of cash but which they know will not last a long time. They then use a part of the incoming cash to fuel the longer term but slower starting projects.

The problem with gap analysis is not uncovering profitable ways to make money, but rather in uncovering too many of them and going crazy.

## Warning

Performing the gap analysis ritual can be intoxicating. It is easy to lose your head when realizing miles and miles of staggering opportunities.

When doing a gap analysis you need to stay steady and remain methodical. If you start to get emotional you may miss important market ideas or build bias into the matrix. The result of these slips is chronic rainbow chasing.

The Gap Analysis Ritual is best performed by two or more people. There seems to be a multiplication effect due to interpersonal interaction often leading to results beyond the sum of individual efforts.

When Rich White's market analysis group discovered the technique they ran into trouble right away. The trouble was the technique worked too well! Their first session was run for 35 marketing executives. In a short time they uncovered 300 viable markets, each with sales potential of more than ten million dollars a year. These discoveries put the R&D departments of their companies into an inverted spin.

Twenty-two of the participants quit their jobs within a year of the session in order to go into business for themselves and eighteen of them became millionaires!

Rich White's consulting group then ran a similar seminar for a computer manufacturing company. The results of this gap analysis session registered 11 on the Richter Scale! In a single day's session they discovered 116 viable markets with a sales potential of more than five million per year, 27 good quick-buck schemes and 87 mirages!

I suppose by now you are wondering how it is done. The first step is to define your business objectives. You should use your own but here is a sample set as an example:

A. You want to be in the microcomputer business.

B. You want a 10:1 minimum markup.

C. You want a market potential of 100 million units per year.

D. There should currently be no competition.

E. You want immediate and enthusiastic product acceptance.

F. You want to sell through existing channels of distribution and have the customer pay their bills quickly.

G. You want a low technology product you can initially job out.

Sounds pretty crazy, huh? We have hardly started. Go on to Step Two. Conceptually divide your industry into major segments. For example, one way the microcomputer business can be segmented is as follows:

1. Hobbyists
2. Business accounting and recordkeeping.
3. Scientific applications
4. Industrial controls
5. Security systems
6. Entertainment
7. Communication
8. Safety systems
9. Educational uses

Now take each one of these categories and divide it into specified categories. As an example, let's take scientific uses of microcomputer systems. How many ways could microcomputers be used in scientific applications?

1. Medical monitoring.
2. Performing complex calculations in the lab.
3. Recording data input from analog devices.
4. Leading a researcher through a complex series of processes of tests requiring calculations before the appropriate next step can be taken.
5. Biochemical or biophysical modeling.
6. Speech synthesis/voice recognition applications.

Now for Step Three: let's take one of these categories and divide it up. Take #6 for example. How many applications an you think of for speech recognition/voice synthesis? Now do you get the picture? In any direction you take, gap analysis leads to more and more real and often unfilled opportunities.

The examples I have given are rather obvious. The beauty of this system is that every group going through the ritual will come up with unique and powerful answers to the questions so often asked by hopeful entrepreneurs: Is there any room left for me in the market? Yes, Barbara, there is a Santa Claus!

## Product Selection

When deciding on your product or service, don't be a "dumb genius." This is a person who knows an incredible amount but is incapable of making it useful. The woods are full of dumb geniuses.

If you design a product so advanced your customers won't understand it or will be afraid of it, the product might as well be from the Stone Age.

If you can't sell your product, it is worse than having no product at all because your R&D, production and marketing investment will be lost.

Stay simple. Select a product that takes very little capital equipment to make. A perfect product has the following characteristics:

### CHARACTERISTICS OF A PERFECT PRODUCT

- It is an essential part of other successful products.
- These products are made by large-well-established companies.
- The product uses specialized materials available to only you.
- Only you can service or provide parts for your product.
- The market is small enough that the manufacturers that your product supports won't go into the business themselves.
- The work involved in making your product is fairly easy only if you know how to do it. This knowledge factor is your insurance policy and will give your product stability. Many times it seems easy to duplicate a competitive product. How many products have seemed easy prior to starting and turned out to be technical nightmares?
- Your modest size will allow you to provide certain products which larger companies find unprofitable.

## Knock-Offs

In the garment industry copying someone's product is called "knocking it off." Garment manufacturers who make the most money are usually the copy-cats.

The reason for this is simple: If you wait for a product to be proven, you may sacrifice some market lead-time but you gain the advantage of accurate aim.

By being a product follower you are able to track a particular idea before you commit yourself to it. This increases your chances of product success and reduces costly misfires.

What about the legal and moral considerations of product copying? Can't you get sued? Yes and no. In the first place a patent or copyright is no good until it has been tested in court.

Many people or corporations hold patents that have never been tested and which couldn't stand up to a court test. Many holders of shaky patent rights know it and won't litigate an infringement.

It is difficult for juries and judges to understand cases involving complicated electronics or programming concepts. Neither side of a litigated issue can be sure of the outcome. If a patent holder sues and loses, it wipes out his protection.

Another factor is the enormous cost of cases like this. The attorneys for both sides often have to spend weeks boning up on the technical issues before preparing the first of a long series of interrogatories and answers. The cost can be enormous and both sides know it.

It is often the case, however, that large companies with a lot to lose have staff attorneys or have budgeted for expensive legal battles in order to protect their business. This is an area where it is worthwhile to spend some money for an attorney.

Your attorney should be able to help you evaluate the risks of crowding someone else's product. Some attorneys are timid souls and so are deal killers. Hopefully you will have already realized this and retained an aggressive, practical-minded, hard-core business attorney who won't get nervous when you want to talk about the possibility of exposing yourself to shellfire.

Your attorney will be able to evaluate the best response if you get a "You better stop or it's big trouble" letter. It is inevitable that other business operators will resent your intrusion into their market. The depth and severity of that intrusion is really a question of how you decide to run your business.

I am *not* talking about moral issues. I *am* talking about a practical, business-minded approach to product selection.

Entrepreneurs' attitudes about product selection range from "I will never step on anyone's toes" to "Devil take the hindmost." I know one guy who copies a product, runs it until he get a "Cease and Desist" letter, and then replies to the aggrieved party's attorney on newsprint-type plain paper, handwritten in pencil.

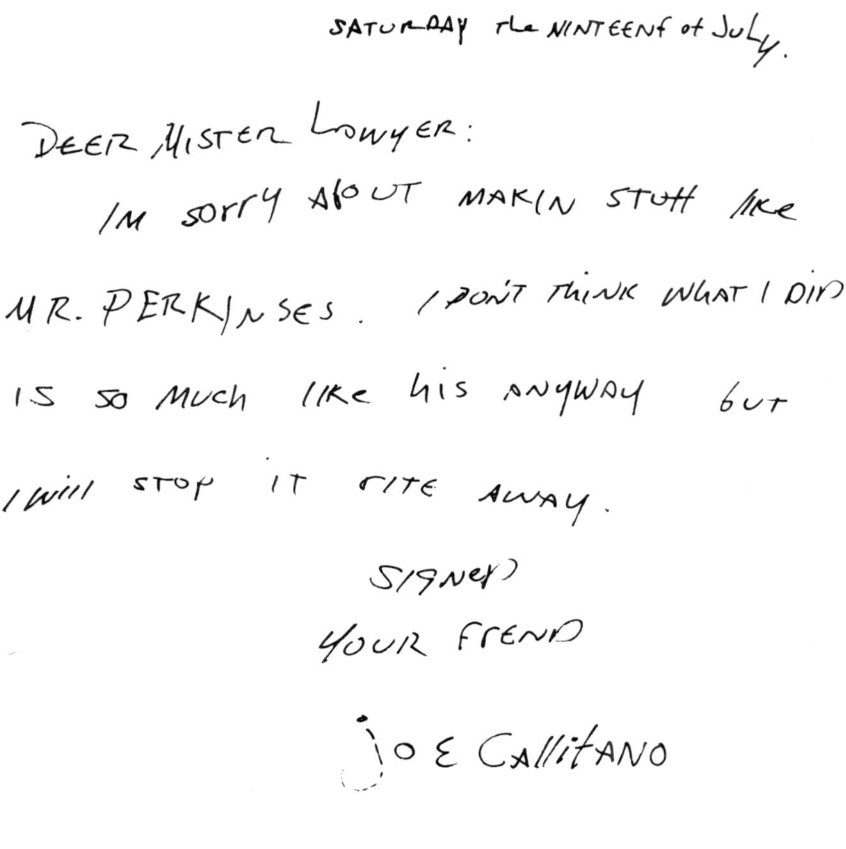

SATURDAY the NINTEENf of July.

DEER MISTER LAWYER:

IM SORRY ABOUT MAKIN STUFF like MR. PERKINSES. I DON'T THINK WHAT I DID IS SO MUCH like his ANYWAY but I will STOP IT RITE AWAY.

SIGNED
YOUR FREND

JOE CALLITANO

Another practical approach to the knock-off situation is to use other's successes as a guide to your own efforts. Borrow ideas and innovations when that is the best way to develop your product, but don't simply copy. If you leave room for doubt there will be skepticism in the mind of the person you "innovated" from and his lawyer.

I am not suggesting the knock-off approach to product development. I am telling you some of the ways products get "developed." At the bottom line you should do what you can live with.

## Pricing

One of the most maddening problems for a struggling businessperson is how much to charge for your product and how flexible you should be when dealing with big users.

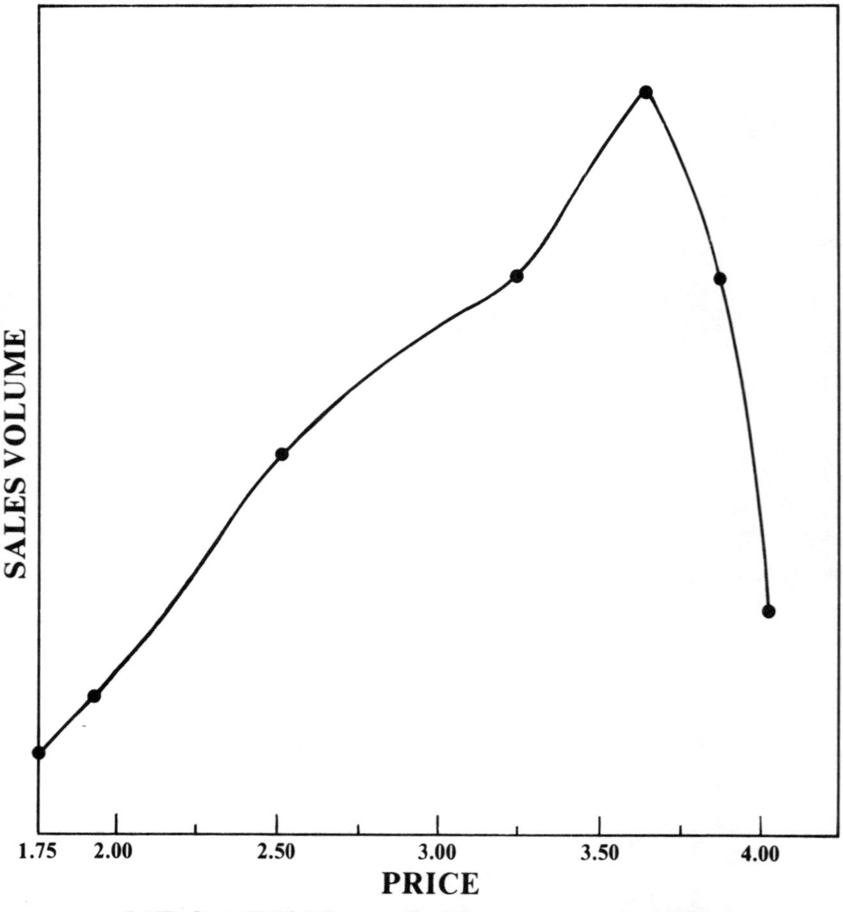


**NEGATIVE PRICE ELASTICITY**

A classic marketing concept is "price elasticity." This means that you will be able to sell more if your price is lower. A perfectly elastic product doubles its sales volume if the price is halved. This is a theory they teach in undergraduate economics classes. Fortunately the real world reacts to many other factors.

Here's an anti-price elasticity example. A merchant I know sold dozens of leather watchbands a week. He originally priced them at $1.50. He *raised* the price to $1.75. Sales increased 10%. He then raised the price in weekly steps to a high of $4.75. The following chart represents his price/volume experience:

This effect is due to *perceived value.* Watchbands were a status item. People wanted to have a high quality, expensive watchband. $3.50 was the price they *expected* to pay for this item. When it was cheaper the item lost its quality appeal because in some instances people equate price with quality.

If you are selling or distributing a quality product that has negative elasticity and the product has enough margin to allow for it, you can offer the retailers a bigger markup. This gives the retailer the incentive to feature the item and makes everyone happy.

If your product is nationally recognized and advertized, the retailers may discount it. This is only a problem if they aren't making enough money on the transaction. The suppliers who contribute the least profits are paid last.

## Gross Margin Pricing

Most entrepreneurs simplify their pricing decisions by deciding what the item costs and adding a standard margin. Retailers use this method and it makes their lives easier. If an item costs $10 and your normal markup is 100% (this is called keystone), then the selling price is twenty bucks.

A twenty dollar selling price gives you ten dollars gross margin. Out of this comes your operating overheads. The difference is your profit or loss.

A manufacturing operation functions in exactly the same way except manufacturers call the cost of the product "Cost of goods sold." CGS is what it costs the factory to produce the item or what it costs to have it made.

Operating overheads such as office expenses, administrative and clerical salaries, shipping room costs, salesman's commissions, and promotional expenses are deducted from the gross margin and the remainder is profit or loss.

$$\text{Gross margin} = \frac{\text{markup}}{\text{selling price}}$$

$$\text{Profit} = \text{gross margin} - \text{operating overheads}$$

## Break-Even Analysis

How many widgets do you have to sell to keep your nose just above the waterline? You need to answer three questions:

1. What are your total operating overheads?
2. What is the price of the product?
3. What is your direct cost for each product?

$$\frac{\text{Total operating expenses}}{\text{unit price} - \text{cost of each unit}} = \text{how many you have to sell to cover your assets}$$

What should you charge for your product? Take everything into consideration, write a lot of numbers on a piece of paper and throw a dart. You'd be surprised how many prices are determined initially by this aspect of the "Marketing Mystique."

PRICE POLICY FACTORS

1. YOUR PRODUCT COST
2. OPERATING OVERHEADS
3. COMPETITION
4. END-USERS'.EXPECTATIONS
5. VOLUME (IF YOU CAN AFFORD IT)
6. PROFIT GOAL
7. INFLATION AND INCREASED OVERHEAD
8. FUTURE POTENTIAL MARKDOWNS AND DEAD ITEMS

# References


Beaumont, John A. et al. *Your Career in Marketing.* McGraw-Hill Book Company, 1976.

Blackwell, Roger. *Knowing Your Image.* Small Marketers Aid #124, Washington, D.C.: SBA, 1967.

Breibart, Joan and Edward Smykay. *Introduction to Marketing: A Programmed Approach,* New York: The MacMillan Company, 1971.

DeBoer, Lloyd M. *National Directories for Use in Marketing,* Small Business Bibliography No. 13, Washington, D.C.: SBA, 1973.

_________. *Marketing Research Procedures,* Small Business Bibliography No. 9, Washington, D.C.: SBA, 1974.

Dutka, Solomon. *Using Census Data in Small Plant Marketing,* Management Aids No. 187, Washington, D.C.: SBA, 1973.

Elton, Revel W. *How Trade Associations Help Small Business,* Management Aids for Small Manufacturers No. 33, Washington, D.C.: SBA, 1973.

Gelb, Betsy and Ben Enis (eds). *Marketing is Everybody's Business,* Pacific Palisades, CA: Goodyear Publishing Company, Inc., 1974.

Janezeck, Elizabeth G. *Basic Library Reference Sources,* Small Business Bibliography No. 18, Washington, D.C.: SBA, 1974.

Pickle, Hal. "Marketing Research for Small Business," *Journal of Small Business Management,* Volume 9, October, 1971, pp. 21-25.

Semon, Thomas T. *Statistics and Maps for National Market Analysis,* Small Business Bibliography No. 12, Washington, D.C.: SBA, 1973.

Stanton, William, *Fundamentals of Marketing,* 4th ed., New York: McGraw-Hill Book Company, 1964.

_________. "Improving Material Handling in Small Business," Small Business Management Series No. 4, Stock No. 045-000-00041-9, Washington, D.C.: Small Business Administration.

_________. "Financial Recordkeeping forSmall Stores," Small Business Management Series No. 32, Stock No. 045-000-00142-3, Washington, D.C.: Small Business Administration.

_________. *Your Business Tax Kit,* Department of the Treasury, Internal Revenue Service.

Desktop Computing
Nº 3
COMPUTE!
The Journal For Progressive Computing
COMPUTER
Dr. Dobb's Journal
the Community Computerist's
Business Computers
Package
MICROCOMPUTING
DataCast
Computer Systems Dealers
Office Products Dealer
creative computing
creative computing
BUYER'S GUIDE
TO PERSONAL COMPUTERS, VIDEO & ELECTRONIC GAMES, AND CONSUMER ELECTRONICS
GAMES
JUMPING JEHOSHAPHAT!
99'er
THE ORIGINAL MAGAZINE FOR TRS-80™ OWNERS
COMPUTRONICS
Desktop Computing
The first plain language computer magazine!
MICRO
Popular Electronics
PERSONAL COMPUTING
It can help you pick the winner
COMPUTING FOR BUSINESS AND HOME
INTERFACE AGE
onComputing
NEW PRODUCTS REPORT
Surviving a Computer Faire
Mattel's Computer for Kids
Eight Chess Programs
Money Market Fantasies
nibble
Micro-computers in the home
'I refuse to be a computer widow!'

# Chapter Thirteen

# PROMOTION, ADVERTISING AND SALES

How are microcomputer products sold? They are sold through direct mail by sending promotional material to selected lists of people. They are sold by mail order through space ads and classified ads in the print media. They are sold by telephone, by independent sales reps or by your own road agents. Best of all, they are sold by word-of-mouth. Many businesses use the most listened-to words of all: editorial mention.

As you can see in the back of this chapter, there are a lot of magazines who owe their existence to computer mania. Most of these magazines select a segment of the market and speak to the inhabitants of that segment. These people listen. In fact, many people who subscribe to specialty magazines read every word in the magazine and are anxious for the next issue.

The magazine publishers and editors know all about the dynamics of their market. They also know magazines live by selling ad space. The price of ads is determined by circulation. Circulation is determined by the market segment size and relevance to the subscribers' interests. Are you starting to get the picture?

**Axiom: The best product or service in the world is useless unless it can be sold.**

Editors are interested in whatever might interest their readers. A new product or company which is important to their readers is important to the magazine. Showcasing new products or industry developments is a sign to the reader the magazine is on the front edge of what's happening. All of this means editors want to talk about your new enterprise.

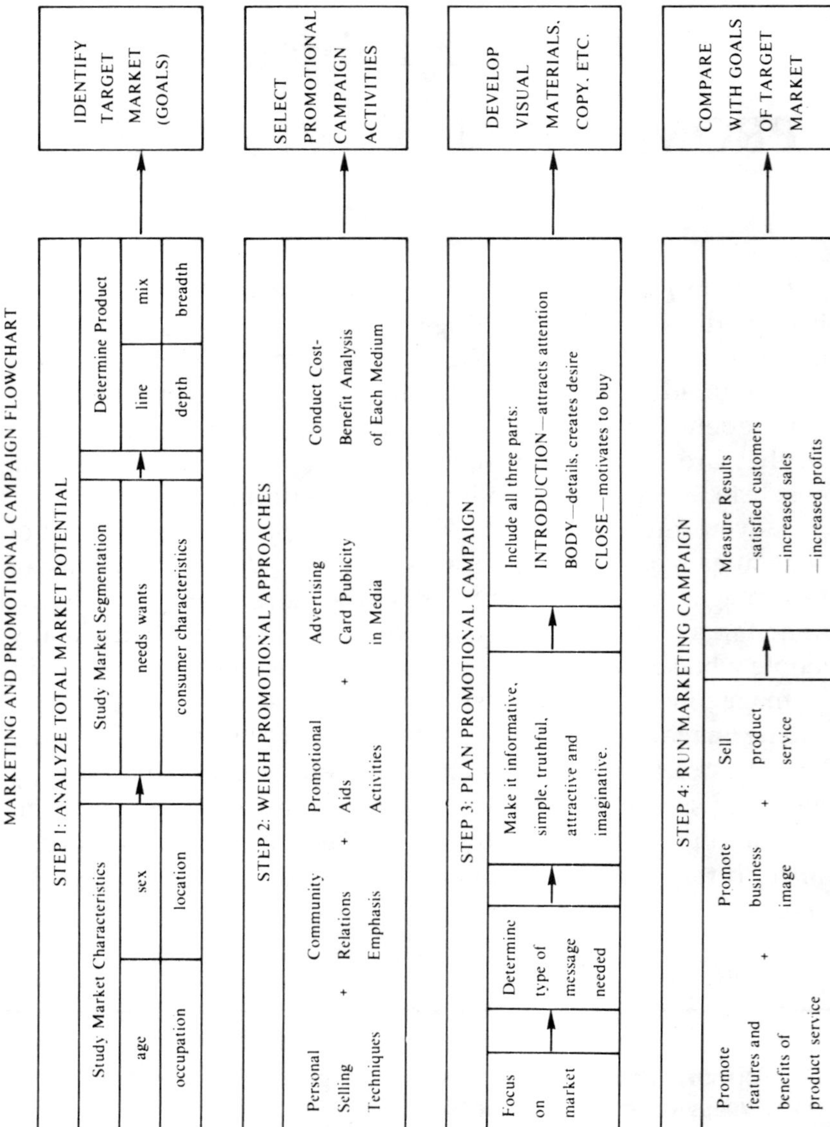

If you want a magazine editor to showcase or make editorial comment on your product or company you need to let him know his readers would be interested. The traditional way to do this is to send a news release to any editor who might conceivably have an interest.

But the news release is only one-third of the promotional package. The other items you must include in order to complete this process are a cover letter and a news release response card.

## The News Release

Copies of news releases are seen throughout this book and there is a copy of a good one in the appendix of this chapter.

To make up your news releases you should spend a few dollars having some type set onto one of your letterheads. This type should say "NEWS RELEASE—for immediate release" and should have a contact name and phone number. The form used by Digital Research shown in the back of this chapter is ideal.

Take your typeset master and run a good copy. *Type* the copy onto the form. You want to give the idea you distribute news releases all the time. The smoother and more professional the news releases, the more you look like a pro and the better your chances are to get your free editorial advertising.

Double-space the text of the release. Write it in newspaper style — keep the sentences short and punchy and make no paragraphs over three sentences long.

RELEASE RESPONSE REPLY CARD

*To:*

*We have received your News Releases about* ____________

______________________________

*We will take the following action:*
*Your product will be featured on (date)* ____________
*Your product will be featured in the near future* ____ *(check)*
*Please send more information* ____ *(check)* *Samples* ____ *(check)*
*Name* ____________
*Title* ____________
*Publication* ____________
*Address* ____________
______________________________
*Comments* ____________
______________________________

*(You type in the appropriate information here)*

# News Release

FOR IMMEDIATE RELEASE October 12, 1981

## DISCOUNT ON NEWLY-RELEASED MP/M-86 T.M.

PACIFIC GROVE, CA: MP/M-86, the high performance multi-user operating system from Digital Research, Inc. is now available for shipment. Based on the CP/M® and MP/M T.M. operating systems for 8-bit microcomputers, MP/M-86 adds new features that take advantage of the 16-bit microprocessor's increased power. As a special offer to Independent Software Vendors, a $50 price reduction is being offered on MP/M-86 through November 30, 1981.

MP/M-86 maintains full compatibility with the CP/M-86 T.M. single-user operating system. CP/M-86 programs can be operated immediately under MP/M-86. Because the file system formats of MP/M-86, CP/M-86, CP/M and MP/M are compatible, conversion from 8-bit single-user application programs running under CP/M through multi-user 16-bit applications is greatly simplified.

MP/M-86 offers multi-user capability with multi-programming for each user. It supports up to 16 logical drives managing up to 512 megabytes each. Other features include record and file locking, date and time stamps as well as password protection on files. Extensive error-handling and reporting and networking capability is also included.

OEMs and Independent Software Vendors will find it easy to convert existing application programs to the new system, making the world of CP/M-based software quickly and economically available to the MP/M-86 user. Contact the Digital Research Marketing Staff for further information. When ordering by mail, please include this release with the order.

For more information call or write:

DIGITAL RESEARCH®

Post Office Box 579 • Pacific Grove, California 93950 • (408) 649-3896 • TWX 910 360 5001

FOR IMMEDIATE RELEASE
(for CALENDAR, also?)

November 16th, 1981

N E W S   R E L E A S E

**Computer Swap America Going Nationwide**

**...to Southern California first**

John Craig's Computer Swap America shows in the San Francisco Bay Area have become high-technology "flea markets" for buyers ranging from die-hard computer hobbyists to businessmen. The most recent event, held in October, 1980 in San Jose, CA, drew a crowd of 5,233 to buy used and new computers, a wide range of software, diskettes, disk drives, printers, books, and other computer-related articles. The "hi-tech-flea-market" flavor was introduced by companies selling items ranging from home satellite receiving systems to automobile computer systems to mobile phone systems.

The highlight of the most recent show was a door prize drawing by Bill Godbout of Compupro systems in which he gave away a $14,000 Compupro system. The lucky winner was Jim Russell in Atwater, CA. Other door prizes, auctions, bargains, "wheelin' & dealin', and the anticipation of finding that certain item, or not knowing what you'll find, add to the air of excitement found at this and past shows. The next scheduled show, in Orange County, CA (see below) will feature seminars by Integrated Services Instruction on making the personal desktop computer purchase decision.

John Craig has announced plans to take Computer Swap America

# The Cover Letter

The most important part of the editorial-mention process is getting your foot in the door. This is done with an appropriate cover letter. Your cover letter is a sales document. The purpose of it is to sell the editor on the idea his readers have an interest in your company and its product.

You should start this letter like a news story. Editors are used to that style and it lends impact to your sales appeal. Here's an example of the kind of letter that makes editors act on your news: (Ms. J is editor of a hobbyist magazine)

Dear Ms. Jones:

Advances in disc drive technology are the hottest news in the microcomputer business.

Until just recently, hobbyists have been held back by the high price of drives with the capacity they need.

A new technology has just brought high-capacity, hard sector Winchester drives into the price range of most computer hobbyists. This new technology is reliable, expandable and will be on the shelf in September.

Enclosed is a News Release announcing a disc system that will excite and encourage your readers. They need to know about this new development. It is something they have been waiting for.

Enclosed is an Editorial Response Card. Please let me know if you plan to use this new information. If you want further details mention it on the card or call me at 305-576-6756.

Very truly yours

Joe Hotshot

Joe Hotshot
Disc Drive Productions

JH/ndg

## Paid Media Advertising

The next step in your promotion is to advertise. Your ad program of course will depend upon how much money you can spend on it.

Advertising is the most powerful sales tool in our culture. It is the backbone of our industrial society and most of it is done poorly.

Before you spend a cent on any ad, please get a copy of John Caple's book, *Tested Advertising Methods,* published by Prentice-Hall, Inc., Englewood Cliffs, NJ, ISBN #0-13-609-909-7. This book is in its seventh printing and is the bible of no-bullshit advertising. This chapter is only a tickler to point you in the right direction. Caple's book tells all the details you need to know to write ads that work!

## Classified Advertising

Classified ads are the cheapest way to buy paid advertisements. Almost all classified ads are "response" ads. This means the ad tells you to send for further information or offers a free booklet, etc.,if you write for the information.

The reason for the response idea is it is difficult to sell anything over $10 with 40 words or less. But forty words can be quite enough to get someone to inquire.

People read classifieds. This advertising method can be a most cost-effective way to get your product rolling.

## Display Advertising

Display advertising is expensive and expensive advertising requires planning. Not only do you need to carefully plan your ad layout, appeal and copy, but you also need to prepare the magazine so they will deal to your advantage.

Discounts, location and review articles are all a matter of negotiation. No one negotiates with more juice than a "qualified" advertising agency.

If you have a big budget start-up you may want to use an outside agency to plan, prepare and place your ads. An agency can take the burden of learning the ad business off of your shoulders so you can have more time to administer the other parts of your business. An agency can also waste your money and blow your introduction campaign.

If you use an outside agency, make sure they have experience

and expertise with your *exact* industry and the type of promotion you want to run. Most agencies are only interested in large accounts who want to run institutional (no coupon) ads and develop batches of promotional material.

If you are spending less than $100,000 a year on ads you aren't going to make them much money and you may be more of a bother than a help.

Agencies make part of their money by adding 15% on to whatever services they provide in your behalf. If they write, typeset, layout and print your brochures, they will either do it in-house or contract it out. The in-house work is charged out at top going rates, and if the work is contracted out the agency adds 15% to the contractor's bill.

Agencies get a 15% discount on ad rates. The magazine bills them and they bill you for the amount the magazine bills. They pay the magazine and discount the invoice 15%.

I don't begrudge an agency its commission. I run an agency

**Ads starting with an "interesting" story not relating to the thing being sold are losers. I recently saw an ad for an airborne particle counter. The headline was EVERY FIVE SECONDS. This headline is meaningless unless you read the body copy, which told how scans are made every five seconds. A better headline would have been something like RED HOT PARTICLE COUNTER. Remember, an ad competes with hundreds of similar ads. The ones that arrest the eye of the *right* person are the winners.**

**John Craig's ad gets its point across clearly. This ad is direct and to-the-point. If you are interested in computer swap meets, you will have no trouble spotting this ad. Ads that pinpoint a definite interest area work best. Have you ever seen small ads with big headlines taking half the ad space saying HEMMORHOIDS or BACK PAIN? They look pretty crude, but only a person with these problems is interested in these specialized products—and if you have one of these particular problems, you *will* notice the ad offering relief.**

Reprinted by permission of John Craig.

myself and I can tell you in most cases commissions are earned by hard work. The problem is most agencies aren't geared to small accounts. Fifteen percent commission on a $500 ad is only $75. How much commission does a $30 classified ad pay?

Many agencies will take a small account because they are hungry or because they think the account will expand. But dollars talk. If you aren't bringing much money into an agency you won't get much attention.

Agencies also dislike coupon ads. Their typical spiel goes something like this: "Let's run image enhancement ads—they will pay off in the future." Image enhancers and other institutional ads have two deficiencies: First, since they have no coupon, you have no direct way to measure the ad's effectiveness. Second, they may help your image but your new business needs sales now!

Coupon ads allow you a measure of the agency and the ad. Most agencies don't like such an effective weathervane and will actively avoid coupon ads.

**DISK DOCTOR– a good headline–the word "automatic" makes the program seem easy to use. The copy is effective–gives a list of benefits. Note Technical Hotline number in lower right. This gives the reader the feeling that *Supersoft* is interested in user's problems and that they are willing and able to help. The illustration detracts from an otherwise very effective ad.**

# FORTRAN IV

## for CP/M

"I needed a FORTRAN with COMPLEX as well as REAL and DOUBLE precision arithmetic, that would produce relocatable code and link in assembly language subroutines. It also had to be a FORTRAN that was easy to use as well as being a complete implementation. SuperSoft/SSS FORTRAN is the only microcomputer FORTRAN that met my requirements."

Supersoft makes full WATFIV FORTRAN IV available to microcomputers. Supersoft/SSS FORTRAN meets and exceeds the ANSI 1966 standard. The compiler supports many advanced features including: variable character strings and recursive subroutines with static variables. Fully compatible RATFOR is also available.

**FEATURES**

| | |
|---|---|
| Code generation: | ROMable ".COM" files or intermediate code files (saves disk space). External routines may be called. Relocatable format. |
| Data types: | Byte, integer, real, double precision, complex, logical, character and varying length strings. |
| Operations: | All standard operations plus string comparisons, assignments, and .XOR. |
| Constants: | Hexadecimal, decimal, and character literals with features to imbed control characters. |
| Statements: | ANSI 1966 standard with multiple statement lines. |
| Controls: | Map, List, and Symbol table output options. |
| I/O: | Read, Write, Append, Rewind, Close, Delete, Rename, Search, Sequential and Random I/O on disk files. Supports all CP/M devices. |

**System Requirements & Prices**

SSS FORTRAN requires a 32k CP/M system. Z80 only.

| | |
|---|---|
| SSS FORTRAN with RATFOR: | $325 |
| SSS FORTRAN alone: | $250 |
| Manual only: | $ 25 |
| RATFOR alone: | $100 |
| Macro Assembler: | $ 80 |

(Sold only with valid SSS FORTRAN license)

CP/M Formats: 8" soft sectored, 5" Northstar, 5" Micropolis Mod II, Vector MZ, Superbrain DD/QD Apple II +

All Orders and General Information:
SUPERSOFT ASSOCIATES
P.O. BOX 1628
CHAMPAIGN, IL 61820
(217) 359-2112
Technical Hot Line: (217) 359-2691
(answered only when technician is available)

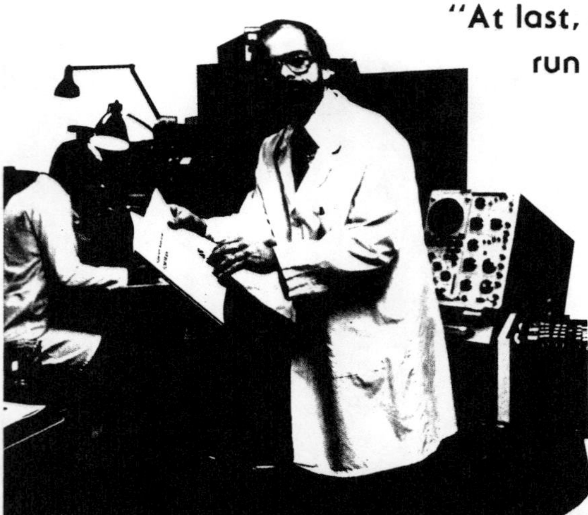

**"At last, a FORTRAN that will run my large mainframe programs."**

**SuperSoft**

*CP/M REGISTERED TRADEMARK DIGITAL RESEARCH
SSS FORTRAN is the copyright of Small Systems Services, Urbana, Illinois

**First in Software Technology**

## Writing Your Own Ads

Why not read John Caple's book and write your own ads? Once you know the basics, producing ads becomes a matter of assembling the details.

I write the ads for all of my own profit centers. Every time I write one of these ads I get out Caple's book and read it cover to cover, making notes relvant to my ad as I go.

Below are some guiding ideas and examples to let you know how you can write better ads for your product. Caple's book gives you the construction instructions. Who knows your product and market better than you?

**FORTRAN FOR CP/M: A good headline—direct and to the point. Testimonial in the copy gives relevance and believability. The illustration of an obvious "scientist" surrounded by sophisticated equipment gives the ad credibility. This ad is direct and gives ethical persuasion. Herb Schildt, president of *Supersoft Associates,* told me they previously ran a FORTRAN ad with an illustration of dancing diskettes. The scientist ad pulled a large multiple of responses compared with "dancing diskettes."**

Reprinted by permission of Countryside Data.

**COUNTRYSIDE DATA—An artistic ad that will catch the eye of someone interested in ag business programs. This ad could be improved by elimination of "white space" and substitution of some body copy.**

**If you have anything to do with small computers, you should be reading the Carl Helmers**

# PERSONAL COMPUTER LETTER

**every month!**

You won't want to miss a single issue of the new Personal Computer Letter... a monthly publication of comprehensive studies on issues affecting design, implementation, and applications of small computer systems. The Personal Computer Letter is a journal compiled and edited by Carl Helmers, co-founder and first editor of **Byte Magazine.** Here is valuable information in professionally prepared format about small computers, software, peripherals, trends in the industry, and new ideas. We accept no advertising, and the information provided is available nowhere else. Written for executives, decision-makers, market strategists, product designers and authors in the small computer field, each 12 to 16-page issue contains analysis and design studies by many of the personal computer industry's foremost experts. For example, the current issue covers: **Intelligent Serial Line Filters:** *Exploring a family of application oriented product ideas.*

Subscribe today. Mail the coupon with your check for $200 for the next 12 monthly issues. Sample issues at $25 per copy, applicable to a full year's subscription.

**NORTH AMERICAN TECHNOLOGY, INC.**
Strand Building
174 Concord St.,
Peterborough, NH 03458
(603) 924-6048

☐ Enclosed is my $200 check or money order for the next 12 issues of the Personal Computer Letter.
☐ Enclosed is my $25 check or money order for a sample issue, applicable to subscription price.

NAME __________
ADDRESS __________
CITY __________
STATE __________ ZIP __________

**PERSONAL COMPUTER LETTER—Nice graphic design; does not interfere with the message. Dotted lines around the coupon increase response. It has also been found the bigger the coupon, the better the response *up to half the ad area.* One mail-order company found a 7% increase when they added a drawing of scissors cutting the coupon corner. Sounds unlikely, but remember, the biggest problem with a direct response ad is to get people to *take action.***

**The primary rules for designing a direct response (coupon) ad are:**

**1. Arrest the reader's eye with a direct specific interest headline.**

**2. COPY SELLS. Testing has repeatedly shown that the longer the copy, the better the response. Long copy has been taken to the extreme of 2000 or more words, and the results were even better. Tests have shown *no limit* to the drawing power of long copy. Artistic ads with lots of white space look nice, but if you cram copy into every available space, your ad will pull better.**

Reprinted by permission of North American Technology Inc.

## Your Own Agency

"Qualified" ad agencies get a 15% discount on advertising. This discount comes right off the top of the advertised ad rates. To be a qualified agency you need to spend about thirty dollars and two hours' time.

Select a name for your agency that doesn't relate to your business. I use GRAYHALL ADVERTISING AGENCY for a name. What could be more neutral and conservative sounding? Also there is a huge agency in Los Angeles with a similar name so my agency's letters and requests get prompt attention.

To form your agency, register the name with the appropriate authorities, put a DBA ad in the local newspaper, and open a commercial bank account in the name of the agency. Get the biggest checks they have (you won't be carrying them around in your hip pocket). Obtain some letterhead stationery and #10 envelopes.Get some 13x15 envelopes with your agency's name printed on them. (NEBS has all this stuff—see Chapter Ten.)

Get a Post Office Box for the Agency. If that is impractical and you have to use the same address as your main company, put "Suite C" or something in the address. The mail will still get to the right place and it creates the idea that both companies are in the same building but not necessarily related.

I have a phone line whose number I reserve to handle the several small businesses (profit centers) I manage. This line is answered "3882" (the number is 688-3882). That way I can use one line for a whole range of calls and the overhead stays low.

All advertising bills should be paid with agency checks. This way there is never a problem with the agency discount. Another interesting thing that happens in connection with having your own agency is you get better treatment than if you are just a poor slob business owner placing his own ads.

When, as a business owner, you try to negotiate price with an ad rep, there will usually be an arm wrestling match. Maybe they will or maybe they won't. When you call them as an agency they will immediately go the mat and give you the net price.

If you represent yourself as an agency and they still won't give you a discount beyond the agency commission, you should say, "The other magazine (name a big one) gives us a 15% 'mail order' discount." Some magazines have a policy to never deviate from the rate card prices. But the "mail order" discount idea lets them give you a break without going off the card.

You can occasionally negotiate a "fer" discount. If you run

**Consultants**

**PROGRAMMER & CONSULTANT NETWORK**

Tired of wasting time looking for a consultant? This organization specializes in getting you together. We match his qualifications to your requirements. We have the best Programmer/Consultant Network in the nation. Send a $25 registration fee and get your information package.

**C & C Data Consultants**
1373 E. Whitton Ave.
Phoenix, Arizona 85014

**Business Opportunities**

**PROGRAMMER & CONSULTANT NETWORK**

Looking for an opportunity? Part-time programmer or full time. Finding clients can be very time consuming. Join our expanding programmer consultant network and save time and money. By registering with us you get the edge over competition. Let us match you to a compatible client. For a yearly fee of $15 you have potential income $$$$. Want recognition? Write today and succeed! Send in now for information to:

**C & C Data Consultants**
1373 E. Whitton Ave.
Phoenix, Arizona 85014

**Which of these ads pulled five times more than the other? They were both run in *Infoworld.* The ad on the right outpulled the one on the left five-to-one. Why? Because of critical aim. Who reads *Infoworld?* Computer consultants and programmers, not people who are looking for a consultant. The ad on the left was aimed at someone who does not read the media it was placed in. The righthand ad was aimed accurately and pulled well as a result.**

Reprinted by permission of C&C Data Consultants.

twice, the third ad can be run free. This is called "one fer two." It's another way to give discounts without going off the card.

Another item of negotiation is editorial mention. Discuss this openly with your ad rep. Deals are commonly negotiated for editorial mention on a "fer" basis .

Always deal with your local ad rep rather than directly with the magazine. Your local ad rep can give you better deals and as you develop a personal relationship there will be many ways they can help you.

The fact you maintain an agency to get discounts for your primary profit center will be an open secret. Once your rep starts placing your ads and learns you pay your bills on time and are reasonable when there is a problem, he won't care whether you are a "real" agency or not. In fact, some magazines give the agency discount routinely to whomever places the ad. But the in-house agency is still a good idea because it opens doors and because some of the big corporate magazines are really sticky about discounts.

## Sales

How your product is sold and how your selling strategy evolves depends strictly on the kind of business you are in.

If you are a consultant or are in a service business, your selling will be largely done by personal phone calls or visits. You may do some direct mailings to a highly qualified mailing list and run a small ad in the trade journals.

If you are in the retail business, your sales will be made on the basis of your signs and displays, local reputation, newspaper ads, and the expertise of your floor sales personnel.

If you are a distributor or manufacturer, your sales will be made by trade ads, direct mail, trade show displays, telephone solicitation, a field sales force and word-of-mouth.

Research is the key to a successful sales effort in any industry segment. Luckily there are many successful retailers in the microcomputer business. By paying careful attention to how they set up their stores, how they recruit and train sales personnel, and how they advertise you can get an idea of where to begin your own efforts.

To find out the best way to go about this is to use the phone. Call the national sales manager of COMPUTER WORLD, THE BYTE SHOPS, etc. Ask them direct questions. You may be surprised at the candid answers you get.

## PRINT MEDIA COMPARISON

**NEWSPAPER ADVERTISING**

- ✓ Reaches a large number of people
- ✓ Has a short life span
- ✓ Cheapest per reader rate
- ✓ Can be placed in a section relevant to your product
- ✓ Choice of formats:
  - Display or classified in regular editions
  - Inserts in regular editions
  - Special editions, such as Shoppers' Guides

**MAGAZINE ADVERTISING**

- ✓ Reaches a selected audience
- ✓ Has a relatively long life span
- ✓ May be shared between several readers
- ✓ Must be planned and purchased a long time in advance
- ✓ Available in various sizes
- ✓ Available in several formats:
  - Display or classified
  - Card inserts
- ✓ Is more expensive than newspaper advertising

**DIRECT MAIL**

- ✓ Reaches a selected audience
- ✓ Higher per person cost
- ✓ Likely to be kept or posted
- ✓ Has many special uses:
  - Soliciting mail order to phone in business
  - Announcing new or changed products, etc.

- ✓ Has many formats:
  - Catalogues
  - Circulars
  - Letters
  - Flyers
  - Brochures
  - Coupons
  - Inserts
  - Cards

The sales managers of these companies are proud of their work and there is always a possibility you will want to buy a franchise.

Talk to the sales managers of the product lines you intend to carry in your store. They have an interest in helping you get started properly.

Talk to the managers of local stores. Be frank with them and they might tell you things you would normally miss in a clandestine investigation. If you start things on the right footing you and your competitors can be a great help to one another.

If you are selling a product through the mail your sales will almost entirely depend on your paid ads and editorial mention. Read John Caple's book. It's better than insurance.

## Testing

A successful ad campaign depends solely on testing. Testing is done by changing only one thing in an ad and comparing returns. Every successful mail order operation increases its sales by systematically testing *every* advertising element. Look at ads that have run for years in magazines like *Popular Mechainics.* The LASALLE TRAINING INSTITUTE has run the same exact ad for twelve years. Why? Because an enormous amount of testing told them that particular ad gives them the best return for their money. Some tests have shown that changing a single word can triple response.

If your company depends upon sales to someone who will use your product as a component of something they make or if they resell your product (distributor or retailer), then research is even more important.

IBM has estimated a typical industrial sales visit costs $127. These visits are preceded by mailed promotional material and letters. They are set up by phone conversations and submission of quotes. All these activities add up to the high cost of industrial selling.

How do you make the expensive sales visit worthwhile? By your own personal investigations. Before you commit yourself to sales policy, brochures, ads, trade show space and the hiring of sales reps, you should do lots of footwork.

This means you should talk to *everyone* who will even grunt back at you. Take a step back to Chapter Two. Go to *every* trade show and get to know everyone there. Stay every hour of every day of the important shows. Go to every show function. Attend the parties and seminars. Talk a little and listen a lot.

## Finding the Right Information

You may have been to these shows and talked to many of these people before. But this time it is different. You have a special purpose and are after selected knowledge. Your subconscious will lead you to the answers you need. You will find yourself tuning-in to information that was there before but not noticed. You will find people's conversations drifting to the subject you need to know about. You will notice items in the newspaper and on TV that were never apparently there before. Our sensory apparatus is so loaded with input that it filters most things out of our conscious awareness. The unconscious is the operating system that does this selecting. When it is programmed to pick up certain information you will be surprised at how much there is that ordinarily goes unnoticed.

Go on the road with a prospective sales rep. Keep your ears to the tracks. Listen to everything. You will hear what you need to know.

## Working With Your Salespeople

I once had a partner who was the best salesman in our industry. He was flamboyant, outrageous and a natural *courtier.* Everyone in the trade knew him and looked forward to his visits. He had the ability to get your attention, keep you laughing and close the deal with unnoticeable transitions and infinite timing. At trade shows his booth was always crowded. What he said, the products showed, and the orders he wrote (called paper in the trade) were inevitably the talk of the show. Customers would call the factory to place an order but would talk only to him.

The business grew about 300% a year and generated enough profits to sustain the cashflow demand of such growth. I became worried that too much of the new business depended on one personality. It was obvious to me our growth would be limited if we depended on one person for all our sales increases, so I began to put pressure on my Superstar partner to become more of an administrator and shift his talents to training a sales group. This group would form the nucleus of a professional sales team and thus we could make the transition from depending upon a single personality to reliance on a broad-based professional sales organization.

In retrospect, this concept was correct but my means of achieving the goal was wrong. The mistake was due to a misassumption about the ability of a born salesman to become an administrative type.

My partner shared by concern about developing sales professionalism and put on the collar of an administrator. He tried hard but things never seemed to run quite right. He recruited and trained some of the best salespeople in the industry, but there were always problems with keeping things organized at the office. Promises were made and not recorded, policies were revised and re-revised, certain sales personnel received special treatment and customers grew restless. There was trouble in paradise.

I saw these problems developing and so put pressure on my partner to get his end of the organization in order. He tried desperately but things only became worse. Worse for him that is. Bookings rose steadily and though customers were beginning to voice dissatisfaction due to unrealistic delivery promises and erratic administration of the discount policy, they continued to order in ever-increasing quantities.

If customers order more but are increasingly dissatisfied with the way you handle them it creates a dangerous situation. In fact this state of affairs is what you should look for when studying potential markets. Dissatisfied but hungry customers will quickly change horses if a good competitor comes along.

Increasing sales proves there is an expanding demand. Increasing customer dissatisfaction indicates the appearance of flaws in the dominant supplier. If you step in with comparable product and price, customers will shift their business to you.

That is what happened to us. The competition soon offered our customers better delivery, smoother sales management and comparable product. Our expansion slowed and my partner blamed himself for our state of affairs. His tension and despair created a severe problem and soon he wanted out.

The rest of this story will be told as an example of the problems faced by a company that grew too fast and lost the market to eager competition yet to go through the same cycle.

I came away from this experience realizing that a person perfectly suited to sales and promotion is not necessarily an administrator. It was a perfect example of the Peter Principle: If a person is very good at something he tends to get promoted until his talents no longer suit his position.

If I were to face the same situation again I would hire an

administrative type to implement our sales policy on a day-to-day basis and would hire an executive assistant to handle details for my partner.

Nothing is ever perfect in business. The solution would have created a new problem: My partner felt he should be the head of sales and marketing. The appearance of an administrator to serve this function would have caused jealousy and insecurity.

## Sales Administration

Salesmen are sometimes hard to teach new tricks. Many old salts believe they know it all and have heard it all at least once. If you try to teach them improved methods in a sales seminar they sometimes listen with half an ear. An exerienced salesman typically rolls his eyes toward heaven when he hears the company is sponsoring a show-and-tell.

A microcomputer manufacturer was experiencing a sales slowdown and took the following approach to upgrade and stimulate his rep organization.

They circulated a monthly newsletter to the sales reps. It was filled with the usual house-organ claptrap, but on the inside front page of every issue there was a feature article titled, *Do You Know How to Close This One?* The article presented a sales call where the manufacturer's equipment was pitted against tough competition. Technical arguments were given for both sides, and while the units were not comparable point-for-point, they were roughly equal. The hitch was that the price for our manufacturer's unit was 10% higher than the competitors. How do you close this sale?

The article was presented as a contest. The best answer was printed in a succeeding newsletter.

Of course only a small percentage of the reps actually sent in answers. But each month some salesperson's solution appeared as the winner. *All* the sales reps read this column and there was much discussion among them about the answers.

Sales increased dramatically. Not only were the salespeople closing better, but their attention had been drawn to the technical aspects of the product. After all, if they were arguing for their method of closing last month's scenario they would have to back up their argument with technical points. As the sales reps became familiar and comfortable with the technical specifications of the product, they thought of new ways to close tough sales and everybody was happy ever after.

## Sales Personalities

1. *Polyesteri iridescentalis.* Usually wears a green-checked iridescent polyester suit with white shoes and belt, usually seen during station breaks on Sunday TV sponsoring old movie reruns. Interesting courting behavior includes pounding fenders and droning repetitions of the mating call "No money down and payments start next year." This species makes a high percentage of its sales on the first call. Second calls are usually laden with difficulties.

2. *Ho-Hummus.* This variety will take orders if the customer phones or sends his order in the mail. This type is not pushy and has no difficulty at all with customers. In fact, customers look forward to seeing this type so they can discuss golf.

Ho-Hummers are not self-starting. Some models require a kick start. Even when started, this variety will not part new grass. He will only do what has become habitual. He will go to see the same people no matter what lines he takes on. If his customer's store has burnt down, a Ho-Hummer will stand around in a daze until the soles of his feet get hot.

Ho-Hummers are useful if you are selling shoe-resoling supplies or dry cleaning plant equipment. They can get the maximum yearly yield from a select and sedentary territory. If the Ho-Hummer sells shoe repair shops and this industry is dying because people want new boots instead of having their old ones' repaired, he will be found staring through the window of the now-empty shoe repair shop with a puzzled expression on his face.

A Ho-Hummer will often take your line but never get it out of the back of the station wagon. And most importantly, he will *never* go to see some new customer for whom the product may be relevant.

3. *Engineerus technicalus.* This rare strain can be identified by a thoroughly technical understanding of the product, an anaylitical and aggressive approach to your customer's needs, active customer orientaton to the capability of your product to satisfy his needs, clean sale closure with no unrealistic promises, and finally technical and service backup after the sale. This type is easily identified by the number of employment offers he gets from competitors and customers.

Though rare, the *Engineerus technicalus* sales type is not shy. You can spot them easily. The older ones are best looked for in the topmost branches of a tall tree. They exhibit rapid movements toward management assignments.

Remember, when sales watching, there is much species diversity. The generalizations above are valid only when applied to classes of people and become invalid the closer you try to apply them to a single individual.

## You Are Your Company's Best Salesperson

An entrepreneur is a born salesperson because of his enthusiasm for the product and the company. When you are in the scouting phase, don't sell; just listen. When you take a salesman, prospective client or customer to dinner order wine and ask the waiter for the cork. Put the cork in your mouth and hold it there for the rest of the evening. Let the other person do the talking. You'll learn more and gain better information.

If you listen carefully and often, you will hear every question answered. You will learn every detail you need to start your sales effort right.

The subject of sales administration is hotly debated by everyone involved in the art. There are hundreds of books on it. The best sales administrative advice I have read is in Rich White's book, *The Entrepreneur's Manual.*

Talk to salespeople, go to shows, interview customers, read Rich White's book and every other one you can stay awake while reading.

After you have gathered all the information possible, have sorted, categorized and utilized the relevant items, you will have your sales plan. You will soon go to the next class and will have the best of all teachers: experience.

Selling the product made by your company is one of the most challenging, exciting and memorable experiences you will ever have. Drop me a line sometime to let me know how you are doing.

# REFERENCES

*Asian Computer Monthly,* 7th Floor, Seabird House, 22-28 Wyndham Street, Hong Kong.

*Byte,* McGraw-Hill Publishing Co., Editor, Mark Haas; Thomas Harvey, Advert. Dir., 70 Main Street, Peterborough, NH 03458. (606) 924-9281. The biggie for everybody in the business.

*Call A.P.P.L.E.,* 6708 39th Avenue S.W., Seattle, WA 98136. (206) 271-4514. Val J. Golding, Editor. For Apple owners and users.

*Computer Instant Ads,* 277 East 6100 South, Salt Lake City, UT 84107. Low cost classified ads. Some display advertising.

*Computer Retailing,* W.R.C. Smith Publishing, 1760 Peachtree Road N.W., Atlanta, GA 30357. 1-800-241-5517. Make Witter, Editor and Ad Director.

*Computer Shopper, Patch Publishing Co., Inc.,* P.O. Box F, Titusville, FL 32780. (305) 269-3211. If you want to buy or sell, this is the place. Also has a growing ad section.

*The Community Computerists Directory,* 15250 River Road, Guernville, CA 95436. Editors and Pulishers, Jeffrey Love and Steven P. Pizzo. Everyone should subscribe to this great directory. Has listings of everyone you need to contact when starting your business.

*Compute!,* Published by Small Systems Services, Inc., P.O. Box 5406, Greensborough, NC 27403. (919) 275-9809. Robert C. Lock, Editor and Publisher. Hobbyist oriented.

*Computer,* IEEE Computer Society, 10662 Los Vaqueros Circle, Los Alamitos, CA 90720, (714) 821-8380. Editor and Publisher, True Seaborn. High level general interest.

*Computronics,* 50 North Pascack Road, Spring Valley,NY 10977. Publisher, Howard Y. Gosman; Editor-in-Chief, Hubert S. Howe, Jr. TRS-80 owners.

*Creative Computing,* 39 East Hanover Avenue, Morris Plains, NJ 07950. (201) 540-0445. Publisher David H. Ahl, Editor Elizabeth Staples. The second hottest magazine in the business.

*Desktop Computing,* Wayne Green, Inc., Petersborough, NH 03458. (605) 924-7138. Managing Editor, David Smith; Advertising Director, Marcia Stone. The plain language computer magazine.

*Data Cast,* Published by Wireless Digital, Inc., 345 Swett Road, Woodside, CA 94062. Jim C. Warren, Jr., Publisher; Cheryl Rhodes, Editor. Software oriented.

*Digital Design,* Bewill Publishing Company, 1050 Commonwealth Avenue, Boston, MA 02215. (617) 232-5470. Paul Sigier, Editor. Aimed at electrical and computer engineering types.

*Dr. Dobbs Joural,* Published by Peoples Computer Company, 1263 El Camino Real, Menlo Park, CA 94025. Editor, Marlin Ouverson. Software oriented for small systems users.

*80 Journal,* 3838 South Warner Street, Tacoma, WA 98409. (206) 475-2219. Publisher and Editor-in-Chief, I. Mike Schmidt. TRS-80 Users Journal.

*Educational Computing,* P.O. Box 535, Cupertino, CA 95015. Joan R. Hiraki, Editor.

*The Electron,* 4781 E. 355th Street, Willoughby, OH 44094. John D. Drinko, Publisher, William L. Bowden, Editor. The bimonthly newspaper of The Cleveland Institute of Electronics.

*Games,* Published by Playboy Enterprises, Inc., 515 Madison Avenue, New York, NY 10022. Editor, Ronnie Shushan. About all kinds of games.

*Hardcore Computing,* Softkey Publishing, 14404 East D Street, Tacoma, WA (no zip given). Bev. R. Haight, Editor. Fun and stuff for Apple users.

*Horsetrader,* P.O. Box 11712, Santa Ana, CA 92711. (714) 832-0628. David Jacobsen, Publisher. Buy and sell computer equipment—inexpensive classifieds.

*Infoworld,* 530 Lytton, Palo Alto, CA 94301. (415) 328-4602. Thomas Hogan,

Editor. News, best priced merchandise.

*Interface Age,* 16704 Marquardt, Cerritos, CA 90701. (213) 926-9544. Robert S. Jones, Publisher and Editor-In-Chief. Home and business topics for beginners.

*Lifelines,* Lifelines Publishing Co., 1651 Third Avenue, New York, NY 10028. (212) 722-1700. Editor-In-Chief, Edward H. Currie. A software magazine.

*Kilobaud MICROCOMPUTING,* A Wayne Green Publication. See *Desktop Computing.*

*Micro,* P.O. Box 6502, Chelmsford, MA 01824. (617) 256-5515. Robert M. Tripp, Editor and Publisher. 6502/6809 Users Journal.

*MIS Week,* Fairchild Publications, 7 E. 12th Street, New York, NY 10003. (212) 741-6484. Aimed at mainframe DP pros.

*Nibble,* Box 325, Lincoln, MA 01773. (617) 259-9710. The referece for Apple computing.

*99er Magazine,* P.O. Box 5537, Eugene, OR 97405. (503) 485-8796. Publisher/ Editor, Gary M. Kaplan. For users of the Texas Instruments TI-99/4 and other 16-bit TMS-9900-Based personal computer systems.

*Office Products Dealer,* Hitchcock Publishing Company, Hitchcock Building, Wheaton, IL 60187. (312) 651-1000. Arnold E. Keller, Publishing Board.

*Pacific Office Dealer,* Allen-Pacific Publications, 41 Sutter Street, Suite 300, San Francisco, CA94104. (415) 986-4323. Robert B. Frier, Editor.

*PEEK 65,* P.O. Box 347, Owings Mills, MD 21117. (301) 363-3267. Al Peabody, Editor. The Unofficial OSI Users Journal.

*Personal Computing,* Hayden Publishing Co., 50 Essex Street, Rochelle Park, NJ 07662. David Gabel, Editor. For newcomers.

*Popular Electronics,* Ziff-Davis Publishing Co., One Park Avenue, New York, NY 10016. (212) 725-3500. Harold A. Rogers, Executive Editor. The oldest magazine in the business; broad appeal.

*Purser's Magazine,* P.O. Box 466, El Dorada, CA 95623. Robert Purser, the guy to talk to. Fun games, etc.

*Robotics Age,* 10049 Commerce Avenue, Tujunga, CA 91042. (213) 352-7937. Joel M. Wilf, Managing Editor. Devoted to robot science and development.

*Small Business Computers,* Published by *Creative Computing.*

*Softalk,* 11021 Magnolia Boulevard, North Hollywood, CA 91601. (213) 890-5074. Margo Comstock Tommervik, Editor. Fun, games and programs for the hobbyist.

## Chapter Fourteen

# KEEPING YOUR HEAD ON STRAIGHT

## A HALF-TIME SUMMARY

The foregoing chapters have been written to give you an idea of the kinds of things you will be dealing with when starting your own business. Starting and successfully operating a business is just the same as programming, circuit design, brushing your teeth or driving a car.

Business skill is learned by reading and reasoning about many fascinating details. But most of all, you learn about business by doing it. Find out all you can about your business before you start. Read, think and talk to anyone who won't walk away.

Your real education begins when you open that commercial bank account and deposit your savings into it. The real education concerning marketing comes on the heels of your own product successes and misfires. The real lessons about production control and cash management come when your product costs get out of hand or you run out of money. The lessons of sales are learned on your feet at trade shows and in your customers' offices. The real lessons of finance are read in the loan officer's crooked smile when you present your loan proposal package.

Most people never take the risk of opening their own business enterprise. The risk of failure and fear of the unknown paralyzes most people and locks them into a life of frustrated gray boredom.

Our fears come from a part of our brains which developed when the world was ruled by tooth, fang and the weather. Our only tools of survival then were a thighbone club and a quick mind. Failure in this world didn't mean going on unemployment or back to the assembly line. Failure meant quick and violent extinction. Our irrational fears were built into us in a time when to fail meant to die.

Quite a few things have changed in the 600 centuries since those times. One of the greatest changes is we have evolved into a society where the result of business failure is that you might loose your boat and Visa Card.

If your business succeeds our society provides rewards reserved previously for kings. Freedom, personal growth, enhanced knowledge and material reward are the inheritance of those who take the risk of starting a business and succeed.

Another powerful but less tangible reward awaits everyone who starts a business enterprise, win or lose. This reward is the fulfillment you get from effort at the outer limit of your ability and knowledge.

When you start your own business you will learn from all the experiences you encounter. You will have successes and setbacks and will learn equally from both. As an older business patriarch once told me, however, that it is better to learn from your own successes and others' setbacks. Whatever the result it's one hell of an experience.

There are two classes of property in this world. The first I call "Primary Property." It is a combination of your talents, intuition and knowledge. Kings, courts or tax agents cannot take away your primary property. "Secondary Property" is all the things subject to the ravages of moths and rust. Secondary Property is all the things that can be bought, sold and traded away. Secondary Property owes its existence to Primary Property. What your Primary Property created once, it can create again in better and more satisfying form.

What do you really have to lose? If your business fails in the most spectacular way you only stand to lose your secondary things. In the worst situation you are left with the most valuable element of all — the source of all wealth and success — your talent, instincts and knowledge. If your first business fails, the experience will make your second business better than anything that has gone before. You will know so much more. You will be an honors graduate of the school of real experiences.

You will learn things from starting your own business you could not possibly learn anywhere else or in any other way. This learning will be valuable to your self-concept and will make you a better, broader and finer person.

Do you really want a better life? Do you really want more freedom? The best way I know to achieve those things is with your own business.

If this book could transmit one message clearly, I would choose the message that starting your own business is an enobling experience which no one should miss.

The foregoing chapters discuss many technical details: How to take a personal inventory. How to analyze the microcomputer market. What steps to take establishing your business legally. How to set up your accounting systems. How to set up your office. How to launch your product and how to begin to make sales.

All the aspects of business discussed here are covered more thoroughly in other books. The biggest problem in writing this particular book was the realization that each chapter could become a library and still not cover the subject entirely. I hope this book has show you where to begin your efforts most effectively.

Volume II of this work looks at the problems and situations you will encounter after your business gets going. It takes a more strategic approach and tries to help you keep perspective on the dynamics of your developing enterprise.

There are innumerable tricks to running a business profitably. I just learned a helpful one today. The phone company has a special information service for 800 numbers. If you dial 1-800-555-1212, a special operator will answer and tell you the 800 number of any company in the country that has one listed. I had to make 25 calls yesterday and 18 of the companies had 800 numbers. The information calls took fifteen minutes and I saved about a hundred dollars in phone charges by calling the listed toll-free numbers.

If you learn an interesting trick like this one please drop me a line about it. I will keep a list of the people who might be interested in information like this and from time-to-time will send out a summary of the new information I have run across.

If you run across any problem you have questions about, write it down and send it to me with a self-addressed stamped envelope. If I don't know the answer, I'll try to find someone who does and let you know.

If you find these volumes have been helpful, please let me know about that also. I am interested to hear what you like or dislike about what I have written and recorded.If you have suggestions for improving these volumes I would also like to hear them.

Keep in touch. I'm interested in what and how you are doing. The microcomputer industry has a vast and important future. With a little luck and some smart work, you and I will be a part of it.